MOVING FROM THE PRIMARY CLASSROOM

Edited by Maurice Galton and
John Willcocks

ROUTLEDGE & KEGAN PAUL
London, Boston, Melbourne and Henley

First published in 1983
by Routledge & Kegan Paul Ltd
39 Store Street, London WC1E 7DD,
9 Park Street, Boston, Mass. 02108, USA,
296 Beaconsfield Parade, Middle Park,
Melbourne, 3206, Australia, and
Broadway House, Newtown Road,
Henley-on-Thames, Oxon RG9 1EN
Printed in Great Britain by
St Edmundsbury Press, Suffolk
Authors' contributions © Paul Croll, Maurice Galton, Brian
Simon, Anne Jasman and John Willcocks 1983
Other contributions © Routledge & Kegan Paul 1983

Library of Congress Cataloging in Publication Data
Moving from the primary classroom.
Bibliography: p.
Includes index.
1. Education, Elementary – Great Britain – Curricula.
2. Transfer students – Great Britain. I. Galton,
Maurice J. II. Willcocks, John.
LA633.M68 1982   372.941   82-18569

ISBN 0-7100-9343-8 (US)

CONTENTS

FIGURES

TABLES

INTRODUCTION

This book marks the completion of the first stage of the ORACLE project. Funds from the Social Science Research Council for a five-year period (1975-80) enabled a series of interrelated studies concerning aspects of primary education to be mounted. The first of these, an evaluation of teaching style and pupil performance in fifty-eight classrooms, was reported in two earlier books, 'Inside the Primary Classroom' and 'Progress and Performance in the Primary Classroom'. A third volume, 'Research and Practice in the Primary Classroom' provided accounts of several smaller-scale studies carried out in conjunction with the main research on teachers' styles.

A five-year funding period, rather than the usual three, greatly increased the scope of the investigation and, most importantly, allowed for replication of the teaching styles with a substantially different sample of teachers. This was a new departure in British classroom research and made it possible to examine the question of the consistency of pupils' behaviour when they changed classes in the primary school. This kind of investigation inevitably raises further questions about what happens to the same pupils when they leave the primary school. After the move to a new school they meet not only many more teachers but also children from other feeder schools. Earlier studies of transfer have documented a number of effects on pupils which are associated with the transition. These include short-term increases in anxiety and, for a sizable minority, a decline in academic performance in the year after transfer. None of the previous large-scale studies has, however, observed children during transfer to seek an explanation of why pupils are affected in this way.

In search of possible explanations, the ORACLE researchers continued to observe the target pupils after transfer. For this part of the research however, participant observation became the main research strategy rather than interaction analysis. The main reason for this change was a practical one; the pupils in the classes observed at the primary stage were now distributed among different ability groupings in different specialist subjects. The task of observing all of them systematically was beyond the resources of even a project as large as ORACLE. However, by retaining some systematic observation after transfer on a sub-group of pupils it was possible to explore ways in which the two different techniques of observation could be used to complement each other. Our experience suggests that this should be

attempted more often in classroom studies.
'Moving from the Primary Classroom' gives an account of what
the ORACLE observers saw when pupils changed teachers in the
feeder schools, and afterwards when they met more new teachers
after transfer. The book's format follows that of 'Progress and
Performance in the Primary Classroom' in that individual members
of the research team have taken responsibility for the various
sections, but the book has been edited in a way which enables
it to be read as a whole. As before, the teachers are generally
referred to as female and the pupils as male except where specific
examples are quoted.

Part I looks at the background of the transfer problem and
argues that the effects on pupils when they meet new teachers
may be more important than the related problems of moving to an
unfamiliar building and learning to cope with a new set of rules.
In Part II the effects on pupils when they move to a new teacher
in the feeder school is contrasted with the way in which they
adapt to the new teachers after transfer. It appears that as
children move up through the school system the range of
approved behaviours becomes more limited. They either conform
to the teacher's demands or do the minimum work required,
while seeking other ways of occupying their time.

Thus after transfer there is increasing polarization between
the hardest workers and the other pupils and this is reflected in
their academic performance. Part III of the book considers pupil
performance both before and after transfer and shows how after
moving on to the new school some pupils drop back in performance for the first time in the study. This decrease is also
accompanied by a decline in their motivation and attitudes. Some
reasons for these dramatic changes can be found in the participant accounts presented in Part IV of the book. Three chapters
describe children's experiences after transfer, the kind of
curriculum offered, the specialist subject teaching they receive
(even in the 9-13 middle school) and the ways they earn their
reputations as 'good' or 'bad' pupils in the eyes of the teacher.

The final section, Part V, attempts to integrate these findings
on transfer with those of the earlier books on the main theme of
the ORACLE research, teaching and learning in the classroom.
It examines how far the ORACLE findings are compatible with
current theoretical explanations of classroom practice and
suggests ways in which headteachers, advisory staff and those
responsible for initial and in-service training can play a part in
helping teachers to evaluate their own work in the light of
ORACLE. It is thus hoped that the book will have something to
offer everyone with an interest in educational practice:
researchers, teachers, parents and those employed by local
authorities in an administrative as well as an advisory capacity.

The book could not have been completed without the help and
support of several groups of people to whom we owe a debt of
gratitude. Foremost among them were the teachers and pupils
who underwent observation. The fact that some of the teachers

are still actively engaged in the second stage of ORACLE is testimony to the friendly co-operation we received. Also deserving of thanks are the observers who collected the data for the transfer studies, Margaret Greig, Linda Hargreaves, Janice Lee and Sarah Tann and the members of the research team, Paul Croll and Anne Jasman. Additional help was provided by Sara Delamont who, although she had left Leicester for the University at Cardiff at the beginning of the project, came back for six weeks in the second and third years to carry out participant observation. The success of the project owes much to the way in which these observers developed the warmest of relationships with the staff of the schools in the study. Both project secretaries must be thanked for their help with the preparation of this manuscript. Jaya Katariya who left at the end of the first stage of the project also punched all the data on to cards for processing. Diana Stroud remains with the project and to her has fallen the main burden of typing and checking the numerous drafts of the book. For the compilation of the index our thanks are due to Elizabeth Willcocks. Finally thanks are also due to Professor Brian Simon, the original project's co-director, who has retained a wathcing brief over the manuscript and has helped with much useful advice at the editorial stage.

During the period in which this research was planned and carried out English primary schools have been the subject of much criticism from those who wish to see a return to what they term 'traditional values'. In spite of this hostile climate and the cutbacks in teachers and resources more schools are becoming interested in using the techniques developed by classroom researchers for evaluating teaching. In so far as the classrooms observed were typical of those in other areas of the country, the message from ORACLE is that the complaints of these critics were largely unjustified. It is to be hoped that the findings presented in the ORACLE books will encourage even more schools to become involved in self-evaluation of classroom practice and thus create the beginnings of a genuine debate about realistic ways in which pupil learning can be improved.

Maurice Galton
John Willcocks
University of Leicester

Part I
PROBLEMS OF TRANSITION
Maurice Galton

1 CHANGING TEACHERS AND CHANGING SCHOOLS

The main subject matter of this book, the fourth to be produced as a result of the ORACLE project, deals with an issue which is of concern to most parents: the effect on their children as they move each year from one teacher to another. If an observer were to mingle with parents waiting for their sons or daughters to come out of school, she might frequently hear it claimed that a particular child had learnt little under Mr A, while in the previous year Miss B could get him to do almost anything. Such statements, if true, are particularly relevant to the primary school where, for a considerable period during the year, pupils have contact with only one teacher.

There are a number of interesting questions to be asked about the effects on pupils when they move to a new class within a school at the beginning of a year. Do teachers change their teaching styles to meet the needs of children in the new intake, as is often claimed, or do the pupils have to change their behaviour to fit in with the demands made on them by the new teacher? Is it the same teachers each year who tend to get the best academic results from their pupils or is it the proportions of certain types of pupil within the class that make the difference? About such questions of consistency of teaching style, pupil behaviour and performance there is no shortage of opinions available but little firm evidence. In this country there has been only one small-scale study where the same teachers were observed at work in the classroom over a period of two years (Gray, 1979). Generally, however, researchers who have shown interest in such problems have chosen to examine what on the surface appears to be a potentially more traumatic change: the transfer from primary school to the secondary stage of education.

PREVIOUS RESEARCH ON TRANSFER

Research into school transfer has been mainly concerned with the changes in anxiety, motivation and achievement after the move to the secondary school. The findings of the most important studies so far undertaken in this country have recently been reviewed by Spelman (1979).

Where the pupils' anxiety has been measured before and after transfer the studies all reach similar conclusions about the effect of the move to the new school. To summarize briefly, the research shows that prior to transfer over two-thirds of the pupils express some measure of anxiety about the change, but that these may be sub-divided into children who are apprehensive and wish to remain with their own teacher and those who look forward but with some trepidation to the challenges provided by the new school. These latter pupils appear to welcome the wider range of subjects and activities which will be on offer after transfer while at the same time expressing a certain disquiet about how they will cope with the new environment. By the end of the first six months, only about 10 per cent of children have not adjusted to the change (Nisbet and Entwistle, 1969; Youngman and Lunzer, 1977). This small minority tends to have learning problems and to remain totally unreconciled to the move away from the primary school.

With respect to achievement the progress that pupils make after transfer has generally been assessed in terms of scores on tests of mathematics and English. The research shows that the progress pupils make after transfer is, for the majority, a reflection of their level of achievement towards the end of their time in the primary school (Youngman, 1980).

The pupils' academic motivation and their attitude to work are also important correlates of improved performance after transfer. It was suggested by Nisbet and Entwistle that although these 'transfer problems' are mainly of a transient nature, to do with settling into the new school, they do seem 'to leave their mark on children's academic performance throughout the first year at secondary school' (Nisbet and Entwistle, 1969).

One study has paid particular attention to the needs of low-achieving pupils after transfer (Youngman, 1978). Three types of poor achievers were identified, two of which made no progress in the year following the move to secondary school. The two groups differed, however, in that only one was worried about poor performance. Youngman suggests that each of these three types of pupil needs to be watched carefully over the first few months after transfer and wherever possible given positive discrimination. There is also evidence for the existence of a small group of children who do much better than expected after transfer (BEDC, 1975). These pupils seem to have outgrown primary school well before leaving it and have often been a nuisance to their teachers there. They have found the curriculum unstimulating, and are excited and challenged by the new range of activities which they experience after transfer. These findings, like those of Youngman, suggest that day-to-day progress of certain children needs to be carefully monitored, particularly during the first six weeks in the new school.

LIMITATIONS OF PREVIOUS RESEARCH

What this research fails to provide, however, is information about the experiences of these pupils during the final year in the old school and the first year in the new one. Without this information it is difficult to be certain of the reasons for the changes which take place during the transfer year as measured by achievement tests and attitude inventories, and without such explanations it is difficult to suggest to teachers how any detrimental effects might be minimized. Thus while Youngman and Lunzer recommend that teachers ought to watch certain pupils carefully, they are unable to direct the teachers' attention to particular aspects of the child's behaviour that would bear scrutiny.

Such information can be obtained only when the researcher spends time in the primary and secondary schools observing the actual transfer process. One early study which did this (Nash, 1973) reported, for example, that children's ideas of what secondary schools were like, prior to entry, were largely misconceived because their teachers in the primary school shared these false impressions and passed them on. The secondary school teachers also had a false picture of activities in the primary school so that the work they set pupils during the first weeks after transfer was very often either inappropriate or repetitive. Pupils were therefore ill prepared for their experience of secondary education and had to adjust their ideas and working methods considerably during the first weeks in their new school. Pupils who failed to adjust quickly began to experience some of the difficulties documented by the other studies. Nash found that, in the primary schools he observed, the curriculum was dominated by the teaching of basic skills, particularly in the final year. All these feeder schools transferred to the same secondary school where in the first two years pupils were housed in a separate base area and the emphasis was on integrated subject teaching and 'activity' methods. In most reports on transfer great emphasis is placed on achieving continuity in the curriculum and the production of suitable records for the correct placement of children in the new school (Sumner and Bradley, 1977). Nash is the only researcher to hint at the possible discontinuity between teaching methods in a way which conflicts with accepted notions of primary and secondary practice.

CLASSROOM ISSUES - CHANGING TEACHERS

Nash's study was a relatively small-scale one and lacks the support of other similar investigations. However, in raising the issue of discontinuity in teaching methods it broadens the debate about transfer considerably. For if Nash is correct and one of the important determinants of pupils' adjustment is the ease with which they adapt to new teaching methods then the 'transfer problem' is not primarily one of changing schools but of changing teachers. In that case many of the difficulties which children face when they move from one teacher to another within a school may be reproduced when they meet new teachers in

different schools. The experience of pupils as they move up
through the primary school may therefore be an important factor
in their adjustment to secondary school. Most studies concerned
with transfer, however, collect information about the pupils for
only a short period before they leave the primary school. Unless
the researcher extends the period of study so that children are
followed for at least two years prior to transfer it is not possible
to say, with any degree of certainty, whether failure to adjust
is chiefly attributable to the change in school or whether it is
more affected by the change of teacher. It may be that many
of the so-called transfer problems are really problems of schooling in general brought about by a move from one class to the
next.

TRANSFER AND THE ROLE OF THE MIDDLE SCHOOL

Another important issue concerned with transfer arises from the
development, in recent years, of the middle school. At the
beginning of 1968 there were no middle schools in the United
Kingdom. Ten years later, there were 1,690 (Hargreaves and
Tickle, 1980). These schools have spawned a variety of ages of
transfer. Although after considering much conflicting evidence
the 1967 Plowden Committee Report came out in favour of the
8-12 pattern, with the advent of 9-13, 10-14 and 11-14 schools
pupils in some parts of the country are preparing to leave one
school for another at any age between 7 and 14. There is little
empirical evidence about what constitutes the 'best' age for
transfer. If Nisbet and Entwistle's (1969) assessment that the
after-effects of transfer leave their mark on children's academic
performance throughout the first year in the new school is
correct then middle schools could exacerbate this problem. The
more transfers a pupil makes during his progression from the
first year in the infant school to the final year in the secondary
one the more disruptions to his academic progress there will be.
   Blyth and Derricott (1977) argue that middle schools were
originally established because they were, for many local authorities, the only viable way of going comprehensive. They have
since been justified on educational grounds as a means of
extending child-centred practice into the secondary sector, but
over the years this *extension* model has been replaced by an
emphasis on the *unique identity* of middle school provision
(Hargreaves, 1980). Schools are no longer viewed as an
administrative necessity providing frequent breaks in the
child's education but as the 'creation of a transition period that
will smooth rather than interrupt the change from what is distinctively 'primary' to work that is distinctively 'secondary',
(Schools Council, 1972, p. 8). According to this argument any
hold up in performance should be decreased as a result. So far
however, there is no systematic body of evidence available about
the effects of transfer in and out of middle schools. The design

of the ORACLE Study makes it possible to obtain such evidence.

THE DESIGN OF THE TRANSFER STUDY

In one important respect the decision to investigate the transfer
of pupils from the primary school was a crucial one. The
selection of the six transfer schools automatically determined the
sample of primary schools in which the main ORACLE studies
would be conducted. Because of the variety of patterns of comprehensive schooling it was decided to observe the transfer
process in three different local authority areas where the three
common types of transfer operated. In local authority A children
attended the first school until the age of 9 and then transferred
to middle schools where they stayed until they were 13. In this
authority the transfer into the 9-13 middle school was observed.
The schools in local authority B followed the more common
pattern where children attended the infants department from 5
until 7 and then transferred to the junior school from 7 until 11.
In local authority B they then transferred to 11-14 middle
schools. In local authority C children stayed in their first
school until 8 and then moved to the middle school until the age
of 12 where they transferred to the high school. In this authority
transfer out of the 8-12 schools was examined.
  In each local authority a pair of schools was selected to which
pupils from the primary sample would eventually transfer. The
schools were chosen mainly because of the contrast in their
approach to the problems of pupil adjustment after transfer.
In broad terms schools tend to adopt, with certain modifications,
one of two main approaches. Some of the schools try to maintain
the organization of the primary school by preserving the idea of
the non-specialist class teacher and giving the first-year pupils
a separate identity by providing special facilities for them. For
example, pupils may have their own special base area in the
school and their own play areas. In contrast to this approach
other schools feel that it is better for the pupils to enjoy a new
status when they move up from the primary school. They therefore integrate new pupils as much as possible into the general
life of the school. There are no separate play areas or first-year
assemblies and the teachers whom the children meet will usually
be specialists in particular subject areas.
  It is also likely that organizational decisions about the arrangements for teaching the first-year pupils will, in part, reflect
more deep-seated ideological differences about the aims and
practices of education in the middle school (Hargreaves and
Tickle, 1980). Schools which maintain the primary organization
will also be more likely to favour an informal style in relation
to such matters as streaming and setting, placing the emphasis
on intrinsic forms of motivation rather than urging children to
compete, and emphasizing social as well as academic outcomes.
Schools which provide a system more akin to the secondary

school will tend to emphasize the academic goals, give tests regularly and favour plenty of competition through the use of stars and house points. Most of these practices are well documented in an earlier study of secondary school values (King, 1973). Bridging as they do the primary and secondary sectors, middle schools, which in many cases have still to develop their own special identities, serve as an ideal environment to study the effects of these different ideologies and practices on children.

Some of the aims of modern primary practice concern long-term outcomes. It is claimed, for example, that informal methods develop greater self-reliance in children so that they can cope all the better with the varied experiences afforded by different secondary schools (Blackie, 1967). It is therefore of interest to see just what are the experiences of pupils in moving to schools where there are distinct ideological differences and practices of the kind described above.

CHARACTERISTICS OF THE TRANSFER SCHOOLS

Accordingly a number of characteristics of the type described by King (compulsory uniform, setting and banding, house systems, etc.) were added to descriptions of the organizational and curriculum arrangements in order to create two contrasting 'ideal' types of transfer school. These descriptions were then sent to the advisers in the three local authorities who were each asked to rate pairs of schools from the same or adjacent catchment areas in terms of the various 'ideal' characteristics. The pair of schools with the largest overall rating difference was then selected and the heads of the schools were invited to participate in the study. Having secured the agreement of the heads of the two nominated schools in each local authority area to take part in the study, all feeder primary schools were invited to take part in the main ORACLE study assessing teacher effectiveness. Only if all the feeder primary schools agreed to participate was it then possible to accept the adviser's nomination. Local authority C was the only case where the original nominations of the advisory team had to be replaced by the second most extreme pair because only some of the feeder schools agreed to participate. In local authority C children in the (8-12) feeder schools could transfer to a number of schools. It was therefore very difficult to predict at the start of the study the exact number of target pupils available two years on. The potential number in the sample became smaller when one of the feeder schools decided not to participate because of their involvement in another project. By the time the headteacher reached this decision it was too late to re-select another pair of transfer schools. The contrast there is not so sharp as in the other two authorities on account of this fact and also because the children were prepared for public examinations so that the secondary influence was stronger in both schools.

Table 1.1 *Main characteristics of the six transfer schools*

Local Authority	A		B		C	
School-type Identity	Secondary (AST)	Primary (APT)	Secondary (BST)	Primary (BPT)	Secondary (CST)	Primary (CPT)
Age-range of pupils	9–13	9–13	11–14	11–14	12–18	12–18
First-year base	No	Yes	No	Yes	No	No
First-year play area	No	Yes	No	Yes	Yes	Yes
First-year assembly	No	Yes	No	Yes	No	Yes
Higher proportion of teaching done by one teacher	No	Yes	No	Yes	No	No
Official school uniform	Yes	No	Yes	Yes	Yes	No
Setting or banding by ability for maths/English	Yes	No	Yes	No	Yes	Yes
Setting or banding in some other subjects e.g. French/science	Yes	No	Yes	No	Yes	No
Stars or conduct marks awarded	Yes	No	No	No	No	No

The main characteristics of the six transfer schools are shown in Table 1.1. A full description of the feeder schools has already been provided in 'Inside the Primary Classroom'. Although the latter were a self-selected sample, all the available evidence suggests that they were reasonably representative of suburban and urban village schools on the outskirts of major conurbations.

In the earlier ORACLE books all schools in the study were referred to as primary. With the discussion of the transfer issue, however, it becomes difficult to retain this simple distinction because transfer schools in local authority A (9 - 13) only extend the age range studied by one year compared to the so-called primary schools in local authority C (8 - 12). Accordingly, throughout this book, all schools to which pupils transfer are called *transfer* schools while all schools from which the pupils moved are referred to as *feeder* schools and sometimes, to clarify a point, *primary feeder* schools.

Within each pair of transfer schools in the three local authorities a further distinction has to be made. In the first volume, 'Inside the Primary Classroom', use of the all-embracing terms traditional and progressive or formal and informal was avoided because, as used by critics of modern primary practice, they failed to represent the complexity of life in the primary classroom. Nevertheless, the transfer schools were chosen to reflect certain differences in the use of practices associated with progressivism. At the same time they were also distinguished by their attempts to retain the primary style of organization, particularly those middle schools in local authorities A and B. For this latter reason it was decided to distinguish between *primary-type* schools and *secondary-type* schools. Consequently a primary-type transfer school in local authority A is referred to as school APT throughout the book while a secondary-type transfer school in local authority C will be known as school CST.

Throughout Chapters 6, 7 and 8 of the book, in particular, there are extended quotations from the accounts written by observers of what the teachers and pupils did and said during lessons. To preserve anonymity all teachers are referred to by a letter from the alphabet, Miss X and Mr Y, or, when the twenty-six letters of the alphabet have been used, by Mrs McA or Mr McB. Pupils, however, were given pseudonyms. None of the names in the book is unbelievable but some are a little unusual. Where a pupil had a striking name, such as Gianetta, a pseudonym such as Estelle was given, but where a name was straightforward, such as John, a plain pseudonym such as Dick was used.

From the data in Table 1.1 it can be seen that the sharpest contrasts are to be found in the 9-13 schools in local authority A. At school AST, a former secondary modern school, pupils were placed in one of two bands on entry as a result of information provided by the feeder schools. The children stayed in their formroom only for those lessons given by the form teacher. The curriculum included a course on librarianship and practice in handwriting, which was labelled theory on the timetable. Pupils could expect to see as many teachers as there were periods during the day. There was much emphasis on the need to wear the correct uniform (no less than three manufacturers exhibited at the parents' evening) and there were stars for work and good and bad marks for conduct. Form captains and monitors were elected and there was even a 'messenger of the day', a solitary pupil who sat in the main hall outside the headmistress's study waiting for the summons to deliver messages to other staff in far-flung outposts of the school.

In contrast school APT was a purpose-built middle school with four base areas built around a central complex containing the gymnasium and the administrative offices. Each base area consisted of three classrooms, but due to changes in the local authority's policy with regard to comprehensive education there had been few occasions previously when the number of pupils fitted exactly into the base area. In the year in which the pupils were observed (1977-8) all the 9-year-olds were contained in the first-year complex in three classes. Although, as will emerge in the later chapters, the children were taught by almost as many teachers as the pupils in AST, the majority of teaching was done by the form teacher. The curriculum was also organized in a very similar way to that in the previous school and as far as possible children were encouraged to organize and plan their own learning. In APT, there was no compulsory school uniform although many children wore jumpers of the same colour. According to the school's prospectus, pupils were encouraged to improve for their own personal satisfaction rather than for the reward of getting more marks than another child.

The two schools in local authority B were built side by side along with a 14-18 upper school to which the pupils would eventually move. Both schools were purpose built and were similar in design. Although the distinctive features found between the two schools in local authority A were less marked, there were still a number of elements which served to distinguish the two. School BPT had a first-year base area with a separate adjacent play area. Although mathematics and science were taught by specialist teachers this school operated a common curriculum for social studies across all the classes and this was taught by the form teacher who in most cases also taught English. As at APT, when the form teacher was not with the class, the majority of periods were taken by other teachers from within the base area so that, for example, the two teachers who were science-trained took all the forms for science and were replaced at these times in their own forms by other teachers from the base area who were French specialists. Thus, in both BPT and APT when the pupils had to have other teachers they tended to come from a small group of the staff who were seen around a great deal within the base area. At BST, as at AST, the pupils moved around the school much more and went to different rooms for different subjects. They shared their

assembly with the second-year pupils and were placed in sets
at the beginning of the year with the aid of an internal examination.

The two schools in local authority C showed much less differentiation in terms of both the school organization and the
curriculum. Here pupils were transferring from middle schools
into ones where choices about 'O' level or CSE courses would be
made one year after entry. The curriculum in both schools was
therefore geared closely towards these examinations. The schools
were much larger and, as a consequence, the organization more
complex, so that decisions about whether pupils should move to
the teacher or the teacher should come to the pupils were made
on administrative grounds. Thus, for example, in school CST
which was rated by the advisers the more formal of the two
schools, the pupils were housed in their own base area consisting of a series of terrapin huts. They tended to play in the
area directly outside these buildings which thus became their
own playground. According to availability of rooms elsewhere in
the school teachers either came to the huts or the pupils went
off to other parts of the school, especially for activities such as
science, languages or craft, requiring specialist equipment.
Some of the craft work was also carried out in an annexe on the
other side of the main road because of the severe shortage of
accommodation. At school CPT the formrooms were scattered all
over the school but the pupils had their own first-year assembly;
although a standard form of dress was highly recommended, it
was not made compulsory. At CST, however, if a pupil turned
up in the wrong coloured shirt or pullover, he could be sent
home. Nevertheless at CPT there was less emphasis on practices
such as streaming so that, for example, French was taught to
mixed-ability groups whereas at CST it was taught in streamed
sets.

RESEARCH METHODS USED IN THE TRANSFER STUDY

The main research technique employed in the ORACLE research
is that of systematic observation or interaction analysis. During
each year of the study a selection of pupils and their teachers
were observed every term and their behaviour coded under a
number of pre-specified categories. The two instruments used in
this study, the Pupil Record and the Teacher Record (Boydell,
1974; 1975) have been described in detail in 'Inside the Primary
Classroom' (pp. 11-21). Copies of the schedules are reproduced
in Appendix A.

In the transfer study, besides systematic observation, another
technique known as participant observation was used. Unlike a
systematic observer who adopts the role of a 'fly on a wall' a
participant observer will take as active a part as possible in the
classroom in order to try to understand what it is like to be part
of this process. The observer writes detailed case notes of all

that is seen and heard and will supplement these with interviews
with both teacher and pupils in order to compare and contrast
different points of view. Details of the method are presented in
the introduction to Part IV of this volume, and a fuller discussion
of the techniques can also be found in Cohen and Manion (1980).

There were sound practical reasons for adopting this participant approach since to have observed pupils during their early
weeks in the transfer school using systematic observation would
have presented severe logistical problems. In the main ORACLE
study eight pupils were selected in each class according to their
scores on the Richmond Tests of basic skills (France and Fraser,
1975). These tests were administered at the beginning of the
research and for each class the scores of the pupils on the combined tests of mathematics, language skills and reading comprehension were divided into four quartiles. One boy and one girl
were randomly selected from each of the top and bottom quartiles.
In the same way another two boys and two girls were selected
from the two middle quartiles, making a total of eight target
children in each class on whom the observations were carried out.
In a primary feeder school with two parallel forms, the sixteen
target pupils who were observed might eventually find themselves allocated to any one of six sets for mathematics after
moving to a secondary transfer school.

To continue to observe all these pupils it would have been
necessary to employ six observers, since in some schools the
lessons tended to take place at the same time in the block
allocated in the timetable. The same would have been true of
English periods in some cases so that the demands on the
observer were considerably increased, not only by the tendency
to set in these subjects at secondary level, but also because,
unlike in the feeder schools, the teaching was done by subject
specialists. Thus the number of teachers needing to be observed
would have rapidly increased. While it was thought necessary
to continue to collect some systematic observation data about
pupils in order to compare their behaviour after transfer with
that seen during the previous two years in the primary feeder
school, this part of the programme had to be tailored to the
manpower and resources available. Accordingly, it was decided
that in each transfer school systematic observation would be
carried out only in the two mathematics and English sets which
contained the highest number of target pupils.

For participant observation two classes were chosen in each
transfer school. In schools where a banding system was not in
use the two classes were those which contained the largest
number of target pupils from the previous year. In schools
where banding was in operation two classes in different bands,
with the highest number of targets were chosen. The practice
in all the transfer schools was not to set for science during the
first year. Some systematic observation was also carried out in
this subject area because, given the well-established disparity
between the sexes when pupils opt for science at secondary level

(Kelly, 1981), it was of interest to see if teachers tended to differentiate in any way between boys and girls during the first lessons in this subject.

OTHER MEASURES USED IN THE STUDY

As in the first year of the research, achievement in basic skills was measured using the Richmond Tests (France and Fraser, 1975). These tests consisting of reading, language skills and mathematics were developed from the American IOWA tests of basic skills and were designed for use with children between the ages of 8 and 13. Each test was divided into six levels corresponding to the six year-groups. Short versions of the tests were used in this research in order to limit the amount of testing which pupils had to undergo. Full details can be found in 'Progress and Performance in the Primary Classroom'.

In addition to these measures of attainment, information about the pupils' liking of school, level of motivation and anxiety was also collected by means of a short questionnaire derived and adapted from that used by Bennett (1976) in the Lancaster study. The shortened version used in this present research was based on an instrument called 'What I Do In School' (WIDIS). The problems of constructing such questionnaires and their limitations were discussed in more detail in 'Progress and Performance in the Primary Classroom' (pp. 150-1).

TIMETABLE OF OBSERVATIONS AND TEST ADMINISTRATION

The ORACLE research programme necessitated fairly complex organization and timetabling. The main study concerned the description of the classroom process and the evaluation of different types of teaching style in terms of the pupils' progress on a variety of achievement measures. The second and third strands of study examined the effects on pupil performance and behaviour when moving class within the primary school (consistency studies) and when moving schools (the transfer study).

In the process-product study, in addition to the Richmond Tests, other achievement measures were used including a series of specially constructed activities designed to tap skills required for independent study. While it would have proved desirable to continue to administer these study skill exercises to the pupils even when they had transferred to the secondary school, this proved impracticable because the teachers involved felt that the presence of two observers carrying out different types of observation during the course of the year made sufficient demands. In consultation with the teachers it was therefore agreed to limit the testing programme to the administration of the tests of basic skills at the end of the year and to administer the WIDIS questionnaire at the beginning of November and again in the summer.

Table 1.2   Timetable for observation and testing in the transfer study

	Local authority A	Local authority B	Local authority C
Sept. 1976	First administration of Richmond Tests plus shortened version of the WIDIS questionnaire		
	Systematic observation of target pupils		
Oct. 1976 onwards	pupils aged 8+	pupils aged 8+ and 9+	pupils aged 10+
June 1977	Second administration of Richmond Tests and WIDIS		
July 1977	Observation of pre-transfer arrangements, parents' meetings, pupil visits, etc.		
Sept. 1977	Participant observation for first weeks after transfer. Two classes in each school		
Oct. 1977	Participant observation plus systematic observation of a sample of target pupils in maths/English and and science lessons	Systematic observation of same target pupils as in previous year	
		pupils aged 9+ and 10+	pupils aged 11+
Nov. 1977	Third administration of WIDIS		
June 1978	Third administration of Richmond Tests and WIDIS (fourth administration of WIDIS for transfer school sample)		
July 1978		Observation of pre-transfer arrangements parents' meeting and pupil visits	
Sept. 1978		Participant observation of first four weeks in the new schools; four schools (two classes per school)	
Oct. 1978 onwards		Participant observation and systematic observation of pupils in transfer schools	
Nov. 1978		Administration of WIDIS in transfer schools	
June 1979		Final administration of Richmond Tests and WIDIS. Pupils' essay on transfer	

The timetable shown in Table 1.2 gives details of the observation procedures and test administrations which were relevant
to the consistency and transfer studies. It will be seen that
in local authority A the transfer study in the 9-13 middle schools
was begun one year earlier than in the other two areas. This
was an attempt to develop a number of hypotheses during the
time spent in these schools which could then be re-examined and
checked during the observations of the following year.

SOME MAJOR THEMES FOR STUDY

This book is therefore about a series of interrelated problems
concerning the effects on pupils' behaviour and achievement
when they change teachers or move schools. These two issues
are interrelated because when pupils transfer from one school
to another they must inevitably also change teachers. It is
possible therefore that some of the effects attributable to the
transfer process can, in part, be accounted for by the difficulties pupils face in adjusting to teachers with different styles.
    Part II of this book concerns an important theme of the
ORACLE study, the behaviour of teachers and pupils in the
primary classroom and the relationship between these interaction
patterns and pupil behaviour after transfer. Here the data from
year 2 of the observation is used to replicate and extend the
findings already presented in two earlier volumes, 'Inside the
Primary Classroom' and 'Progress and Performance in the Primary
Classroom'. Previous research on transfer has reported that the
effects on pupils are mainly short term, but primary teachers
must surely hope that what their pupils learn while with them
will continue to be of benefit throughout the time these pupils
spend at secondary school. When pupils transfer out of the
primary school they are expected not only to have mastered the
basic skills of mathematics, reading and writing but also to have
acquired good habits of independent study and to have developed
social and personal skills. The results reported in previous
volumes, however, suggest that in the average primary classroom, containing upwards of thirty children, these objectives
are difficult if not impossible to achieve, particularly when
pupils are taught individually rather than as a class or in
groups.
    There is little reason to think that the management of children's
learning in the transfer school classrooms is any less difficult
than the ORACLE research found it to be in the feeder schools.
On the other hand, there may be pupils whose patterns of
working and interaction enable them to cope more easily with
such difficulties even while they are still at primary school and
it is of interest to see whether they then cope more easily with
similar effects after transfer. Thus in Chapter 2, where changes
in pupils' behaviour as they move up in the primary school are
examined, an attempt is made to identify those pupils who seem

to be less affected by changes in teaching style as they move
from one year to the next.

In Chapter 3 the attention is directed to the behaviour of the
same pupils after they have transferred to the new schools and
encountered new teachers. The extent to which teaching styles
differ in the transfer schools will be investigated, as will the
effect of such styles on the pupils. In the earlier volumes it was
strongly argued that the teaching style was a dominant influence
on pupils' behaviour and it is therefore of interest to see how
children cope when they begin to have different subject teachers
who use different styles.

Part III concerns the progress that pupils make before and
after transfer which is dealt with in Chapters 4 and 5 respectively. Earlier studies have claimed that a number of children,
although adjusting quickly to the new school, nevertheless do
less well academically during the first year. With the growth of
middle schools this raises important issues about the best age
for transfer and the wisdom of increasing the number of such
transitions throughout a child's time at school. The data
presented here is clearly relevant to these issues since it compares the progress that pupils make at different ages of transfer
with that of pupils who, though of similar age, were not involved
in a move.

Part IV of the book concerns the manner in which the children
adjust to the work, the teachers and the pupils from other
feeder schools. Participant observation is used for this purpose,
providing qualitative descriptions of the experiences of different
pupils after transfer to different types of school. Earlier studies
have all shown that children who adjust badly to transfer
develop considerable anxiety coping with the work and getting on
with the teachers. Chapter 6 describes the curriculum which the
child experiences on entry to the new school, while Chapter 7
examines how teachers begin to establish a relationship with the
pupils and initiate them into new ways of working. Then in
Chapter 8 the pupil's view of his experience is described.

The final part of the book reviews and brings up to date many
of the ideas developed in the earlier volumes. It seeks to explain
the findings in terms of existing explanations of classroom practice and goes on to suggest how these might be modified to
accommodate data coming from the ORACLE study. The problems
of making use of these findings within current programmes of
initial and in-service training, a recurrent theme of this series,
will again be discussed.

At the end of the book an earlier conclusion that in the primary
school teaching style is one of the most important determinants
of pupil progress will be shown to remain true after transfer
also. This result is an important one. It suggests that many of
the difficulties experienced by children, which teachers attribute
to the effects of the transfer, may have more to do with problems
of schooling and teaching in general than with transition in
particular.

Part II
PUPILS IN TRANSITION

John Willcocks

2 TEACHERS AND PUPILS BEFORE TRANSFER

The two chapters in this section concern the main theme of this book: what happens to pupils when they move to new teachers.

The present chapter examines the effects on the children in the ORACLE study when they changed classes within their primary feeder schools, while Chapter 3 looks at a potentially more disturbing change in which a sub-sample of pupils was observed after their move to the more complex organizational structure of the transfer schools.

In 'Progress and Performance in the Primary Classroom' it was shown that the behaviour and achievement levels of pupils are significantly influenced by their teacher's style. It was not possible in the context of that study of a single year's data to do more than raise the question of the extent to which the teacher's style is in turn influenced by the balance of pupil types in her class. However, the children who took part in the study were observed for a further two years during the course of which most of them moved to new teachers and some of them moved to new schools. The accumulated data from three years of observation permit an examination of the extent to which various types of pupil continue to behave in a consistent way when they move to the class of a new teacher, and the extent to which the new teacher's style influences this consistency. It is now also possible to examine whether a teacher's style is pre-dominantly a determinant of or a response to pupil activity, and which of these in turn exerts the greater influence on pupil achievement.

TEACHING STYLES

As defined in the ORACLE study, teaching style is basically a matter of the teacher's preferred kinds of task-oriented and managerial interaction with the pupils in her class. These inter-actions may involve conversation or they may be silent. Task-oriented interactions range from probing, open-ended questions to simple guidance about what to do next or the silent demonstra-tion of a piece of equipment. Managerial interactions range from carefully planned sets of instructions to entirely reactive com-ments like 'Stop this silly noise!' or pregnant pauses calculated to influence pupil behaviour.

Faced with a class of pupils, a teacher must make a series of choices about how to deal with the many different kinds of demand they make on her, and how to impose her own demands upon them. At any given moment some of the children may be clamouring for her attention, some working steadily on their own or in groups, and some chattering, looking out of the window or otherwise avoiding approved activities. Among those in this last category, some may be incorrigible time-wasters while others may simply have got stuck with their work and grown tired of trying to attract the teacher's attention, or have been temporarily distracted by their neighbours. For her part the teacher may be wanting to teach a new skill, start a campaign against untidiness, get a display of work ready for open day, or organize any one of a large number of activities.

Among the first of her choices must be a decision about whether to respond or initiate, to meet demands or impose them; and leading from this will come a decision about her prevailing mode of interaction. She must decide whether she will try on the whole to deal with the children individually, in groups or as a whole class; or whether she will switch from one of these modes to another as the occasion seems to demand. In principle any kind of task-oriented or managerial interaction can take place within any mode, although in practice the preferred strategies for classroom organization of the teachers in the ORACLE sample tended to impose limitations upon the range of kinds of interaction which they generally used.

Individual monitors

As reported in 'Inside the Primary Classroom' (Chapter 7), teachers who made considerable use of individual attention very rarely developed probing, challenging exchanges with their pupils. The reason for this seems very straightforward, since teachers who opted for a largely individual approach set themselves an enormous if not insuperable problem. However hard they worked they found themselves constantly in a situation where every child but one in the class was unattended. The pressure upon them therefore was constantly to move on to another child, and then to another and another, so that pupils would not be kept waiting too long. This being so, their interactions with children tended to be brief, and were generally concerned with the checking of work, often in silence, and the giving of instructions for the next task. Because of this great emphasis on the simple monitoring of work the teachers who adopted this style were termed *individual monitors*.

Class enquirers

Those who went to the other extreme devoted about a third of their time to class teaching, and less time than the other groups to individual interactions. They also spent very little time dealing with pupils in groups. This strategy freed them from the constant pressure faced by the individual monitors and enabled them to devote time to the development of an extended enquiry approach to the teaching and development of pupil skills.

They asked more questions than other teachers, particularly in relation to class work. Specifically they made maximum use of questions and statements of ideas and problems rather than of simple straightforward facts. Their emphasis on problem-solving and ideas led to their title of *class enquirers*.

Group instructors
A third set of teachers favoured the strategy of interaction with their pupils in groups, and on average they made about three times as much use of group work as the rest of the sample. It might have been expected that this policy would have freed them to develop the kind of enquiry approach which was common among the class enquirers and to encourage co-operative work among their pupils. However, on the whole this did not seem to happen. The interactions of a number of them were largely didactic or concerned with feedback on work already accomplished. Although co-operation on tasks was higher among their pupils than among those of teachers using other styles, it still accounted for only 6.5 per cent of all observations. Thus group work seems often to have been used for its organizational advantages rather than for the educational possibilities which it has been thought to offer (Plowden, 1967). This finding is mirrored in the report 'Primary Education in England', in which HM Inspectors describe a tendency, in a number of classes where children often sat in ability groups, for individual assignments to be set when 'it would have been more appropriate to draw the group together' (HMI, 1978). It may be that for many teachers the pressure of unattended groups in a class turns out to be as great as the pressure of children working individually. Certainly the possibilities for co-operative endeavour which are offered by group work seem to be difficult to put into practice. Because of their emphasis on information giving, the teachers who favoured group interaction were termed *group instructors*.

Infrequent changers
Almost half of the teachers adopted the strategy of changing their modes of interaction, using the interactional characteristics of a specific style when they switched to its pattern of organization. Three main types of *style changers* were identified. Teachers in the first sub-group began the year by using one of the three styles already mentioned, but later on, when they felt they could achieve more by a change of organizational strategy, they switched to one of the other styles. For example, one teacher began the year as an individual monitor, but realizing that this style was depriving her of time to develop stimulating exchanges with her pupils, she began to devote more time to whole-class teaching, thus becoming a class enquirer. Another teacher began the year as a class enquirer, but later, when he felt he had trained the children in the discipline of working on their own, spent more time on individual assignments and thus became an individual monitor. Teachers in this sub-

group achieved the highest level of interaction of all styles,
including the highest overall level of questioning, and a relatively
high proportion of statements of ideas and of feedback to the
pupils. The flexibility of these teachers paid handsome dividends
in terms of their pupils' achievement levels; and to distinguish
them from the other two sub-groups who changed their style
rather frequently, they were termed *infrequent changers*.

Rotating and habitual changers
The teachers in the other two sub-groups were much more like
each other than they were like infrequent changers, in that
they were much less successful and they changed style far more
often. However, they did differ from each other both in their
organizational strategies and their interaction patterns. One
sub-group placed their pupils in groups which rotated from one
curricular area to the next by moving bodily to the relevant
table, the whole class shifting position at given points during
the day. Among this sub-group, who were termed *rotating
changers,* there was a high level of questions relating to task
supervision, and of 'critical control' in response to disciplinary
problems. The other sub-group made irregular and apparently
unplanned changes between class and individualized instruction,
often as a response to pupils whose behaviour was causing
difficulties. This sub-group, who were termed *habitual changers*,
made relatively little use of questions (particularly those of an
open-ended or probing nature) or of statements of ideas. The
time spent in interaction with pupils was the lowest of the entire
sample.

REPLICATION OF TEACHING STYLES

The identification of the four main teaching styles was carried
out by means of a cluster analysis of the first year's data from
the systematic observation schedule, the Teacher Record, which
is comprehensively described in 'Inside the Primary Classroom'.
Cluster analysis is a numerical technique which sorts people into
groups in such a way that each individual has more characteristics in common with fellow members of his own group than with
people belonging to other groups.
    When the observational data from the second year became
available, they were subjected to the same kind of analysis, in
order to discover whether the first year's teaching styles would
be replicated. A full account of this replication study is to be
found in Appendix B of 'Progress and Performance in the Primary
Classroom': in summary it can be said that the two cluster
analyses gave similar groupings of teachers in the two years.
The relationship between the audience and content of interactions remained much the same. The single exception to this was
the discovery of a number of teachers using group interaction
in a different, and possibly more interesting and challenging,

fashion from those in the first year's sample, although this change was not accompanied by any increase in the amount of co-operative group work.

The numbers and relative proportions of teachers using each of the teaching styles in the first and second years of observation is shown in Table 2.1. Because of their general similarity to each other the rotating and habitual changers are combined in this analysis.

Table 2.1 Numbers and proportions of teachers using each teaching style during the first and second years of observation

	Year 1		Year 2	
	N	%	N	%
Individual monitors	13	22.4	4	10.0
Class enquirers	9	15.5	5	12.5
Group instructors	7	12.1	15	37.5
Infrequent changers	6	10.3	4	10.0
Other changers	23	39.6	12	30.0
	58	100.0	40	100.0

The principal difference between the two years' data is the greatly increased proportion of group instructors in the second year, and the corresponding decrease in the proportions of the other styles, in particular of individual monitors and rotating and habitual changers. It should be emphasized that whereas the same pupils were observed throughout the three-year period of the study, the teacher data considered here are in the main from different teachers each year. Only fourteen of the forty teachers observed during the first year were also observed during the second; the remaining twenty-six teachers were new-comers to the study. This being so, there would be no reason to expect that the relative proportions of the various styles would be similar in the two samples. One advantage of the change in proportions of teaching styles in the second year is that it permits an examination of the effect on pupils of a change in the balance of teaching styles, and thus highlights the teachers' influence on their pupils' work and behaviour patterns.

PUPIL TYPES

The data derived from the first year's observation of the pupils' behaviour were subjected to the same kind of cluster analysis as that used on the Teacher Record data. Four groups (or pupil types) emerged, characterized chiefly by their varying amounts of work and interaction with other pupils, and by both the quantity and the quality of their interactions with the teacher. Again, a replication study was carried out on the second year's data, and this confirmed the main findings of the first year, yielding the same four distinctive patterns of classroom behaviour.

However, since the sample of pupils, unlike the sample of teachers, included in the second year only individuals who had been observed in the first year, any marked change in the balance of the four pupil types will require an examination of the factors which may have brought it about.

Before penetrating further into this matter it is necessary to outline the characteristic behaviour of each pupil type. Detailed descriptions are given in 'Inside the Primary Classroom', and also in 'Progress and Performance in the Primary Classroom'.

In general, it is the children in the first two groups who have the most active relationship with the teacher. Those in the first group, the *attention seekers,* seem to seek her out, while those in the second group, the *intermittent workers,* persistently avoid her. The pupils in the other two groups, the *solitary workers* and the *quiet collaborators* seem to fade into the background for much of the time, the main difference between them lying in the extent to which they work on their own or with other pupils.

The attention seekers

Although the typical *attention seeker* is busily occupied on his task or on associated routine activities for two-thirds of the time, he will seek out the teacher far more frequently than will the typical member of any other group, consequently spending a great deal of time moving about the classroom or waiting at the teacher's desk. He is not trying to avoid work, but rather seeking constant feedback, and he returns to the teacher again and again for each bit of work to be checked, discussed and done again if necessary.

Within this general pupil type there is a sub-group of children who differ in one respect from the main group in that they respond to, rather than initiate, the large amount of teacher-pupil interaction in which they are involved. In terms of their conversations with the teacher, they might be more accurately described as attention getters than attention seekers. In terms of their more general behaviour, however, it seems valid to retain the label attention seekers, since the teacher's opening words are often a response to the kind of overt behaviour which looks remarkably like a bid for the teacher's attention.

An attention seeker of either of the two kinds described is likely to have a much less intense relationship with his fellow pupils than he does with the teacher; he neither pursues them nor avoids them, and his level of interaction with them is average.

The intermittent workers
The typical *intermittent worker* avoids rather than seeks or
provokes the teacher's attention. He characteristically spends
most of his time in his work base, and if the teacher looks in
his direction she is likely to see him working; but the moment
her back is turned he will probably continue talking with his
neighbours. His conversation is more likely to be about the
previous evening's television programmes, or some such topic,
than about the task in hand, but it must not be supposed that
he is an unremitting time-waster. Although he spends more time
talking to other pupils than do children of any other type, he
still manages to spend almost two-thirds of the time working on
his task or on associated routine activities, and his achievement
levels are not significantly lower than those of other pupil types.
The observers' accounts suggest that he particularly enjoys
lessons such as painting, where he can work and talk about
other things at the same time. The over-riding impression one
gets when observing him is that he lacks application. However,
in some cases this masks the fact that, for him, the work is not
sufficiently demanding to require much effort.

The solitary workers
Solitary workers are characterized by the infrequency of their
interactions with other pupils and the teacher, and by the high
proportion of the time they spend working. The typical solitary
worker spends most of his time in his work base, and is busy
with work or with associated routine activities for more than
three-quarters of his time (a higher proportion than in any of
the other pupil types). He has very little conversation with his
fellow pupils, and even with the teacher his interactions are
limited. Most of his dealings with her are as a member of the
whole class, or of the group to which she is talking, and most
of his feedback is from simply listening rather than asking
questions. At first glance he may seem an ideal pupil: hard-
working, rarely distracted, academically successful, quiet and
unobtrusive. However, the extreme solitary worker is curiously
one-sided, purchasing his undoubted success at the expense of
a kind of isolation within the group.

The quiet collaborators
In many ways the *quiet collaborators* resemble solitary workers.
Their work output is almost as high, and their verbal contact
with the teacher and their fellow pupils almost as low. The
teacher spends more of her time with these pupils than with
those of the other three types, but this is because most of her
contact with them is in a group or a whole-class setting. Once
she has gone, they show a tendency to revert to the work
patterns of solitary workers. When they do co-operate it is
likely to be at the non-verbal level of sharing apparatus and
materials rather than through conversation. They spend more
time than the other types on routine activities, and in waiting

for the teacher to return with further instructions. Some of the observers formed a clear impression that for many of these children their pattern of work was something imposed upon them rather than something they would have chosen.

CHANGES IN PUPIL TYPE

Table 2.2 shows the numbers and proportions of pupils of each type during the first and second years of observation. It should be remembered that the observation was of the same children in both years, but that many of them had a change of teacher at the end of the first year. Of the 486 children originally observed some moved to a transfer school at the end of the first year, and a few more were lost from the sample because of reorganization of classes within primary schools. In all, 334 pupils remained in primary schools and were observed again during the second year. The first two columns of values in the table relate to the full first-year sample, and the next two columns only to those children who were observed in both years.

Table 2.2 Numbers and proportions of pupils of each type during the first and second years of observation

	Year 1 pupils		Year 2 pupils in Year 1		Year 2 pupils	
	N	%	N	%	N	%
Attention seekers	96	19.5	67	20.0	54	16.2
Intermittent workers	174	35.7	129	38.6	77	23.1
Solitary workers	156	32.5	98	29.3	114	34.1
Quiet collaborators	60	12.3	40	12.0	89	26.6
	486	100.0	334	100.0	334	100.0

It will be seen that in these four columns of the table the relative proportions of the four groups are very similar, intermittent workers being the largest group in each case, followed by solitary workers, attention seekers and quiet collaborators in that order. Thus, the sub-sample of pupils who were observed again the second year is broadly representative of the full original sample. In the second year, however, as indicated in the last two columns of figures in the table, the proportions of children in the four groups are markedly different, there now being fewer attention seekers and intermittent workers, and more solitary workers and quiet collaborators.

RELATIONSHIPS BETWEEN TEACHING STYLE AND PUPIL TYPE

Referring back to Table 2.1, it will be seen that the marked
shift towards quiet collaboration among the pupils was accompanied by a large increase in the proportion of group instructors, while the tendency of pupils to give up intermittent work
patterns and attention-seeking behaviour went along with a
decrease in the proportions of individual monitors and rotating
and habitual changers. The reasons for these relationships
seem clear. It has already been indicated that, in the main,
collaboration on tasks was not popular among the children and
that they tended to revert to individual work patterns when the
teacher's back was turned; in other words, quiet collaboration
was a strategy imposed upon them rather than freely chosen.
It is therefore in no way surprising that with more teachers
adopting the style of group instruction, more pupils were
manoeuvred into the pattern of quiet collaboration. Attention
seekers flourished in classes where teachers gave the most
individual attention or were extremely sensitive to pupils'
demands and made frequent changes of style in an attempt to
meet them; and intermittent workers were able to follow their
preferred pattern of behaviour only in those classes where the
teacher's attention was generally focused on some other child,
or where the organization was so fluid that there were many
opportunities to remain unnoticed in the general mêlée. With
fewer individual monitors and rotating and habitual changers in
the second year of the study, it was predictable that these types
of pupil behaviour would be less frequently observed.

The relationship between teaching style and pupil type is
illustrated in more detail in Table 2.3, which shows the distribution of pupil types in the classes of teachers using each style.

It is apparent from this table that in classes subjected to at
least some of the teaching styles, pupils of some types are
greatly and consistently under- or over-represented. However,
the sizes of these discrepancies are not immediately clear since,
as was shown in Table 2.2, the proportions of each pupil type
were by no means equal in the total sample. Thus, a superficial
comparison of the proportions of attention seekers and intermittent workers in the classes of infrequent changers in year 1,
for example, may suggest that the latter are over-represented,
since they make up 35.3 per cent of the classes while the former
account for only 27.5 per cent. However, in the sample as a
whole, 35.7 per cent were intermittent workers, and only 19.5
per cent were attention seekers, so that in fact intermittent
workers are neither over- nor under-represented in these
particular classes, while attention seekers are over-represented.

To clarify the extent to which each pupil type is over- or
under-represented in the classes of teachers of each style, it is
helpful to arrange the same data in a different way. If the overall sample percentages from columns 2 and 6 of Table 2.2 are
subtracted in turn from each figure in the relevant rows of

Table 2.3 Distribution of pupil types in the classes of teachers using each style (%)

	Individual monitors		Class enquirers		Group instructors		Infrequent changers		Other changers	
	Year 1	Year 2	Year 1	Year 2	Year 1	Year 2	Year 1	Year 2	Year 1	Year 2
Attention seekers	19.0	17.5	18.4	20.0	5.4	0.9	27.5	35.8	22.3	22.7
Intermittent workers	47.6	45.0	9.2	11.4	32.1	25.4	35.3	17.9	41.8	18.2
Solitary workers	31.4	37.5	64.5	54.3	25.0	29.1	33.3	17.9	22.2	37.3
Quiet collaborators	1.9	0.0	7.9	14.3	37.5	44.5	3.9	28.2	13.8	21.8
	100.0	100.0	100.0	100.0	100.0	100.0	100.0	100.0	100.0	100.0

Table 2.3, the resulting values will indicate the *percentage* by which each pupil type is over- or under-represented, (and the values in each column will sum to zero, since an over-representation of some types must be matched by an under-representation of the others). The data are presented in this way in Table 2.4 which dramatically illustrates an important finding of this consistency study. For the most part the links between teaching style and pupil type can be clearly seen to be consistent from one year to the next; and this greatly strengthens the case for asserting that teaching style is a major influence upon pupil type. On the basis of Table 2.4 one can make several speculations about the nature of this influence.

Table 2.4 Over-representation and under-representation of pupil types in classes subjected to each teaching style (%)

	Individual monitors		Class enquirers		Group instructors		Infrequent changers		Other changers	
	Year 1	Year 2	Year 1	Year 2	Year 1	Year 2	Year 1	Year 2	Year 1	Year 2
Attention seekers	-0.5	+1.3	-1.1	+3.8	-14.1	-15.3	+8.0	+19.6	+2.8	+6.5
Intermittent workers	+11.9	+21.9	-26.5	-11.7	-3.6	+2.3	-0.4	-5.2	+6.1	-4.9
Solitary workers	-1.1	+3.4	+32.0	+20.2	-7.5	-5.0	+0.8	-16.2	-10.3	+3.2
Quiet collaborators	-10.4	-26.6	-4.4	-12.3	+25.2	+17.9	-8.4	+1.6	+1.5	-4.8
	00.0	00.0	00.0	00.0	00.0	00.0	00.0	00.0	00.0	00.0

It seems quite clear that individual monitors act in a way which discourages group collaboration: it is quite alien to their emphasis on individual attention. The price they pay for this is that a high proportion of their pupils work only intermittently, doing just enough to keep up with their classmates, and allowing themselves to become distracted rather than seeking further work during the long periods when the teacher's attention is elsewhere. Class enquirers are very successful at overcoming intermittent work patterns among their pupils, and like the individual monitors they also discourage group collaboration, though not so strongly. The kind of pupil behaviour they approve and encourage is solitary work; they tend to teach the class as a whole, and then set the children to work individually. Group instructors, as their label suggests tend to give their pupils work as a group and to interact with them as a group. It has been reported in 'Progress and Performance in the Primary Classroom' that much of the subsequent pupil effort is not in fact collaborative, though there is certainly more pupil collaboration than takes place in the classes of teachers using other styles. Although pupils within a group may spend a good deal of the time working on their own, the teaching unit is the group, and it is for this reason that comparatively few children adopt attention-seeking patterns of behaviour. The teacher is unlikely to call out individuals to have their work checked, preferring to go to the group and address it as a unit; and the individual pupil is unlikely to leave the group and seek the teacher's attention, preferring to stay put and await her next visit to the group. As would be expected, in these classes solitary workers are somewhat under-represented.

No such clear and consistent patterns emerge or should be expected for the style changers, since the teachers who fell into these groups had in common simply the fact that they changed their styles. In each of the two years, and from one year to the next, the styles with which they started and the styles to which they changed were varied. The exception to this was the infrequent changers who generally changed their style in order to increase their levels of interaction with their pupils. It should be noted that in both years their classes contained more attention seekers than did those subjected to any other teaching style. Just as infrequent changers had very high levels of interaction with pupils, and high levels of questioning and feedback, so attention seekers were generally characterized by their high levels of interaction with their teachers and their constant quest for feedback. It has already been suggested in 'Progress and Performance in the Primary Classroom' (p. 145) that the way in which these teachers changed their approach seems to be a response to the perceived needs of the particular children who happen to be in the class, rather than a temperamental need for variety or the mechanical following of a pre-arranged plan; and that with this kind of teacher the hard-working attention seeker might be expected to experience a particularly tolerant hearing, followed by a change of teaching method designed to bring out the best in the class as a whole. Those suggestions were made on the basis of the first year's data only; in the data from the second year the relationship between this pupil type and teaching style emerges even more strongly.

CONSISTENCY OF TEACHING STYLE

The pattern of relationships described not only highlights the influence of teaching style upon pupil type, but also makes it clear that at least some teachers are influenced in their choice of style by the behaviour of their pupils. However, there can be no doubt that the dominant influence is that of teaching style. A second major finding of the present study is that not a single teacher changed to a different style when taking on a new class of children, although changes would have been expected if teaching style were very susceptible to influence from the balance of pupil types within a class. Of the fourteen teachers who were observed in both of the two consecutive years, all those who maintained a single style throughout the first year continued with that same style throughout the second year even when they were teaching different children; and all those who were style changers during the first year continued with the same pattern of style changing during the second. Thus in no case did the balance of pupil types in a class impose a change of style on a reluctant teacher. Some teachers were dedicated to a style and stuck to it while others changed style whenever the need arose, either after careful consideration or in an apparently impulsive way. To call the former group rigid and the latter flexible implies a value judgment which is not entirely justified; to use the terms consistent and inconsistent presents the same problem with the value judgement reversed. Whatever labels are used, however, it seems clear that a teachers' tendency to stick to one style or to change from one style to another is a temperamental trait rather than a yearly reaction to a new set of children, and this in itself dramatically highlights the dominance of teaching style over pupil type.

CONSISTENCY OF PUPIL TYPE

The pupils were quite different. It has already been shown that many of them changed to a new type when they moved to a new class (and hence came under the influence of a new teacher). The question which arises is whether their changes of type were purely a response to the new teacher's style. If this were so, it would be expected that pupils who moved to a teacher whose style was generally supportive of their current mode of behaviour would be very unlikely to change type, while most of those who moved to a teacher whose style did not positively encourage their current behaviour would change to fit in with the new teacher's style. It can be readily seen from Table 2.4 which teaching styles are supportive of the various pupil types. In both years attention seekers were over-represented in the

classes of all style changers, and an explanation has been offered
of why the characteristic behaviour of the style changers should
be supportive of attention-seeking behaviour in pupils. Similarly,
individual monitors have been shown to support intermittent work
patterns in that their attention is so divided that they are
generally unable to secure from their pupils more than the
minimum amount of work necessary to reach their required
standard. Solitary workers and quiet collaborators thrive best
in the classes of class enquirers and group instructors respectively, and it has been suggested that pupils become quiet
collaborators only if their teacher adopts the strategy of imposing
group work upon them. At other times, like solitary workers,
they prefer to work on their own. It therefore seems appropriate
to amalgamate the two types in the analysis which follows.

Table 2.5 explores the question of changes in pupil type when
children come under the influence of teachers using supportive
and unsupportive styles.

*Table 2.5 Consistency of pupil type under supportive and
non-supportive teaching styles*

First-year-type	N (second year)	Number taught in second year by		Pupils staying in same type	
				N	%
Attention seekers	67	All style changers:	32	14	43.8
		All other styles:	35	5	14.3
Intermittent workers	129	Individual monitors:	8	3	37.5
		All other styles:	121	32	26.4
Solitary workers and Quiet collaborators	138	Class enquirers or group instructors	50	45	90.0
		All other styles:	88	52	59.1

It will be seen, for example, that of the children who had been
attention seekers in the first year and who were taught in the
second year by style changers (who adopt the teaching styles
most supportive of attention-seeking behaviour) 43.8 per cent
remained attention seekers, while of those taught by less
supportive styles, only 14.3 per cent stayed true to type.
Indeed as one would expect, for each of the pupil types the
same pattern was repeated. More interesting, however, are the
sizes of the various proportions. Nearly all of the solitary
workers and quiet collaborators stayed in one of these two
groups when taught by class enquirers or group instructors,
as did well over a half of those who moved to teachers using
other, less supportive styles. This last finding strongly
suggests that pupils of these two types have generally found a
way of conforming to the demands of school which is satisfactory
both to themselves and their teachers, and also that the work
habits they develop tend to stay with them even when they move
to classes where they could get away with less. It is as if they

have learned the rules of the game and decided that they will
play it.

Attention seekers and intermittent workers are much more
likely to change type, and well under a half of them stay constant even when they move to teachers whose style is supportive
of their characteristic behaviour patterns. With less supportive
teachers only one attention seeker in seven and about one intermittent worker in four maintain their types. Bearing in mind
the age range of these pupils, it is tempting to see in the
characteristics of attention seekers and intermittent workers
the lingering traces of a younger more immature stage. However,
it should be remembered that, as shown in 'Progress and Performance in the Primary Classroom', intermittent workers are
second only to solitary workers in their levels of achievement.
It may be that for some of them the work offered is generally
far too easy, and if this is so, then the technique of spinning
it out to fill the time available by taking frequent breaks for
idle chatter, though possibly not admirable, is scarcely a sign
of immaturity. It was suggested earlier that solitary workers
and quiet collaborators have discovered the rules of the game
and decided to play it. Among both the attention seekers and
the intermittent workers there are undoubtedly children who
have not yet learned the rules of the game; in addition there
seem to be those who have learned the rules but bend them when
they play, and possibly a few who, having learned the rules,
make a calculated decision not to play at all.

It is now clear that in spite of the strong influence of teaching
style upon pupil type, other factors must also be at work. If
the relationship were a straightforward matter of cause and
effect it would be expected that virtually all the pupils in a
class would switch to the types most encouraged by the teacher's
style, yet clearly this does not happen. Many pupils stick to a
type of which the teacher's style is not supportive, and many
others switch away from a type which is generally encouraged
by their teacher's style. The analogy already offered, of learning the rules of the game, offers a clue to the process which
seems to take place.

LEARNING THE ETHOS OF THE CLASSROOM

An examination of the proportion of pupils of each type who
changed to a new type at the end of the first year shows that
of the four types, solitary workers were the least likely to
change (Table 2.6). It has already been suggested that these
were the pupils who had learned the rules and decided to play
the game. The other three groups were much more alike in their
strong tendency to change type, with this tendency at its
strongest among those pupils who had been forced into quiet
collaboration. In this last group it seems as if pupils had learned
the rules, but were reluctantly playing an unpopular game. To

Table 2.6 Proportions of pupils who changed type after one year of observation (%)

| Second-year type | First-year pupil type | | | |
	Attention seekers	Intermittent workers	Solitary workers	Quiet collaborators
Same	28.4	27.1	44.9	22.5
Different	71.6	72.9	55.1	77.5
	100.0	100.0	100.0	100.0

evaluate this explanation, and to gain more insight into what was happening with the attention seekers and the intermittent workers, it is illuminating to consider only those children who changed type, and discover the types to which pupils in each group were most likely to change.

Table 2.7 Subsequent type of pupils who changed type after one year of observation (%)

| Second-year type | First-year pupil type | | | |
	Attention seekers	Intermittent workers	Solitary workers	Quiet collaborators
Attention seekers	–	18.1	20.4	22.6
Intermittent workers	39.6	–	25.9	29.0
Solitary workers	35.4	40.4	–	48.4
Quiet collaborators	25.0	41.5	53.7	–
	100.0	100.0	100.0	100.0

The relevant data are presented in Table 2.7, where it will be seen, for example, that of the 72.9 per cent of intermittent workers who changed type after one year (cf. Table 2.6), about a fifth (18.1 per cent) became attention seekers while about two-fifths became solitary workers and the remaining two-fifths became quiet collaborators.

This table highlights the strong relationship between solitary workers and quiet collaborators, showing that about half the

pupils who changed from either of these two groups moved into
the other. It seems reasonable to conclude that both of these
two groups of pupils have adjusted themselves to the work
demands of school. To continue with the analogy, both groups
have learned the rules, and both groups play the game. Which
game they play depends on the organization imposed by the
teacher, but once they have become players, there is a strong
chance that they will remain so. Intermittent workers, on the
other hand, may be seen as children who have not yet adjusted
themselves to the teacher's demands in the way the teacher
would wish. Those who move out of the group generally do so in
order to become solitary workers or group collaborators; that
is to say, they learn or are taught to play the game strictly by
the rules which apply in the classroom in which they find themselves. They are unlikely to become attention seekers, as are
children from all the groups: the three lowest percentages in the
table are all on the top row, which denotes changes to this type
from the other three groups. Thus attention-seeking may be
seen as pre-eminently the pupil type which derives from temperamental factors. An attention seeker can be weaned away from
this kind of behaviour, but a non-attention seeker is rather
unlikely to become one. Attention seekers who leave the group
tend to become intermittent workers or solitary workers rather
than quiet collaborators since the co-operation implicit in this
last pupil type might be thought particularly uncongenial to
children who have been accustomed to a great deal of individual
teacher attention. In terms of the analogy, those who become
solitary workers can be seen as pupils who decide they will
play the game strictly according to the rules, while those who
become intermittent workers play the game but get away with
bending the rules. In any case the demands of the new teacher
may be assumed largely to determine which of these two groups
the ex-attention seeker joins.

In general terms, then, the modern primary classroom can be
seen as a setting in which children have to learn to work by
themselves for quite long periods. The teachers intentionally
or otherwise foster this ability, ranging from those who have a
preferred style of interaction and a matching organizational
strategy to which they stick from one year to the next, to those
who change their strategies, either impulsively or after detailed
consideration, to meet the needs of the moment.

Over the course of their period in the primary school most
pupils come to understand what is required of them, and
gradually learn to see solitary working as the preferred mode.
Some find the work uncongenial, and seek to relieve the mon-
otony through idle chatter and other distractions, but this is
largely dependent on the room for manoeuvre they are given by
the teacher. In doing just enough work to keep up with their
more diligent fellows, these pupils show a high level of adaptation
to institutional demands, which is echoed in the work behaviour
to be found in many adult settings. Other pupils demand or

attract more than their fair share of attention from the teacher, but the evidence presented suggests that the persistence of this kind of behaviour is related to the flexibility of the teacher's approach. Style-changing teachers are often able to find time to deal with these pupils, and to pick up clues from their attention-seeking behaviour which help to determine the direction of their own flexibility. With other kinds of teacher, however, such pupils generally come to learn that what is required is something rather different; and once they have acquired the habit of getting on busily with the tasks which are set for them, pupils of any type are rather unlikely to revert to a less conforming way of meeting the demands of the day, so long as the teacher's organizational strategies permit her to give the necessary support.

This examination of the data derived from two consecutive years of systematic observation of pupils and teachers in primary classrooms has revealed three dramatic and important findings relating to what happens when the same children move up to new classes at the end of a school year.

First, the dominant influence of teaching style upon pupil type was consistent from year to year. The replication study rules out the possibility that the apparent relationship between, say, individual monitors and intermittent workers, or class enquirers and solitary workers might be a meaningless random occurrence.

Second, whatever the ways may be in which the behaviour of pupils influences that of their teachers, pupil type itself is not a strong influence on teaching style. Not one of the teachers who were observed in both years of the study was driven by a different balance of pupil types in a new class to change from the style she had adopted with her old class.

Finally, many pupils switched from one type to another when they moved to a new class; and the move was generally in the direction of a closer conformity with the class ethos and a greater emphasis on task-oriented behaviour whenever the teacher's style did not positively discourage such a development.

3 PUPIL AND TEACHER BEHAVIOUR AFTER TRANSFER

On the basis of data derived from systematic observation, it was argued in the previous chapter that as pupils progress through the primary school they tend for the most part towards a more work-orientated kind of behaviour, making fewer idiosyncratic demands on the teacher and conforming more and more to the patterns of work and behaviour laid down by her. With this argument in mind it is now time to consider what happens to them when they transfer from primary school to the next stage of their education. In considering first the data from systematic observation, perhaps the most basic question to be asked concerns the extent and direction of any overall change in their work and interaction patterns after the move from primary school, to discover whether the trend already observed continues, or whether it is altered or reversed. In examining this rather complex matter, it is relevant to consider first the general overall picture before looking in detail at any variations which appear between different kinds of schools and different curricular areas.

To avoid cumbersome repetition and thus to keep the description as simple as possible, all schools from which the children transferred will here be termed *feeder schools* while the term *transfer schools* will be used as a convenient generic term for the various kinds of school to which the children moved when they left their primary schools.

Table 3.1 indicates overall differences in activity and interaction at feeder and transfer school. The pupils involved were all those who were observed both before and after transfer, and the figures in columns 2 and 3 represent mean raw scores based on all observations made of these pupils at pre- and post-transfer levels respectively. It will be seen that in general they spent considerably more of their time on task work in the transfer schools. Both before and after transfer they stayed in their work base for most of the time, but after transfer they were even less likely to be observed out of it. The most usual kind of work base after transfer was a desk or table at which there were two pupils of the same sex; about half the pupils were seated in this way, while just over a third were to be found in single-sex groups of more than two. This pattern is in sharp contrast to that found in the feeder schools were the most popular system was for children to be seated in groups of mixed sex, and where seating in single-sex pairs was not at all common.

Following transfer there was no significant change in the overall amount of interaction *between pupils,* but the total amount of *pupil teacher* interaction more than doubled. This enormous increase was entirely in terms of interaction between the teacher and the class as a whole; the amount of interaction between the teacher and individual pupils or groups within the class was in both cases significantly less after transfer than before. Among the pupils themselves, although the overall amount of inter-action scarcely changed, its pattern was markedly different. In the first place significantly more of it concerned the task in hand, rather than other peripheral or irrelevant matters; in the second place, significantly less of it involved pupils of the opposite sex, and significantly more of it involved more than two pupils of the same sex.

Table 3.1 Mean raw scores on major categories of the Pupil Record, before and after transfer

Observation† category	Feeder schools	Transfer schools	Significance of difference
Activity			
COOP TK	59.1	67.7	**
COOP R	11.4	10.7	
P IN	86.1	91.9	*
Pupil-teacher interaction			
TOTAL	15.2	33.0	**
IND ATT	2.2	1.3	**
GROUP	1.8	0.8	**
CLASS	11.2	30.9	**
INIT	1.2	1.2	
Pupil-pupil interaction			
TOTAL	18.5	17.4	
SS	13.1	11.4	
OS	2.2	0.8	*
SEV SS	2.1	4.7	*
SEV OS	1.1	0.5	*
ON TASK	5.2	7.0	*
Base			
ALONE	4.8	5.3	
2SS	14.0	48.6	**
2OS	2.1	1.1	*
SEV SS	32.5	36.6	*
SEV OS	44.2	7.3	**

* Significant between 5 per cent and 1 per cent levels.
** Significant beyond 1 per cent level.

† The abbreviations in this column are explained in Appendix A1 on page 203, and the observation schedule is described in detail in Chapter 1 of *Inside the Primary Classroom*, pp. 11-16.

. Thus the picture which emerges from this initial analysis is of a shift towards greater emphasis on clearly defined task work in a more traditional setting of class teaching, with pupils seated in pairs, and a greater segregation of the sexes. So far, the primary-level trend towards a more conforming and work-oriented kind of behaviour seem to continue after transfer.

DIFFERENCES BETWEEN TYPES OF TRANSFER SCHOOL

Against this background it is particularly interesting to compare those transfer schools which were selected because they were said to be of a primary type with those which were said to be of a secondary type. In Table 3.2 the data from the second column of Table 3.1 are divided so that the mean raw scores of primary-type and secondary-type schools are presented separately. It is immediately apparent that on the activity categories the two types of school are very similar. In the secondary-type schools pupils spent slightly more time on task-oriented and associated routine activities, and consequently slightly more time in their work bases; but the differences are all very small and in no case reach statistical significance. There were, however, marked differences between the nature of the work bases in the two kinds of school, and also in the patterns of interaction both among the pupils themselves, and between the pupils and the teachers.

The seating arrangement in single-sex pairs, which in the earlier table seemed dramatically characteristic of transfer schools, can now be seen to be very much more common in secondary-type schools than in the primary type, although it is worth remarking that even in the latter this particular arrangement of seating was more than twice as common as it had been in the feeder schools. Groups of more than two, on the other hand, were significantly more common in primary type than in secondary type of transfer school; and within these larger groups the balance of sexes was interesting. Single-sex groups were certainly far more common in the primary type than in the secondary type or indeed than in the feeder schools from which the children had come. Groups of mixed sex were much less common at either kind of transfer school than they had been at the feeder schools; where they did appear they were more likely to be in the primary type than in the secondary type of school, but here there was a great deal of variation within each of the two types of school, so that the contrast between the types is not nearly so clear-cut as is that for single-sex groups. In summary then, seating in pairs was much more common at transfer level and as might be expected, very much more common in the secondary type of transfer school; seating in single-sex groups was much more common in primary-type transfer schools than in either secondary-type transfer schools or feeder schools.

The impact upon the pupils of these differences in seating can

Table 3.2 Comparisons between progressive and traditional secondary schools

Observation category	Primary type	Secondary type	Significance of difference	eta^{2}†
Activity				
COOP TK	66.9	68.8		
COOP R	10.3	11.1		
P IN	90.7	93.1		
Pupil-teacher interaction				
TOTAL	25.8	40.8	**	0.25
IND ATT	1.5	1.0	*	0.05
GROUP	1.0	0.5	*	0.05
CLASS	23.3	39.3	**	0.44
INIT	0.9	1.5	**	0.07
Pupil-pupil interaction				
TOTAL	20.6	14.2	**	0.20
SS	12.6	10.4	*	0.04
OS	0.7	1.1		
SEV SS	6.9	2.2	**	0.16
SEV OS	0.5	0.5		
ON TASK	8.4	5.7		
Base				
ALONE	5.6	5.0		
2SS	29.2	69.6	**	0.43
2OS	0.7	1.7		
SEV SS	53.3	18.2	**	0.34
SEV OS	9.9	4.5	*	0.04

* Significant between 5 per cent and 1 per cent levels.

** Significant beyond 1 per cent level.

† Eta^{2} indicates the proportion of the variation in the set of scores explained by the categories in the analysis of variance. It can take values from 1.0, indicating that all the variation is explained to 0 indicating that none of the variation is explained.

be seen from the fact that in the primary-type transfer schools there was significantly more interaction among them, and in particular, significantly more interaction involving several pupils of the same sex. It is worth noting, however, that even though pupils in the secondary-type transfer schools were character-istically seated in single-sex pairs, there was significantly less interaction between single-sex pairs in those schools than in those of the primary type (but also a great deal of variation

within schools of the same kind). Thus although the seating
arrangements will inevitably have had an influence on the number
of participants in an interaction, the tendency for children in the
primary type of transfer school to interact more with each other
cannot be seen simply as a consequence of the characteristic
seating arrangements in the two kinds of school, but is much
more likely to be directly connected with the teachers' tolerance
of pupil-pupil interaction, and with their own preferred patterns
of interaction with their pupils.

A particularly dramatic feature of Table 3.2 is that in both
kinds of transfer school virtually all the interactions between
teachers and their pupils involved the whole class rather than
groups or individuals. Certainly the teachers in the primary
type of transfer school spent a little more of their time in individual or small-group interaction than did their colleagues in the
secondary type of school; but in both kinds of school this
accounted for only a very small proportion of total teacher-pupil
interaction, and there was in any case considerable variation
within schools of the same kind. The big difference between the
two kinds of school lay not so much in the precise pattern of
teacher-pupil interaction as in the overall amount of it. Children
in the secondary-type schools spent significantly more of their
time interacting with their teachers, and this in itself goes a
long way towards explaining why they spent so much less of their
time interacting with each other. In both kinds of school nearly
all teacher-pupil interaction was initiated by the teacher (and,
given the characteristic pattern of whole-class interaction described, it is hard to see how this could have been otherwise).
What little pupil-initiated interaction there was took place significantly more often in the secondary-type transfer schools where
the pupils' day was far more intensively oriented towards the
teacher.

There is then a marked overall contrast between the primary-
and secondary-type schools: in the latter the pupils sit in single-
sex pairs, either working on their own or engaged in a fairly
constant whole-class dialogue with their teachers, and talking
rather infrequently to each other; in the primary type of transfer school, on the other hand, the pupils sit in larger groups
and spend far more of their time working on their own, drawing
on each other almost as much as on the teacher for the interactions of the day. That these very different modes of behaviour
were intended by the teachers is to some extent suggested by
the fact that in both kinds of school there were virtually identical amounts of task-oriented and associated routine behaviour.
By definition task-oriented behaviour (COOP TK) is the performance of whatever task the teacher has set or whatever task
the pupil has chosen from the range of options open to him. In
this sense there is neither more nor less work done in one kind
of school than in the other, and therefore the prevailing patterns
of interaction in the two kinds of school could in each case be
seen as part of the preferred work ethic of the teachers.

However, nothing has so far been said about differences in pupil and teacher behaviour across the various curricular areas, although it must be remembered that, unlike their colleagues in the feeder primary schools, all but two of these teachers were subject specialists. Furthermore, no reference has yet been made in this chapter to the different teaching styles outlined earlier. Before any general conclusions can be reached it is necessary to examine differences between teachers of mathematics, English and science, and to consider the balance of teaching styles in the two kinds of school, relating that balance to the other data presented.

DIFFERENCES BETWEEN SUBJECTS AFTER TRANSFER

Turning first to the question of the various subjects or curricular areas, it will be seen from Table 3.3 that there were a number of large and statistically significant differences between them. This table shows not only the differences between feeder-school and transfer-school activity and interaction patterns for mathematics, English and science separately, but also differences between the three subjects at transfer level.

In an earlier section on overall differences between feeder and transfer patterns it was reported that pupils spent significantly more of their time after transfer engaged in task work, and it can now be seen that this held for all three subjects. The tendency of pupils to spend more time in their work base, however, was restricted to mathematics and English lessons; after transfer the pupils spent as much time out of their base in science lessons as they had done in general studies in the feeder schools. This is in no way surprising, since the science lessons involved many specialized activities which had to be performed where particular pieces of apparatus were to be found. A comparison of the three subjects at transfer level (from the last three columns of the table) confirms that significantly less time was spent in the work base in science than in the other two subjects, but also shows that English lessons were significantly different from the other two subjects in that a greater proportion of lesson time was spent in task work. This may have been because of the nature of the tasks set in English, and further consideration will be given to this matter later.

Turning to teacher-pupil interaction, the table shows that the tendency for this to increase dramatically after transfer held for all three subjects, as did the tendency for the increase to be entirely in terms of the whole-class interaction. However, within this overall pattern there were marked differences between the various subjects. The most striking of these differences was that in mathematics there was far less overall teacher-pupil interaction, and hence far less whole-class interaction than in either English or science. The pattern was very much for the teacher to explain a technique and to set the task, and for the pupils to

Table 3.3 Mean raw scores on major categories of the Pupil Record for mathematics, English and science/general studies

OBSERVATION CATEGORY	MATHS			ENGLISH			SCIENCE/GENERAL STUDIES			SUBJECT DIFFERENCES IN TRANSFER SCHOOLS		
	Feeder Schools	Transfer Schools	Diff-erence	Feeder Schools	Transfer Schools	Diff-erence	Feeder Schools	Transfer Schools	Diff-erence	Maths/ English	Maths/ Science	English/ Science
Activity												
COOP TK	57.0	62.5	**	59.5	73.0	**	57.9	67.2	**	*-*		**
COOP R	11.2	11.9	*	11.5	8.1	*	11.6	10.9		**	*	
PUP IN	86.3	92.4		86.1	95.3	**	86.0	86.1			*	**
Pupil-teacher interaction												
TOTAL	16.3	19.5	*	13.8	41.9	**	17.2	43.4	**	**	**	
INDIV	2.4	1.7	*	2.3	1.2	*	1.8	0.8	*		*	
GROUP	2.9	0.6	**	1.5	0.8	*	1.4	0.8	*	**	**	
CLASS	9.9	17.2	**	10.0	39.9	**	14.0	41.8	**	**	**	
INIT	1.1	1.3		1.2	1.0		1.3	1.2				
Pupil-pupil interaction												
TOTAL	17.2	19.2		19.3	17.4		19.0	16.8	*			
SS	12.3	15.2		12.8	9.3		13.6	11.5		**		*
OS	2.0	0.8	*	3.1	1.1	*	2.0	0.8	*			
SSS	1.9	2.7		2.0	6.7	*	2.3	3.7	*	**		*
SOS	1.0	0.5		1.4	0.3	*	1.1	0.8				
ON TASK	5.1	5.1		4.7	10.1	*	6.1	6.0		**	**	**

*   Significant between 5 per cent and 1 per cent levels.
** Significant beyond 1 per cent level.

work on their own for most of the lesson, while the teacher
offered help to individual pupils. Whereas there was less *overall*
teacher-pupil interaction in mathematics, there was in fact more
interaction between the teacher and *individual* pupils than in
either of the other two subjects, although only between mathematics and science does the difference reach statistical significance.

With regard to pupil-pupil interaction the general picture
reported earlier was for pupils to interact neither more nor less
with each other after transfer than they had done in the feeder
schools, but for more of the interaction to be about the task in
hand, for less of it to involve both sexes together and for more
of it to involve groups of children rather than pairs. Again,
there are subject differences revealed by Table 3.3. There was
less pupil-pupil interaction in science lessons in the transfer
schools than there had been in general studies lessons in the
feeder schools, although it must of course be remembered that
the match between science and general studies is not exact, and
that general studies in the primary schools included a range of
rather nebulous activities in which a discussion between pupils
of what they should do and how they might set about doing it
fairly frequently formed part of the task itself. The tendency to
interact less with the opposite sex held for all subjects, although
the differences did not always reach statistical significance;
and the same thing applied to the tendency for increased interaction among single-sex groups. However, in mathematics lessons
the trend away from interaction between pairs of pupils of the
same sex did not hold; although the difference was not statistically significant, there was in fact more of such interaction
after transfer than there had been at feeder level, presumably
reflecting the fact that for the most part the pupils were sitting
in single-sex pairs and working individually. Any whispered
asides or requests for help would in such a setting be most
likely to involve a pupil's immediate neighbour.

The major difference between subjects in this area involves
on-task interaction. It will be seen from the table that the
tendency towards more such interaction in the transfer schools
was entirely restricted to English lessons, while in mathematics
and science the amounts of on-task interaction did not change
after transfer. Again the anomalous position of English in this
respect arose from the subject matter of the lessons, since in
some cases a discussion of the task formed part of the task,
while in others, notably drama, the pupil-pupil interaction *was*
the task. Turning to the last three columns of the table, it will
be seen that at transfer level, English was very much the odd
man out as far as pupil-pupil interaction was concerned, since
there were no significant differences between mathematics and
science, while in three respects English differed significantly
from both: it involved more task-oriented interaction, less interaction between single-sex pairs and more among single-sex
groups.

In summary then, lessons in the three subjects can be characterized as follows:

science lessons differ from those in the other two subjects
chiefly in the *mobility of the pupils,* who spend a comparatively
large amount of time out of their work bases;

mathematic lessons differ from those in the other two subjects
chiefly in the small amount of *teacher-pupil interaction* they
involve;

English lessons differ from those in the other two subjects chiefly
in the large amount of *task-oriented behaviour and interaction
among the pupils.*

Clearly then, after transfer pupils tend to behave and interact in rather different ways depending on the curricular content
of the particular lesson in which they find themselves. This
raises the question of the behaviour or teaching style of their
teachers, for if teaching *style* is a dominant influence on pupil
behaviour, it is pertinent to ask which, if any, of the six
ORACLE styles the transfer teachers employ, and whether the
behaviour of the three groups of subject specialists differs in
ways which can be described as characteristic of the subjects
they teach.

TEACHING STYLES IN THE TRANSFER SCHOOLS

We have seen that the original ORACLE teaching styles were
derived from cluster analysis of teachers' behaviour and interactions as categorized on the systematic observation schedule.
In order to discover whether the teaching styles of the transfer
teachers were like those of the teachers in the feeder schools,
the cluster analysis was repeated, but now the data from all the
88 primary teachers who had been included in the original
analysis were combined with new data from the 28 transfer
teachers. The results of this new analysis are set out in Table
3.4. The analysis yielded two clusters, which have been termed
simply 1 and 2; that is to say, the differences between the
original clusters (or teaching styles) were now completely
overshadowed by a single basic difference between two groups
of teachers. Those in cluster 1 were characterized by their
comparatively low levels of interaction with their pupils. When
they did interact, it was often about routine or organizational
matters, and generally with individuals or small groups rather
than with the whole class. With the teachers in cluster 2 the
situation was reversed. Much more of their time was spent interacting with their pupils, and their dealings were generally with
the whole class rather than with individuals. For the most part
their conversations concerned the subject matter of the task in
hand rather than routine or organizational matters. Strikingly,

Table 3.4   Cluster analysis of systematic observation data from all teachers (primary and transfer) observed at some time during the three years of the ORACLE study

	Teachers				
	Feeder schools		Transfer schools		Total
	N	%	N	%	N
Cluster 1	76	86.4	8	28.6	84
Cluster 2	12	13.6	20	71.4	32
Total	88	100.0	28	100.0	116

more than 85 per cent of the teachers from the feeder schools fell into cluster 1, while over 70 per cent of the transfer teachers were in cluster 2, suggesting that the basic difference which emerged was between two quite different approaches to teaching which are broadly characteristic of most teachers in the feeder and transfer schools respectively. The very tentative nature of this analysis needs to be emphasised here, as does the fact that there were teachers from each kind of school whose behaviour seemed, in the terms of the analysis, more appropriate to the other. In relation to the eight transfer teachers whose behaviour placed them in the 'primary' cluster, several kinds of hypothesis can be examined.

It might be thought that primary teaching methods would be likely to linger on in 9-13 middle schools in which the younger children are of the same age as their fellows in traditional junior schools. Table 3.5 shows the distribution of the eight teachers under discussion in relation to the type of school in which they were observed. It will be seen that two of the eight were teach-

Table 3.5   Distribution of the eight transfer teachers employing cluster 1 (primary-style) teaching

LEA	Age range of school	Type	Subject speciality (if any)	N
A	9-13	Secondary (AS)	Mathematics	1
A	9-13	Primary (AP)	Class teacher	1
B	11-14	Secondary (BS)	Mathematics	1
B	11-14	Primary (BP)	English	1
C	12-18	Secondary (CS)	Mathematics	2
C	12-18	Primary (CP)	Mathematics	2

ing in 9-13 middle schools, two more in 11-14 middle schools,
and the remaining four in 12-18 secondary comprehensive
schools; all, of course, were teaching the youngest pupils in
their respective schools. Clearly, whatever influenced the choice
of primary-style teaching in transfer schools, it was not a
question of a primary ethos among teachers of very young
transfer children tempting them to defer the adoption of a transfer (or 'secondary') style until later. Indeed, the oldest transfer
children in the study experienced more primary-style teaching
than did the children in either of the two younger age-groups.

An alternative hypothesis is that the more closely the organization of a transfer school resembles the informal primary
feeder school, the more likely will the teachers be to borrow
their teaching style from their colleagues in the feeder schools.
However, the present group of eight anomalous teachers was
equally divided between transfer schools which had been deemed
to be of primary and of secondary types; and this was true not
only for the sample as a whole, but also within each separate
local authority, where the numbers of such teachers were in
each case equal in the two types of school. On the basis of the
evidence available, this hypothesis must also be rejected.

A third approach is to investigate the links between primary-
style teaching in transfer schools and subject specialism. Here
a marked relationship is apparent. Of the eight teachers in the
group, one was a class teacher in a 9-13 school, and one an
English teacher. The remaining six were all mathematics teachers,
and came from both secondary and primary types of transfer
schools catering for each of the three different age-ranges. The
strength of this link between the subject taught, on the one
hand, and the predominantly primary or secondary teaching
style, on the other, is further illustrated in Table 3.6. It must
be remembered that in all cases the numbers are small so that
too much should not be read into the exact size of the proportions in each cluster. Of the class teachers little can be said
with confidence, since there were only two in the entire sample.

*Table 3.6 Subject specialities of the transfer teachers in
clusters 1 and 2*

		Subject speciality (if any)			
	Class teachers	Mathematics	English	Science	TOTAL
Cluster 1 (primary style)	1	6	1	0	8
Cluster 2 (second-ary style)	1	4	10	5	20
TOTAL	2	10	11	5	28

Bearing in mind the fact that they were both not only 'class teachers' rather than 'subject teachers' but also dealing with the youngest of the children in the study, it may seem remarkable that they were not both in cluster 1. However it should not be overlooked that more than a tenth of the primary teachers were in cluster 2, and without a larger sample of class teachers from transfer schools it is not possible to enquire further into the teaching behaviours of this very interesting group. Turning to the subject specialists, it is clear that the only teachers who exibited a marked and unequivocal tendency to employ the teaching behaviours characteristic of their colleagues in the feeder schools were the mathematics teachers, of whom at a conservative estimate about half fell into this category. Among the science teachers on the other hand, such behaviours were unknown, while the English teachers were seemingly in an intermediate position, only one of them making use of primary-style teaching.

This basic difference between primary and transfer styles of teaching clearly over-rides all others: in the cluster analysis the teaching styles which had so clearly differentiated the primary teachers earlier were completely submerged when the transfer teachers were added to the sample. Nevertheless these differences in style between primary teachers do remain, and are plainly paralleled among the transfer teachers by equally strong differences of style which are closely bound to the subjects of curriculum. An account has already been given of the large and statistically significant differences between mathematics, English and science lessons in such areas as organization and interaction between pupils and the teacher, and the dominance of teaching style in such matters has already been emphasized.

In summary it can be said that most of the transfer teachers differed markedly from most of the primary teachers in the feeder schools in their general style of teaching, although six of the ten mathematics teachers were more like the primary teachers in this respect than they were like their colleagues who taught other subjects in the transfer schools. While there were certainly variations of style among the teachers of each subject, the major variation at transfer level was across subjects.

In view of these subject-based differences of style among transfer teachers, and of the dominance of teaching style over pupil type described at length in Chapter 2 of this volume, it is time to consider in more detail the effects on the pupils of one very basic change of approach after their transfer from primary school. Before transfer they had all been taught by class teachers; that is to say, during a single school year each child had come under the influence of a single teacher for most of his time in school. An account has already been provided of how this influence affected the child's gradual acquisition of his characteristic mode of behaviour in school, and of how when he moved to a new teacher's class at the beginning of a new school

year, his behaviour would be likely to change until he had
achieved a style of behaviour which enabled him to cope with
the general 'rules of the game' in school in the way best suited
to his temperament. After transfer however, most of the pupils
were subjected to a quite new situation, for now, instead of
being with the same teacher all day long, they were taught by
several in a single day; and as we have seen, the several would
be unlikely all to be using the same teaching style. The question
to be asked is whether this tended to produce a chameleon-like
response in the children, with changes of behaviour each time
the bell went for a new lesson, or whether it seems rather to
have speeded up the formation in each pupil of a temperamentally-
based all-purpose way of coping with the fluctuating demands of
the day.

PUPIL BEHAVIOUR IN THE TRANSFER SCHOOLS

To investigate this question a cluster analysis was conducted of
data from the 103 pupils who were systematically observed during
their first year after transfer. In this particular analysis the
data from each child were separated into the three sets which
had been collected during mathematics, English and science
lessons, so that in effect each pupil was treated in the analysis
as if he were three pupils: himself studying mathematics, himself studying English and himself studying science. This procedure made it possible to examine the extent to which pupils'
behaviour tended to be consistent across all three subjects.
Purely for the purposes of this exposition, the observed
behaviour of pupils in each subject will be called their personae.

*Table 3.7 Cluster analysis of pupil observation data derived
from mathematics, English and science lessons separately (as a
percentage of total observations)*

Observation category		Cluster			
		1	2	3	4
Teacher-pupil interactions:	pupil-initiated	1.2	1.1	0.9	6.2
	individual	1.3	0.6	1.1	7.6
	group	5.1	0.3	0.3	0.7
	whole-class	11.8	64.3	16.0	11.0
Pupil-pupil interactions:	total	27.2	12.2	19.2	13.0
	task-related	18.0	4.1	7.1	2.7
Activity:	task work	78.1	73.5	63.7	58.0
	approved routine	5.6	8.7	11.4	13.6
	totally distracted	7.7	11.1	12.8	10.1
Location:	in work base	92.9	93.3	90.3	82.5
	N =	24	78	176	12

The term as employed here bears no more than a superficial
resemblance to the persona in Jungian psychology. It is used

simply to reflect the fact that people often behave differently in different settings. The question to be considered is how far this was true of the ORACLE sample of pupils as they faced the varying demands of lessons in these different subjects.

The results of the cluster analysis are set out in Table 3.7. The table indicates the relative frequency of each behaviour category within each cluster, as well as the range across the clusters. Since 19 of the 103 pupils were not observed during lessons in one or other of the three subjects the total number of personae is 290 rather than the 309 which would have resulted if every one of the pupils had been observed in all three subjects. It is apparent from an examination of the row of n values at the bottom of the table that cluster 3 and the smaller cluster 2 are between them sufficiently dominant to encompass the great majority of the personae, cluster 3 alone accounting for 60.7 per cent, and the two clusters together for 87.6 per cent. The same data are represented in a different way in Figure 3.1.

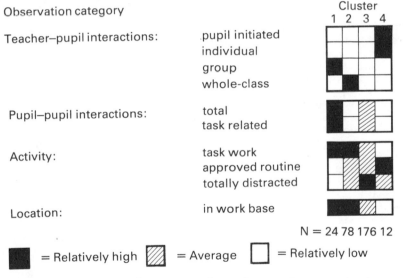

Figure 3.1 Relative frequency of pupil record categories in each of the clusters detailed in Table 3.8

Here, as for the derivation of the pupil types in Chapter 8 of 'Inside the Primary Classroom', for each observation category the range between the highest and lowest incidence has been divided into four equal parts. Wherever the incidence of a particular category falls within the top quartile of the range, the grid is shaded to indicate a relatively high frequency. A value within the bottom quartile is described as relatively low, while those falling between these two extremes are described as average.

Between them, the table and the figure permit an easy and
straightforward analysis of the patterns of behaviour representative of the four clusters.

PUPIL PERSONAE AFTER TRANSFER

Looking first at cluster 3, which is the largest, it can be seen
that when wearing this persona the pupils have relatively little
to do with their teachers; that their levels of work on set tasks
and approved routine activities, and their interactions with
other pupils, are average; and that they are non-involved and
totally distracted from all work for a relatively large amount of
the time, although it should be emphasized that this degree of
distraction, while being relatively high, accounts for only about
one-eighth of lesson time. Perhaps it is neither unkind nor
unreasonable to nickname the pupils in their cluster 3 persona
the *easy riders*. This does not mean that they are simply
passengers, or that they do not work; on the contrary, they are
engaged in approved task work for well over 60 per cent of the
time. Nevertheless they meet the demands of the classroom at a
leisurely pace, sitting well back, as it were, to enjoy the ride,
and doing just enough to avoid the teacher's attention. When
they turn to their cluster 2 persona, however, they seem more
like *hard grinders*, for now they stay in their work bases and
stick at their task work for a relatively large amount of the time,
having comparatively little to do with their fellow pupils or with
the teacher, except as part of her whole-class audience.

In the infrequently used cluster 1 persona one can see a
variation of the hard grinder upon whom group work and hence
group interaction has been imposed so that the pupil becomes a
group toiler; and behind the cluster 4 persona there lurks that
tiny handful of pupils who take the opportunity to indulge in a
brand of *m'as-tu-vu* helpfulness which is often merely a spec-
tacular cover for very little work. This is the *fusspot* persona.
For the most part, however, and for most pupils, the choice of
personae is between that of the easy rider and that of the hard
grinder, with the former choice being by far the more popular.

An indication of the extent to which children adopt a new
persona as they move from one subject specialist to another is
conveyed in Table 3.8; and the same data are represented in
pie-chart form in Figure 3.2. The startling difference across
subjects relates to the variations between the second cluster,
the hard grinder persona and the third cluster, the easy rider
persona. In mathematics the hard grinder persona is adopted
by a very small proportion of the pupils, while in science it is
adopted by almost as large a proportion as is the easy rider
persona, and in English by a proportion which might be considered neither high nor low.

It is worth noting here that clusters 1 and 2 together account
for virtually identical proportions of the pupils in English and

Table 3.8 Distribution of pupil personae across curricular subjects

Cluster	Mathematics N	Mathematics %	English N	English %	Science N	Science %
1 (group toilers)	5	5.1	12	12.4	7	7.4
2 (hard grinders)	6	6.1	34	35.1	38	40.0
3 (easy riders)	80	81.6	50	51.5	46	48.4
4 (fusspots)	7	7.1	1	1.0	4	4.2
Total observed	98	100.0	97	100.0	95	100.0
Not observed	5		6		8	
Total pupils	103		103		103	

science, science lending itself more readily to individual hard
work and English to group effort: an explanation of the high
proportion of on-task interaction in English has already been
offered (p. 49). In these two subjects, cluster 3 also accounts
for very similar proportions of the pupils, so that if clusters 1
and 2 are grouped together as toilers it is found that there are
almost exactly the same number of toilers in English as in science,
as well as almost exactly the same number of easy riders in each
of the two subjects. This raises the question of whether these
proportions are virtually identical because they are made up for
the most part of the same children. If so, then this would seem
to lend support to the idea of the formation in each pupil of a
temperamentally based all-purpose way of coping with the fluc-

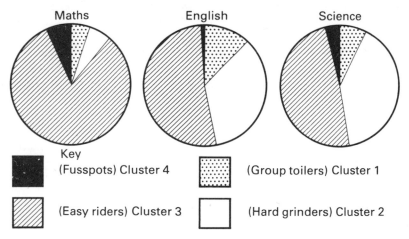

Figure 3.2 Distribution of pupil personae across subjects

Table 3.9 Membership of clusters 1 or 2 (toilers) and cluster 3 (easy riders) in English and science lessons

		Boys Science			Girls Science			All Science		
		1 or 2	3		1 or 2	3		1 or 2	3	
English	1 or 2	6 (14.3%)	11 (26.2%)	17 (40.5%)	10 (22.2%)	15 (33.3%)	25 (55.6%)	16 (18.4%)	26 (29.9%)	42 (48.3%)
English	3	16 (38.1%)	9 (21.4%)	25 (59.5%)	9 (20.0%)	11 (24.4%)	20 (44.4%)	25 (28.7%)	20 (23.0%)	45 (51.7%)
		22 (52.4%)	20 (47.6%)	42 (100%)	19 (42.2%)	26 (57.8%)	45 (100%)	41 (47.1%)	46 (52.9%)	87 (100%)

tuating demands of the day, and would put mathematics in a very isolated and somewhat anomalous position among the range of subjects investigated. If, on the other hand, the pupils making up the similar proportions of toilers and easy riders across curricular divisions are to a large extent different children, so that toilers in English are quite likely to be easy riders in science and vice versa, this supports the notion we have introduced of the personae within which the pupils act out the differing roles which seem to them appropriate in the various subjects of the curriculum.

PUPIL PERSONAE ACROSS SUBJECT AREAS

The relationships between membership of these clusters in English and science are presented in Table 3.9, and the data from boys and girls are presented first separately and then together.

Considering first the part of the table on the extreme right where the data from both sexes are combined, it will be seen that there is no tendency for toilers in either of the two subjects to be toilers in the other: indeed, if there is a tendency at all, it goes in the opposite direction. More than 60 per cent of the toilers in each subject were easy riders in the other, and well over a half of the easy riders in each subject were toilers in the other. So far the concept of pupil personae retains its usefulness, and this being so it is important to consider the data from each of the sexes separately, since there is (not to put it more strongly) a long hearsay tradition that girls do not, in general, see themselves as scientific, and that boys generally find at least some aspects of the English curriculum out of tune with their pseudo-masculine interests. The relevant parts of Table 3.9 show that the data from the present study support that tradition. Among the boys there are in English lessons more easy riders than toilers (59.5 against 40.5 per cent), and in science lessons more toilers than easy riders (52.4 against 47.6 per cent). Among the girls the situation is unequivocally reversed with more toilers than easy riders in English lessons (55.6 against 44.4 per cent) and more easy riders than toilers in science (57.8 against 42.2 per cent). However, that the sex difference is not the only factor involved is clear from the modest size of the overlap between boys and girls in this respect. It is clearly not a case of all boys liking science and all girls liking English, but rather a matter of pupil personae commonly adopted by pupils of either sex, with a clear predisposition for children of a given sex to adopt a particular persona for a particular subject.

In mathematics, as has already been shown, the great majority of children become easy riders, and it is clear that in these lessons there is generally rather little pressure towards toil either individually or in groups. The pupils who seem to merit the closest scrutiny here are those unusual children who, against

the very strong trend, maintain (or even take up) the persona
of either a hard grinder or a group toiler in this subject. It will
be seen from Table 3.8 that only 11 pupils are involved, 5 of
them being group toilers and 6 hard grinders.

For the most part these 11 pupils were toilers of one kind or
another across the board: all 11 were in clusters 1 or 2 in English,
while 9 of them were in these clusters in science (no science
data were available for one of the remaining 2). The general
point can therefore be made that only toilers by temperament
toil in mathematics. For a hard-working mathematics persona to
be adopted by pupils of otherwise easy-riding temperament is a
theoretical possibility, but was not found in practice.

Of the 11 mathematical toilers, 4 were girls and 7 were boys.
Here again, then, is the tendency for one sex to seem more in
tune than the other with a particular subject: in this case it
seems that rare as it is to be a toiler in mathematics lessons, it
is slightly less rare among boys than among girls.

Finally it seems important to pose the question: who are the
mathematical toilers in terms of primary pupil types? It has been
argued earlier that from year to year pupils seem to move towards
a strategy for survival in school, and that in general, once they
have found a way of coping which is acceptable to their teachers
they are rather unlikely to regress to a less acceptable pattern
of behaviour.

In relation to the 11 mathematical toilers, data on primary
pupil type one year earlier are available for all 11, and data on
pupil type two years earlier for 8 (since the remaining 3 pupils
were from local authority A where observation before transfer
was carried out for one year only). Two years before transfer,
4 of the 8 mathematical toilers on whom there are data were
intermittent workers, 1 was an attention seeker, 2 were solitary
workers and 1 was a quiet collaborator. Thus they were distributed amongst all four clusters with half of them character-
istically working at a very leisurely pace indeed. One year
before transfer, 3 of the 11 were solitary workers and the
remaining 8 were quiet collaborators. This shift is very clearly
consistent with the general trend which was argued earlier as
well as seeming to indicate that pupils who have previously
developed habits of working together with other children are
more likely to be able to deal constructively with the very small
amounts of teacher-pupil interaction which they will find in
mathematics lessons after transfer.

It is reasonable to see in the lack of involvement between
teacher and pupils which characterizes mathematics lessons and
differentiates them from lessons in science and English the
carte blanche which allows the majority of pupils a leisurely work-
rate in this subject. It seems likely that those few pupils who
have been termed here mathematical toilers are the mathematics
enthusiasts whose driving force comes from within rather than
from the teacher's insistence. It is noteworthy also that the fusspot persona comes into its own in mathematics lessons; although

not common even here, it appears much more frequently than in English, where it is virtually unknown, or even in science, where it is not difficult to find genuine opportunities to be helpful, for example, in fetching or washing bits of apparatus. It seems as if a small number of children are unable to tolerate the lack of teacher contact which is such a common feature of mathematics lessons, and set about making themselves noticed even at the expense of their task work.

COMPARISONS WITH PUPIL TYPES BEFORE TRANSFER

This analysis of pupil personae has illustrated the flexibility with which many pupils after transfer set about coping with the differing demands which face them as they move from one curricular area to another. With very few exceptions they settle down to intensive uninterrupted task work when the teacher demands it, and to a rather more free-and-easy mixture of work and sociability whenever they can get away with it. It must be said that in this their behaviour is remarkably like that of their elders in any situation where a group is responsible to a foreman, tutor, supervisor or other person in authority.

It is not difficult to see in these four pupil personae echoes of the four pupil types of the primary school. Group toilers are rather like the quiet collaborators; fusspots bear some relation ship to the attention seekers, and the hard grinders are an even more extreme version of the solitary workers. However, a detailed examination of the primary pupil clusters in 'Inside the Primary Classroom' (p. 144, Fig 8.1) shows too many points of divergence for the two sets to be completely equated.

One major difference concerns two of the dominant groups, the intermittent worker in the primary classroom and the easy rider persona in the transfer school. Whereas the intermittent worker tended to work as hard as solitary workers for part of the time and then break off for conversation when the teacher was engaged elsewhere, easy riders cannot do this so often because with more whole-class teaching the teacher remains at the front of the room for longer periods, keeping her eye upon them. Consequently they develop strategies for passing the time giving the appearance of working but dawdling over each task. Compared to hard grinders it takes them longer to find the correct page, copy notes or complete worksheets and they spend a lot of time on such activities as pencil-sharpening and ruling lines. Descriptions of these activities are to be found in the participants' accounts in Part IV of this volume. Faced with such behaviour, a teacher who wishes to keep the class together has either to get more work from the easy riders or slow down the hard grinders. Chapters 6 and 7 offer several samples of how teachers tackle this dilemma.

It should also be borne in mind that the pupil types derived from the data from the feeder schools refer to the overall behaviour of pupils, whereas the pupil personae were created from aspects of behaviour selected by the pupils as appropriate to the demands of specific subject lessons. Nevertheless, when each pupil's three personae were combined before carrying out a cluster analysis about a quarter of the transfer children appeared to adopt an extreme version of the easy rider's behaviour across all subjects. They were totally distracted from their work for a far greater proportion of their time than the other pupils, spent a comparatively large part of the lesson out of their work base and seemed to devote much of their effort in school to avoiding doing more than the minimum amount of work necessary to get by. The portrait of Wayne Douglas, (p. 147ff) exemplifies one form of this extreme behaviour.

Thus the examination of pupils after transfer has shown some modification of the characteristic pupil types of the primary school. In particular, the differing demands of the various subject specialists can be seen to bring about a matching flexibility in some of the pupils. Depending on their temperament and to some extent on their sex, they may maintain a hard-working or an easy-going form of behaviour whatever the subject may be; but for many of them a major lesson which they have learned in school by this stage is to give to each subject only as much effort as the particular teacher demands.

Part III
TRANSFER AND PUPIL PERFORMANCE

Paul Croll

4 PUPIL PROGRESS BEFORE TRANSFER

The main purpose of this section of the book is to explore the
extent to which the academic progress of the pupils after
transfer was influenced by the patterns of behaviour described
in Chapter 3. However, before dealing with this issue, it is
necessary to look at the pupils' performance during their second
year of observation at their feeder schools. In seeking to
evaluate their progress immediately after transfer, it is clearly
important to know whether they were making consistent gains
from year to year before transfer. This short chapter is concerned with replication, and examines whether the teaching
styles which were successful in the first year of the study were
equally successful in the second. It also seeks to answer the
question whether teachers who were observed during both years
in the feeder schools obtained consistent levels of performance
from their successive classes.

THE STUDY OF TEACHER EFFECTIVENESS - REPEATING AND DEVELOPING THE ORACLE FINDINGS

Replication is an important principle in the natural sciences but
is not very often conducted in social and educational research.
This neglect is unfortunate in an area where it is often difficult
to obtain truly representative samples of the population being
studied. The ORACLE teachers, for example, were self-selected
in the sense that once pairs of transfer schools had been chosen
all the teachers in the feeder schools whose pupils reached
transfer age during the course of the study were approached to
take part. Although these teachers seem fairly representative
of those who work in primary schools, considerable caution must
be exercised when attempting to generalize from these particular
schools to those in other parts of the country. Such caution is
all the more important when powerful multivariate techniques
such as factor analysis and cluster analysis are used, because
they can create apparently meaningful patterns out of chance
fluctuations. In this kind of situation it is essential to build into
the research design as many checks on each of the findings as
possible, especially with studies like ORACLE which do not begin
with clear-cut hypotheses to be tested but rather set out to
investigate possible relationships between different variables in
an exploratory fashion.
 On the basis of the first wave of data collection certain relation-

ships between pupil and teacher behaviour and pupil performance were reported. If subsequent waves of data collection reveal the same or very similar patterns then confidence that these are real results rather than statistical artefacts is greatly strengthened. This confidence is based on the fact that if the samples of teachers in the two consecutive years of the study were both unrepresentative of the population, then the chances of two such atypical samples yielding similar patterns of variation in the data would be infinitesimal.

One of the major findings of the ORACLE study, reported in detail in 'Inside the Primary Classroom', was the delineation of teaching styles based on detailed observation of teachers and pupils in classrooms. The typology of patterns of teaching behaviour which was created has been described in detail in Chapter 2. This kind of analysis of teaching style, basing both the overall description and the classification system on an analysis of the moment-by-moment behaviours and interactions of teachers and pupils, was a new departure in British research. Consequently the attempt to replicate these results was of particular interest. The statistical analysis used to produce the descriptions of teaching style was discussed fully in 'Inside the Primary Classroom' where the results were based on one year's observation of 58 classrooms. The following year a further 40 classrooms were observed using identical procedures. Only a third of the 40 teachers involved had been included in the previous year's sample and the analysis of this second year's data has been summarized in Chapter 2. Overall patterns of pupil and teacher behaviour and interaction were virtually identical in the second year, and a very similar typology of teaching styles emerged. However, two of the styles, the rotating changers and the habitual changers were not clearly distinguished in the second year's analysis and were therefore combined. This example illustrates the way in which a longitudinal design enables replication of data to take place and greatly increases confidence in the original results.

The developmental aspect of a longitudinal study is also illustrated, again with respect to teaching styles, in Chapter 2. As the pupils in the sample move into classrooms taught by different teachers it is possible to study the interaction between teaching styles and pupil behaviour in a developmental fashion, by analysing the behaviours of the pupils over the two years in the context of the styles of the teachers in whose classes they find themselves. As Chapter 2 shows that pupils change their behaviour more often than teachers, this analysis tends to emphasize the importance of the teacher and to suggest that teaching style is something that has considerable impact on the behaviours of pupils in the classes studied.

TEACHING STYLES AND PUPIL PROGRESS: YEAR 2

The design of the ORACLE study allowed for the replication both
of the typology of teaching styles and of the process-product
analysis of the gains made by pupils taught by the various
styles. The second year's analysis is based on those pupils who
were observed for two years in primary classrooms. As some of
the pupils transferred to secondary schools at the end of the
first year, this is a smaller sample than was used in the original
process study; as indicated above, observation and testing
were carried out in 40 primary classes in the second year of the
study. The pupils observed and tested were the same ones who
had been studied in the first year. The teachers were mostly
different because the selection of teachers was not under control
of the researchers but was governed by the school head who
allocated teachers to particular classes. However, 14 of the 40
second-year teachers happened to have also been observed in
the first year of the study. It is possible to repeat the analysis
of pupil progress, comparing the gains made by pupils taught by
different styles in the same fashion as in the first year of the
study.

The gains in scores on basic skills made by pupils taught by
different styles in the second year of the study were compared
using an analysis of co-variance, a technique which allows for
the fact that pupils start with different levels of achievement.
Each pupil's initial score is used to predict his performance at
the end of the year and this prediction then compared with the
actual performance on the final achievement test. Pupils who
do better than predicted are judged to have made progress. The
analysis was conducted using both individual pupil scores and
average class scores. For the interested reader the statistical
issues are discussed in detail in Chapters 5, 6 and 9 of 'Progress
and Performance in the Primary Classroom' where detailed
results are also presented.

*Table 4.1 Teaching styles and progress in the basic skills
(class mean scores, Year 1 and Year 2 data)*

Residual scores	Individual monitors		Class enquirers		Group instruc-tors		Infrequent Changers		Rotating & Habitual Changers		Statistically significant	
	Yr 1	Yr 2	Yr 1	Yr 2	Yr 1	Yr 2	Yr 1	Yr 2	Yr 1	Yr 2	Yr 1	Yr 2
Mathematics	-0.5	-1.6	1.4	2.4	0	-0.4	0.6	0	-0.4	-0.1		
Language	-0.8	-0.3	1.7	1.1	0.5	-0.3	1.1	0.9	-0.7	-0.3	*	
Reading	0.8	-0.2	0.8	-0.2	0.3	-0.2	1.3	1.6	-1.1	-0.2	*	
N =	13	4	9	5	7	15	6	4	23	12		

*Statistically significant at 5 per cent level.

The scores for the various styles are presented as residual
gains in Table 4.1 and 4.2. In Table 4.1 residual gains using
class means scores as the unit of analysis are presented and in
Table 4.2 residual gains using individual scores are given.

*Table 4.2   Teaching styles and progress in the basic skills
(individual scores, Year 1 and Year 2)*

Residual scores	Individual monitors		Class enquirers		Group instruc- tors		Infrequent Changers		Rotating & Habitual Changers		Statistically significant	
	Yr 1	Yr 2	Yr 1	Yr 2	Yr 1	Yr 2	Yr 1	Yr 2	Yr 1	Yr 2	Yr 1	Yr 2
Mathe- matics	-0.5	-2.1	1.8	1.2	0.2	0.2	0.4	0.8	0.6	-0.1	**	*
Language	-0.5	-0.3	1.5	1.1	1.2	0.1	0.5	1.1	-0.9	-0.4	**	
Reading	0.5	0.2	0	-0.4	-0.1	0.1	2.7	1.1	-1.0	-0.2	**	
N =	97	27	67	26	49	68	43	18	153	118		

* Statistically significant at 5 per cent level.
** Statistically significant at 1 per cent level.

These can be compared with the first-year results also presented
in these tables. Unlike the first-year results, in none of the
three areas of basic skills does the analysis of class mean scores
give statistically significant results and in the analysis of
individual scores only the results for mathematics are statistically
significant.

However, more important than the question of statistical significance is that in every case the direction of the differences is
the same as was found in the original analysis. For mathematics
and language skills the class enquirers achieved the best results,
while for reading the pupils of the infrequent changers made the
most progress. Pupils taught by individual monitors had below-
average results in general but had better results for reading.
The new combined group of rotating and habitual changers
produced below-average results in all three areas.

These results come from mainly different teachers from those
in the first year of the study and consequently constitute a
genuine replication of the findings. Although the differences
between styles are mostly smaller than in the first year and so
do not generally reach statistical significance, the overall pattern
is strikingly similar.

In 'Progress and Performance in the Primary Classroom' pupil
performance was not confined solely to progress on basic skills.
A series of activities designed to tap skills of independent study
were also completed by the pupils. Some of these activities were
structured exercises concerned with important aims of primary
education such as communicating clearly, listening with concentration and acquiring information by other means than reading.
There were also a number of study skill exercises derived in
part from the work of Dorothy Gardner (1966) which assessed
the pupils' ability to make a model of a clock face, draw a map

of a classroom and construct a block graph. However, it was
not possible in the second year to repeat these exercises
because by this point in the study considerable demands were
already being made upon the teachers and their pupils. Instead
the subject of the teacher assessments for the second year consisted mainly of a series of exercises related to the primary
teachers' aim that children should be able to make use of the
four rules in arithmetic in order to solve everyday problems in
mathematics (Ashton et al., 1975). A full description of how
these exercises were constructed by a group of teachers is
given by Jasman in Chapter 11 of the third ORACLE volume,
'Research and Practice in the Primary Classroom'. All the
exercises were administered on a single occasion and thus no
direct measure of progress is possible. However, as with the
treatment of study skills in 'Progress and Performance in the
Primary Classroom', analysis of co-variance can be used to look
at the performance of children in the use of the four rules compared with the performance that would have been expected on
the basis of their score on the Richmond Tests of mathematics at
the end of the first year of the research. The results are presented separately for each of the four rules of arithmetic and
for the total mathematics exercise in Table 4.3.

*Table 4.3 Teaching styles and performance in structured
mathematics exercises (individual scores, Year 2 data)*

Residual score using previous year's Richmond Test score as co-variate	Individual monitors	Class enquirers	Group instructors	Infrequent changers	Other changers	
Use of four rules	-0.9	1.54	-0.8	0.1	0.5	*
Use in practical maths exercises	-2.9	6.00	-0.8	6.1	-0.9	
N =	30	19	78	22	120	

*Statistically significant at the 5 per cent level.

As will probably be anticipated from the results of the conventional mathematics tests, this analysis also confirms the first-
year ORACLE findings. The pupils who in the second year were
taught by class enquirers now do better in exercises concerned
with the four rules of arithmetic than would have been anticipated
from their results in the mathematics test at the end of their
previous year of schooling. In the case of the practical mathematics exercises pupils taught by class enquirers and infrequent
changers do very much better than would have been anticipated.
In the case of the four rules of arithmetic but not the practical
mathematics exercises these results are statistically significant.

PUPIL PROGRESS AND PUPIL TYPE

In 'Progress and Performance in the Primary Classroom' a key
issue concerns the influence of different teaching styles on
pupils' progress, particularly in relation to different types of
pupils. The general conclusion was that teaching style was the
dominant influence in that if this variable was omitted from the
analysis then few differences were observed between the different types of pupils which had been identified. An important
finding concerned the differences between two particular types,
the solitary worker and the intermittent worker. It was estimated
that whereas on average intermittent workers were distracted
from their set tasks for one out of the five days each week,
solitary workers tended to avoid such distractions and work
much harder. Much of the recent research conducted in the
United States has suggested that the time that children spend
on their task is one of the most important determinants in
estimating a pupil's progress, particularly in basic skills.
According to these predictions solitary workers should make
more progress than intermittent workers. However, the analysis
of the first-year data showed that, overall, there were no
significant differences in the progress made by the two types of
pupil. This suggests that rather than being lazy pupils, who
find difficulty in concentrating, many of the intermittent workers
are fully capable of doing the work but choose instead to make
it last for longer than necessary. Presumably they are aware
that if they complete a particular worksheet quickly their reward
will be another with similar but more difficult examples and they
choose to make the first one last for as long as possible.

These pupil types, described originally on the basis of the
first year's observation data, emerge again from the analysis of
the second-year observations, as shown in chapter 2 of this
volume. When the progress made by different types of pupil was
investigated in 'Progress and Performance in the Primary Classroom' there was very little evidence to suggest that different
types of pupil made progress independent of the particular classroom in which they were taught. Solitary workers made good
progress not because they were this type of pupil but because
they were taught by teachers who were class enquirers. Being
a solitary worker in a class of a habitual changer or a rotating
changer, the two weakest styles, did not result in the same
levels of progress. It is of interest to see how far this is true
of the differences between pupils in the second year of the
study.

Table 4.4 shows the progress made by different types for both
Year 1 and Year 2. For the first year's data the results of this
analysis suggest that although there was an association between
pupil types and pupil progress, it was a very weak one.

On the basis of the first year's progress data solitary workers
were the only group of pupils to make better than predicted
rates of progress in all three of the test areas while intermittent

workers and quiet collaborators made lower than average rates
of progress. However, these differences were very small and
despite the relatively large sample size involved only in language
skills did the difference reach statistical significance. Moreover,
when the effect of teaching style was introduced into the analysis
controlling for teaching style reduced the effects of pupil type
still further so that in no case were they statistically significant
while the reversed form of this analysis, looking at the effects
of teaching style when controlling for pupil types, produced no

*Table 4.4 Pupil types and progress in the basic skills (Year 1
data compared with Year 2)*

Residual scores	Attention seekers		Intermittent workers		Solitary workers		Quiet collaborators		Statistically significant	
	Yr 1	Yr 2	Yr 1	Yr 2	Yr 1	Yr 2	Yr 1	Yr 2	Yr 1	Yr 2
Mathematics	-0.25	0.01	-0.30	0.99	0.54	-0.08	-0.21	-0.37		
Language	-1.06	-0.32	-0.06	-0.81	0.75	0.18	-0.22	0.44	*	
Reading	0.28	0.02	-0.57	-0.31	0.69	0.40	-0.69	-0.18		
N =	77	62	144	40	138	69	48	91		

*Statistically significant at the 5 per cent level.

difference in the effect that teaching style made. This analysis
led to the conclusion that there was an effect of teaching style
upon pupil's progress but that there was little or no effect of
pupil type as defined by characteristics measured by the observation instruments. The small apparent effect of pupil type on
progress in the original analysis occurred because of the
association between particular pupil types and particular teaching styles and all but disappeared when teaching style was
controlled. There were no interactions between teaching style
and pupil type which would have meant, for example, that
certain teaching styles achieved better results with certain types
of pupil but poorer results with other types.

The second-year progress data provides an opportunity to
repeat the analysis of pupil types in the same way as was done
earlier with the analysis of teaching styles. This replication is
presented in Table 4.4. In the second year's data the residual
gain scores of the different pupil types can be seen to be even
smaller than those for Year 1 and in no case statistically significant. No pupil type is associated with better than predicted
gains in all three areas of the basis skills and in no case is a
pupil type associated with a better than predicted gain of one
mark on any one of the tests. These very small differences, and
the fact that none of them is statistically significant despite
relatively large sample sizes, confirm the view presented in the
original analysis that teaching style rather than pupil type is a
major determinant of a pupil's level of achievement in the basic
skills.

TEACHERS MAKE A DIFFERENCE

The main theme of this chapter and of the previous ones is that
primary school teachers can be classified according to differences
and similarities in their patterns of minute-by-minute interactions
with pupils in their classes and that the teaching style of the
teacher characterized in this way makes a difference to the
pupils in her class both in terms of their behaviour and of their
progress in the basic skills. It therefore addresses the familiar
issue in contemporary educational research of whether schools
and teachers really make a difference to the level of achievement
and rates of progress of their pupils. The commonsense answer
to this question is that of course they do; it seems obvious that
if pupils are well taught and if they are at good schools they
will make more progress than if they are badly taught and are
at bad schools. Nevertheless in recent years there has developed
a degree of scepticism among educational researchers and others
about this apparently obvious conclusion, and it is worth considering the reasons why this is so.

In part it can be related to a general disillusion with the
possibilities of education and in particular with the optimism
associated with the educational reforms and expansion of the
1960s. The title of a recently published collection of essays on
education is 'Schooling in Decline'. Its editor writes: 'During
this period (1950s and 1960s) liberal dogmas urged variously
that in advanced industrial societies educational expansion and
change could be used as a vehicle for bringing about the worthwhile objectives of greater economic efficiency and greater social
justice (Bernbaum, 1979).' The apparent failure of these hopes
and in particular the failure of educational systems to compensate for the disadvantages suffered by pupils from working-class
and ethnic-minority backgrounds has been well documented,
especially in the United States. The major studies of Coleman
et al. (1966) and Jencks et al. (1972) concluded that the influence
of school on achievement was slight compared with the effects of
pupils and their family characteristics (Jencks et. al., 1972 p.159).

> We have shown that the most important determinant of edu-
> cational attainment is family background. Except for family
> background the most important determinant of educational
> attainment is probably cognitive skill. Qualitative differences
> between high schools seem to explain about 2% of the variation
> in students' educational attainment. Unfortunately we cannot
> say what qualities of a high school boost its college entrance
> rates and what qualities lower it. School resources do not
> appear to influence students' educational attainment at all.

In a similar fashion early evaluations of the Head Start programme of intensive early intervention and compensatory
education for young children from disadvantaged and ethnic-
minority backgrounds found few lasting effects of participation

in the programme (Bronfenbrenner, 1974). In Britain research conducted for the Plowden Committee concluded that the influence of a pupil's home background (and especially of his parents' attitudes to education) was very much more important for achievement than were school influences.

Of particular concern in Britain has been the failure of the educational system to bring about a greater measure of social equality. Educational researchers in the 1950s and 1960s were also very often educational reformers. It was hoped that the expansion of educational opportunities and the abolition of selection at 11+ would equalize provision and in consequence equalize educational achievement between pupils from different social backgrounds. In general this has not occurred. The increased opportunities have largely been taken up by pupils from middle- and upper-class backgrounds and the proportion of working-class pupils entering universities has actually decreased in recent years (Halsey et al., 1980; UCCA, 1981). The failure of these reforming hopes and the growing realization that, in Bernstein's phrase, 'education cannot compensate for society' (Bernstein, 1970) have been characterized as 'a retreat from optimism and a decline not only in the value placed upon education but also in the scale of the enterprise' (Bernbaum, 1979). It seems likely that this mood is in part responsible for current scepticism about the effects of school and of teachers.

Another factor in this scepticism is the debate over what are the characteristics of good schools and good teachers. Although most people concerned with education probably feel intuitively that schools and teachers do make a difference, there is far less agreement about what it is about teachers that makes this differ- ence and even about whether particular characteristics should be valued or discouraged. Different commentators and, to some extent, different researchers have provided widely different prescriptions for effective teaching. The most obvious examples of this are the claims made by proponents of progressive and traditional teaching methods.

Researchers have generally treated the question of school effects and of teacher effects separately. The American studies by Coleman and Jencks were concerned with school effects, but there is also a large body of American research which is con- cerned with teacher effects (Brophy, 1979a). In Britain research has usually been either on schools (Rutter et al., 1979) or on teachers (Bennett, 1976).

Recent research has tended to support the commonsense view that both schools and teachers do make a difference and it has recently been pointed out that although Jencks and Coleman emphasize the dominance of the effects of individual character- istics and the ineffectiveness of the educational system in reduc- ing social inequalities, they did not entirely deny the influence of schools (Gray, 1981). Later work on the Head Start programme has also suggested that it was more effective than early evalu- ations suggested (Zigler and Valentine, 1979). A major British

study of education and social mobility has also come to the conclusion that type of school attended in its broadest sense
(grammar school, secondary modern school, technical school)
'for boys of similar ability and background allocation between
the three main types of state school was enormously consequen-
tial.' The authors also conclude that, although educational
expansion has not resulted in greater equality of educational
opportunity, further expansion would make these reforming
aims possible (Halsey et al., 1980, pp. 212, 217-18).

An important advance in recent years in educational research
has been the development of process-product studies. These are
studies which compare schools or classes not only on achievement
measures such as test scores (products) but also in terms of
what actually happens in educational settings (process). The
process data are typically gathered by means of systematic
observation of teachers and pupils in school classrooms. In this
way it is possible to link teacher and pupil behaviour and interactions to outcome measures such as test scores. In a recent
review of these studies Brophy (1979a) claims that they show
that teachers do make a difference: 'Certain teachers elicit much
more student learning than others and their success is linked to
consistent differences in teaching behaviour,' said to be related
to forms of 'direct instruction'. An appraisal of this American
evidence will be made in the final section of this volume.

The only process-product study of this kind, utilizing detailed
systematic observation of pupils and teachers, in Britain, is the
ORACLE project on which the present discussion is based. However, two other recent British studies have also linked descriptive accounts of teachers and schools with measures of the
progress made by their pupils. These studies conducted by
Bennett and by Rutter have also come to the conclusion that
respectively teachers and schools make a difference. The study
by Bennett (1976), 'Teaching Styles and Pupil Progress', constructed a typology of teaching styles based on teachers' replies
to a questionnaire eliciting details of their classroom practice.
These details included the curriculum (integrated versus single-
subject teaching), testing, discipline (smacking, sending pupils
from the room) and classroom organization (choice of seats,
insisting on quiet). On this basis teachers were categorized into
three basic styles: formal, informal and mixed teaching styles.
The progress made by pupils taught by these styles was then
compared by means of techniques similar to those used in the
present study. The main (and highly controversial) finding was
that teachers using formal or traditional methods achieved the
greatest pupil gains and that teachers using progressive or
informal methods achieved the least gains. Re-analysis of the
data has led to some modification of these findings (Aitkin et al.,
1981). However this modification is still in accord with the view
that what teachers do makes a difference to pupil progress.
The other recent study is that of Rutter and his colleagues
conducted in twelve secondary schools in London (Rutter et al.,

1979). This study, entitled 'Fifteen Thousand Hours', was concerned with the effects of schools as institutions rather than of
individual teachers. The study found differences between the
schools in terms of levels of achievement, truancy, behaviour
and delinquency. These differences were related to characteristics of the schools as social institutions, to organizational
arrangements and to 'school ethos'.

These two studies, although very different and not using the
detailed classroom observation of the American research, both
reinforced the view that differences in the schooling pupils
received makes a difference to learning and to other outcomes.
The ORACLE research also supports this view. Although
Bennett's distinction between formal and informal teaching
methods was rejected as a result of detailed analysis of the
observational data, the ORACLE results like Bennett's show that
what goes on in classrooms makes a difference to the attainment
of pupils. No direct comparisons between the ORACLE study and
the American observational studies are possible as the data-
gathering procedures and the typologies of teaching styles are
different, probably as a result of the different context of British
and American education. However, certain similarities do exist,
particularly in the common finding that giving feedback, discussing the children's work both when it is right and when it is
wrong, is an important part of the learning process. Explanations
of this differ and will be examined in the final section of this
book.

DIFFERENT TYPES OF REPLICATION: REPLICATING STYLES AND RE-STUDYING PEOPLE

The analysis described earlier in the chapter consists of a conventional replication in which a new group of teachers was
studied, a new analysis of teaching styles was carried out and
when the first year's teaching styles were reproduced a new
comparison between them made. Rather than attempting to repeat
teaching styles with a new group of teachers, a different
approach is to follow the same group of teachers for a further
year and to compare the progress made by their classes over the
two-year period. A recent British study using this method
questions the conclusion that teaching makes a difference. Gray
(1979) points out that if some types of teaching produce better
results than others then it is reasonable to suggest that more
successful teachers will be consistently more effective, that is,
teachers whose classes make above-average progress in one year
should also produce above-average results in classes they teach
in other years. Gray tested this inference by measuring the
reading gains of top infant age pupils in the classes of 41
teachers in one year and comparing them with the gains made by
different pupils taught by the same teachers the following year.
This analysis showed no correlation between the gains made

(using the residual gains scores in the analysis), over the two years. Although Gray is cautious about interpreting his results and does not have systematic information about the methods used by the various teachers in the two years, his findings clearly do not support the assumption that teachers make a difference.

The ORACLE study was not mainly designed to conduct this type of analysis, but the accident of having 14 teachers who took part in both the first and second year of the study allows a limited comparison to be made. These 14 teachers all fell into the same teaching style in the cluster analysis of the second year's data as they had in the first, most of them in the group of rotating and habitual changers.

In order to examine the consistency of the gains made by pupils taught by these 14 teachers across the two years, residual gains were calculated for their pupils for both years. These residuals were separately calculated using the scores from these 14 teachers only. This is because the residual gain is the extent to which pupils or teachers do better or worse than expected and this expectation is a purely statistical one, as it is made in comparison with other pupils or teachers in the sample. Consequently, the inclusion of new teachers in the analysis may influence a teacher's relative position even if her actual performance is unchanged. The residuals used were therefore measures of the teacher's performance relative to the other 13 teachers who were studied over two years.

The rank order correlation between the teachers over the two years was -0.25, indicating a negative, but not statistically significant, correlation between the two sets of gains. This failure to find a positive correlation indicates no consistent teacher effects among these 14 teachers over the two years and in this respect supports the findings of Gray. However, it should be emphasized that such a result is not incompatible with the conclusions about the effects of teacher style made earlier. Eleven of the 14 teachers came from a single teaching style, the mixture of the rotating and habitual changers. It may be remembered that this was the most unsuccessful group of teachers, so that what the data demonstrate is that there is no consistency among the teachers whose pupils made less than average progress in basic skills. It may have been that if this small group of teachers had contained a higher proportion of the more successful styles a relationship might have emerged, since the analysis of the teaching style data in 'Progress and Performance in the Primary Classroom' tended to suggest that the successful styles influence pupil behaviour in different ways from unsuccessful ones. For example, teachers using the successful styles were able to raise the levels of achievement of even poorly motivated pupils while those teachers using the unsuccessful styles were not. Consistency of teacher performance may also therefore be a function of a particular style.

However, it is a fact that the variation in performance between the 11 teachers from the changers style is one which the ORACLE analysis has not explained. But the consistency of an individual teacher's performance is a separate question from that of the consistency of the effects of a particular teaching style. It is reasonable to suppose that although one given teaching style may produce more pupil progress than another nevertheless the performance of individual teachers in that style will vary according to the pupils who make up the class in a given year. The analysis of these 14 teachers raises questions about the consistency of individual teacher performance, but it is not relevant to the question of the effects of teaching style discussed earlier.

PUPIL DIFFERENCES AFTER TRANSFER

The clear picture which has emerged from the foregoing examinations of teacher and pupil behaviour and pupil progress from year to year before transfer is of a situation in which the teacher's style is unmistakably dominant. From one year to the next individual pupils may dramatically change their behaviour, and in doing so many move from one type to another. The types themselves remain remarkably stable in terms of relative pupil progress, irrespective of which individual pupils they contain.

The principal theme of this section, however, is the relationship between the factors which affect pupil progress and the behaviours which pupils adopt after transfer. This will be taken up in the next chapter.

5 PUPIL PERFORMANCE IN THE TRANSFER SCHOOLS

This chapter is concerned with pupil progress in the basic skills during the first year after transfer. The progress pupils made when they transferred to their new schools was assessed by means of the scores on the tests of mathematics, language skills and reading, administered during the final term in the feeder school and at the end of their first year in the transfer school. However, the analysis of pupil progress over this period will not follow the same pattern as that adopted for the analysis of progress during the primary school years. The reasons for this have to do with the very much smaller number of pupils and teachers who are being studied in the transfer schools, the more complex teaching arrangements which exist in these schools and the results of the analysis of teacher and pupil behaviours described in the previous section, where it was shown that pupils faced a basic choice of working hard or taking it easy. At one extreme, about a quarter of the pupils favoured the easy rider persona in all the three subjects observed, while a smaller group adopted an extreme form of across-the-board dedicated hard work first encountered among the solitary workers in the primary schools. Before transfer differences in the amounts of work done had a very limited effect on the pupils' progress. It is of interest to see whether this is also the case after transfer.

The analysis to be conducted here will therefore look at some general themes relevant to the problem of transfer between the feeder and transfer schools. This will be done by examining the careers of particular children and groups of children as they move between the two school systems. It will look at patterns of continuity between the children at secondary schools as well as at elements of disjunction between the two sets of school experiences.

CONTINUITIES IN RELATIVE CLASS STATUS

At the beginning of the ORACLE programme of research pupils were grouped according to their relative standing in the class on tests of the basic skills in order to increase the efficiency of sampling for observation. In each of the 58 primary classes included in the study eight children were to be selected for detailed observation. These children were selected by dividing the class up according to two factors, their sex and their score on tests of basic skills as described in Chapter 1 (p. 17).

Consequently, every child in the study was initially categorized with regard to his standing in the class relative to his fellow pupils. A comparison of this initial situation with the child's position in the class at the end of his first year in secondary school provides an indication of continuity with regard to this aspect of classroom experience. This is a different question to that of continuity in absolute levels of achievement as measured, at least in part, by the scores on tests of basic skills. It refers more to the subjective experience of classroom life and the position in which a pupil finds himself in comparison with his fellow pupils. Other research has shown that children are very aware of their relative standing with regard to achievement in their class and are very accurate in their assessment of it. Relative academic position has been shown to be one of the basic structuring arrangements by which a class is understood by the pupils as well as by the teacher (Nash, 1973).

Table 5.1 Relative class position of target pupils before and after transfer: local authority A

		End of first year in middle school			
		Top quartile	Middle	Bottom quartile	
Beginning of last year in lower school	Top quartile	6	1	0	7
	Middle	3	12	4	19
	Bottom quartile	0	2	4	6
		9	15	8	32

Top quartile pupils remaining in top quartile: 85.7% (6/7)
Bottom quartile pupils remaining in bottom quartile: 66.7% (4/6)
Top quartile pupils coming from top quartile: 66.7% (6/9)
Bottom quartile pupils coming from bottom quartile: 50% (4/8)

A comparison of relative class position at the beginning of the ORACLE study and at the end of the first year in the transfer school has been made separately for local authority A and for local authority B and C combined. In local authority A pupils were studied from the beginning of their last year in the lower school and followed, in the second year of the research, into their first year in a 9-13 middle school. The continuities in relative position given in Table 5.1 refer to tests administered nearly two years apart and in different schools. As Table 5.1 shows, there is considerable continuity in the subjective experience of pupils with regard to their relative standing in class. Of the seven pupils who began their final year in the lower school in the top quarter of their class with regard to achievement, six were in the top quartile of their class at the end of

their first year in middle school. Four of the six pupils in the
bottom quartile of their class at the beginning of their final year
at lower school were still in the bottom quartile of their class at
the end of their first year at middle school. Put another way,
two-thirds of the top pupils at the end of the first year in the
middle schools were pupils who had been in the top quartile in
the first school and half of the bottom pupils at the end of this
first year at middle school were pupils who had been in the
bottom quartile in their previous school. Inevitably, similar
patterns of continuity hold for the pupils in the middle quartile
groups.

Table 5.2 presents a similar analysis for local authority areas
B and C but over a longer period of time. These data refer to
pupils initially categorized at the beginning of their penultimate
year in primary schools and compares this relative position with

*Table 5.2 Relative class position of target pupils before and
after transfer: local authorities B and C*

		End of first year in middle school			
		Top quartile	Middle	Bottom quartile	
Beginning of penultimate year in primary school	Top quartile	10	2	1	13
	Middle	5	21	5	31
	Bottom quartile	1	4	8	13
		16	27	14	57

Top quartile pupils remaining in top quartile: 76.9% (10/13)
Bottom quartile pupils remaining in bottom quartile: 61.5% (8/13)
Top quartile pupils coming from top quartile: 62.5% (10/16)
Bottom quartile pupils coming from bottom quartile: 57.1% (8/14)

that at the end of the first year in secondary schools. That is, it
compares relative position on tests separated by almost three
years. Very similar patterns emerge as were found in local
authority A. More than three-quarters of the original top pupils
were still in the top quartile in a different class in a different
school almost three years later. More than six in ten of the
bottom quartile were also in the same relative position. These
figures are the more striking if it is recognized that they reflect
not only continuity in levels of achievement, but have persisted
while children have been mixed into new classes with children
from different classes and different schools to the ones in which
their relative standing was originally measured, and that true
levels of continuity of this sort are probably under-estimated by
imposing the arbitrary cut-off point used in this analysis. These
figures show clearly that the experience of success and failure

in school which, particularly among these age-groups, is judged relative to other pupils and which other studies have shown are extremely important to children are ones which remain largely unchanged as children move between the upper levels of the primary school to the first year in secondary school.

DISJUNCTIONS IN ACHIEVEMENT BETWEEN FEEDER AND TRANSFER SCHOOLS

The previous analysis has concentrated on continuity between different stages of the educational system. There is in some cases, however, a substantial lack of continuity between the two stages. In respect to pupil performance as measured by tests of achievement this lack of continuity is shown by a marked decrease in the levels of progress made by pupils in their first years in the transfer school compared with their progress throughout the feeder school and the progress that many of them will presumably continue to make as they prepare for public examinations towards the end of the secondary stage. The primary school classrooms in the ORACLE study were the settings for continuous progress on the part of almost all their pupils. The analysis of pupil progress and the comparisons of the progress made by pupils taught by different teachers contained in previous volumes and summarized here in Chapter 4 were all made in the context of this steady progress in absolute terms, throughout the sample. The statistical technique used utilizes the notion of residual gain, and consequently these gains are sometimes expressed as negative quantities. It was, however, made clear that these negative residual gains are negative only in the sense that they are less than the child or the class might have been expected to achieve given their original level of achievement relative to other children and classes in the study. They are not negative in an absolute sense; all classes and almost all children in the primary schools made progress. However, this was not so in the first year of transfer to secondary education. Not only were average levels of progress a good deal lower in the first year after transfer than they were during the primary years but for the first time substantial numbers of pupils made losses in absolute terms, that is, they achieved lower scores in the tests of basic skills at the end of their first year in the transfer school than they had at the end of their last year in the feeder school.

These findings are presented in Table 5.3. In local authority A pupils were tested only during their final year in the feeder school, and then again during their first year in the transfer school. Of the 29 pupils from whom all the relevant data are available all made gains during their last year in lower school. However, only just over half made gains during their first year in the transfer school. Similar results were obtained in local authority B and C where children were studied for two years in

Table 5.3 Gains and losses in scores on the basic skills after transfer

Local authority		Pupils making gains	Pupils making no change	Pupils making losses
A	Year 1 (Last year in lower school)	29 (100%)	0	0
	Year 2 (First year in middle school)	15 (51.7%)	1 (3.4%)	13 (44.8%)
	Year 1 (Penultimate year in primary school)	50 (96.2%)	0	2 (3.8%)
B and C	Year 2 (Last year in primary school)	42 (91.3%)	2 (4.3%)	2 (4.3%)
	Year 3 (First year in secondary school)	36 (69.2%)	5 (9.6%)	11 (21.2%)
	All changes before transfer*	121 (95.3%)	2 (1.6%)	4 (3.1%)
A and B and C	All changers after transfer	51 (63.0%)	6 (7.4%)	24 (29.6%)

*Some pupils appear twice in the figures in this row because they were seen over three years.

their feeder schools as well as during their first year after transfer. In the penultimate primary year 96 per cent of the 52 pupils for whom all the relevant information was available made progress. In their last primary school year 91 per cent made progress, but in the first year in the secondary school 69 per cent made progress and 30 per cent either did not change or fell back. For the three local authorities combined all possible comparisons before transfer show that 95 per cent of possible gains were actually made. In comparison after transfer only 63 per cent of pupils had continued to gain by the end of their first year.

Table 5.4 Average raw score gains by type of transfer school and by local authority

Local authority	A		B		C		Total
Transfer school type	Primary (APT)	Secondary (AST)	Primary (BPT)	Secondary (BST)	Primary (CPT)	Secondary (CST)	
Average gains	2.67	0.09	4.1	7.61	1.29	5.49	3.4
Percentage of pupils making gains	57.1	46.7	57.1	86.7	62.5	71.4	63.0

These results are shown school by school and together with the actual average raw score gains in Table 5.4. The average gain on scores on the basic skills during the first year in secondary education was 3.4 marks. This compares with an average gain during the year in primary education of 12.2 marks a year (not shown in the table). The degree of progress in the six schools in the study ranges from an average gain of virtually nothing to one of over 7.5 marks. The percentage of pupils actually making gains ranges from under a half to over 85 per cent. There are a number of further conclusions which can be drawn from Table 5.4. First, it shows that the phenomenon of decreased levels of performance is a general feature of transfer, at least amongst the schools studied. Even in the most success-ful of the transfer schools a far higher proportion of children were losing ground than did so in any of the years in the feeder schools. Second, the problems of pupils after transfer did not relate in any straightforward fashion to whether the schools attempted to maintain a progressive primary-type ethos or a traditional secondary one. Both the most and the least successful of the transfer schools belonged to the traditional, secondary type. Third, the decrease in rates of progress and the absolute loss of ground by certain children was not a result of pupils' scores being affected by any ceiling effects on the tests. The school which achieved almost zero gains was in local authority A where the lowest age of transfer was studied. Consequently the pupils were among the youngest in the sample and their test scores were some way from the maximum possible.

Table 5.5 Gains and losses at different levels of achievement and by sex

		Pupils making gains	Pupils making no change	Pupils making losses	N
Score at end of last year before transfer	60+	15 (39.5%)	5 (13.2%)	18 (47.4%)	38
	40 – 59	26 (81.3%)	1 (3.1%)	5 (15.6%)	32
	below 40	10 (90.9%)	0	1 (9.1%)	11
Sex	Boys	19 (47.5%)	3 (7.5%)	18 (45.0%)	40
	Girls	32 (78.0%)	3 (7.3%)	6 (14.6%)	41

This question of ceiling effects is taken up again in Table 5.5. Here the gains and losses of pupils in the first year in the trans-fer school are considered separately for children with different levels of achievement and also by sex. Not surprisingly losses

are more frequent among the higher-achieving pupils but the
problem still exists among lower achievers. In fact, on a set of
tests having a combined top score of 90, the highest-achieving
pupil in the present sample scored 79 at the end of his last
year in primary school and only 9 of the 81 pupils scored over
70.

A striking difference emerges between progress before and
after transfer between boys and girls. In the analysis of the
primary feeder school scores it was shown that both absolute
levels of achievement and rates of progress were virtually
identical for both sexes. In the transfer schools, however, it
is boys who are less likely to make progress. Table 5.5 shows
that fewer than half the boys in the sample made gains on the
tests of basic skills during their first year in the transfer
school and 45 per cent fell below their feeder school score. In
contrast over three-quarters of the girls made gains and a frac-
tion under 15 per cent made losses.

CLASSROOM INTERACTION AND ACHIEVEMENT IN BASIC SKILLS

The systematic observation conducted in the transfer school
classes and reported in the previous chapter makes possible a
comparison of the behaviours and interactions of pupils who were
relatively successful in their first year after transfer with those
who were not. Table 5.6 presents the results from some of the
categories of the pupil observation schedule for the 51 pupils
who made gains in their first year in the transfer schools and
for the 24 pupils who made losses. For each group of pupils two
sets of figures are presented. The columns (1) and (3) give the
results from the Pupil Record for the pupils for all the occasions
on which they were observed before they transferred. For some
of the pupils these will be observations made over two years
and for some pupils they will be made over one year. Columns
(2) and (4) give the results for the pupils in their first year
at the transfer school. Consequently, it is possible to compare
the behaviours and interactions of pupils who made gains with
those who made losses, both before and after the transfer to the
next stage of education. It is also possible to compare the results
of each group before and after transfer.

As has already been established in Chapter 3, there were
differences in interactions and behaviour between the feeder
and transfer schools. Two results which were described in
Chapter 3 and which are presented again here are the much
higher levels of class teaching in the transfer schools compared
with the primary feeder schools and the rather high levels of
pupil involvement in their work. The categories of the Pupil
Record presented in Table 5.6 include various types of interaction with the teacher, total interaction with other pupils, task-
oriented interaction with other pupils and the time spent on task.

Table 5.6 Classroom behaviour and interaction of 'gainers' and 'losers' after transfer

Percentage of total observations	Pupils making gains after transfer		Pupils making losses after transfer	
Interaction with teacher	(1) Before transfer	(2) After transfer	(3) Before transfer	(4) After transfer
Individual	1.0	1.1	1.0	1.2
Group	1.5	0.8	1.1	0.6
Class	12.1	27.6	11.8	29.8
Total	14.6	29.5	13.9	31.6
Interaction with pupils				
Total	17.9	17.9	17.9	15.0
Task-oriented	4.3	7.6*	6.4	3.9*
Total time spent on task	59.5	69.6*	58.5	61.8*
N =		51		24

*Differences between 'gainers' and 'losers' after transfer (columns 2 and 4) significant at 5 per cent level.

In the feeder schools the two groups of pupils, that is, the 51 pupils who later made gains in their transfer schools and the 24 pupils who lost ground on the tests of basic skills during their first year in the new school, showed very similar patterns both with regard to interaction with teacher, interaction with other pupils and the amount of time they spent engaged on their work. The two 'before' columns, (1) and (3), are virtually identical and are also almost identical to the overall pattern of primary school interaction and behaviour presented in 'Inside the Primary Classroom'.

In the transfer year, however, some differences emerge which can be identified by comparing the two 'after' columns, (2) and (4). Levels of interaction with the teacher remain the same for the two groups. Both change in line with the general change in transfer school teacher-pupil interaction so that there is now considerably more whole-class teaching and consequently higher overall levels of contact between teacher and class. Total levels of interaction with other pupils are also fairly similar in the transfer school although they are slightly lower for the pupils

making losses. With regard to time spent on task, however, and
with regard to task-oriented pupil-pupil interaction, there are
differences in the behaviour of the two groups after transfer
which were not present at feeder school level. At the primary
feeder school level there was only a 1 per cent difference
between the two groups with regard to the amount of time they
spent on task. In the secondary school this gap has increased
to 8 per cent with pupils who made gains doing considerably
more work than those who made losses. What appears to have
happened is that the pupils who made gains have successfully
raised their level of engagement on task to the higher level
demanded in the transfer schools, whilst those pupils who made
losses in their first year after transfer have not managed to
increase their engaged time much above the level they sustained
in primary school. This greater engagement on task is also
reflected in the difference between the two groups in co-operative
task work with other pupils. Here, the pupils making gains
spend almost twice the amount of time engaged in such co-operative
task work as do those making losses, although at the primary
level their engagement in such co-operative work was lower.

PUPIL PROGRESS IN MATHEMATICS, READING AND LANGUAGE SKILLS

So far the discussion of pupil progress in the basic skills has
been concerned with the overall scores of the pupils on the tests
administered. The three tests of mathematics, language skills
and reading were fully described in Chapter 3 of 'Progress and
Performance in the Primary Classroom'. An analysis of the gains
or losses made in these three different curriculum areas throws
more light upon the hiatus in academic progress which seems to
occur when children transfer out of the primary classroom. In
one sense it makes this hiatus even more striking than before.
When the three tests are considered separately it emerges that
although 63.0 per cent of pupils made gains overall in their
first year in the transfer schools only 28.4 per cent of pupils
made gains on every single test. In fact, 36.6 per cent of the
girls in the sample and 22.5 per cent of the boys made progress
in each of the tests.

   In Table 5.7 the proportions of boys and girls making progress
on the various tests after transfer are presented. Mathematics
is the area where the highest proportion of pupils made progress.
55 per cent of the boys and 65 per cent of the girls had positive
gains over the year, and 60 per cent of the whole sample had
gains. The next most successful subject area overall was reading
where 58 per cent of the whole sample made progress on the test.
However, here the difference between boys and girls was much
more dramatic than in the case of mathematics; nearly three-
quarters of the girls (73 per cent) made further progress in
reading compared with only 42.5 per cent of the boys. In the

case of language skills only half of the total sample made positive
gains on this test over the year (56.1 per cent of the girls and
43.9 per cent of the boys). These findings demonstrate yet
again that the lack of progress in the first year at the transfer
school is not a function of pupils achieving scores on the test
where ceiling effects may begin to operate. As was shown in
'Progress and Performance in the Primary Classroom' the test of
language skills was the one pupils found hardest and where
they obtained the lowest scores. Yet this is the test where
progress in the transfer school is also least likely to occur.

*Table 5.7 Progress of boys and girls in mathematics, language
and reading after transfer*

Subject areas	Percentage of pupils making progress		
	Boys	Girls	All
Mathematics	55.0%	65.0%	60.0%
N =	40	40	80
Language skills	43.9%	56.1%	50.0%
N =	41	41	82
Reading	42.5%	73.0%	58.0%
N =	40	41	81

PUPIL MOTIVATION AFTER TRANSFER

The results presented so far in this chapter have not been
encouraging ones for those concerned with the effects of school
transfer on pupils' academic careers. Despite the fact that pupils
in their transfer schools are spending more of their lesson times
involved in work than the already high levels obtained in primary
schools, the steady rate of progress in tests of basic skills
which were a feature of the primary classrooms studied in the
present research has not been maintained in the transfer schools.
In looking for explanations for this lack of progress, it seems
natural to consider aspects of children's attitudes towards school.
Throughout the project pupils were given questionnaires
designed to measure some aspects of their attitude towards and
enjoyment of school. The questionnaire, described in Chapter
8 of 'Progress and Performance in the Primary Classroom', consisted of a series of statements to be rated on a five-point scale.
A number of these statements related to a child's motivation to
do well at school such as 'I always try my best', or 'I like to be
the first to put my hand up with the answer', etc.
    This questionnaire was given to pupils a number of times dur-
ing the project including the summer term before they moved to

the transfer school, about the middle of their first term in their
new school and during the summer term towards the end of their
first year of transfer. On the basis of the eight items concerned
with motivation a total motivation score was computed for each
child. This score is reported here in terms of a percentage of
the possible maximum score for motivation. For example, if a
child replied 'always' to all the questions concerned with motivation ('I always try my hardest' or 'I like to get the answer right
first', etc.) then he would score 100 per cent. If he answered
'never' to all these questions he would score 0 per cent.

*Table 5.8 Motivation and enjoyment of school of 'gainers' and
'losers' before and after transfer(%)*

Scale	Period	All pupils	Gainers	Losers
Motivation	Before transfer	72.7	73.4	71.2
	November of transfer year	73.4	73.5	73.3
	June of transfer year	69.2	71.9	63.5*
Enjoyment	Before transfer	70.3	70.0	70.8
	November of transfer year	75.4	76.6	72.8
	June of transfer year	69.8	73.6	61.8*
N =		75	51	24

All figures are percentages of the possible maximum score on the
relevant questionnaire items. A score of 100 per cent would
indicate that a child had answered 'always' to all the motivation
items. A score of 0 per cent would indicate answers of 'never'
to all the items.

*Statistically significant at the 5 per cent level.

In Table 5.8 the motivation scores of pupils making gains on
the basic skills during their first year in the transfer school
are compared with the motivation scores for pupils making losses.
The first point to note is that overall levels of motivation were
remarkably high. In the first column, which gives the combined
scores for 'gainers' and 'losers' in the summer before transfer
and in the first term after transfer, motivation scores were
around 70 per cent of the possible maximum and in the summer
term after transfer they have only just dropped below this figure.

It would not seem that the relative average lack of success of pupils in their first year in the transfer schools can be attributed to lower levels of motivation.

However, differences can be found between the expressed levels of motivation of pupils who made gains during their first year in the transfer school and pupils who lost ground on the tests of basic skills. Before the transfer to the new school these two groups had very similar levels of motivation, the future 'losers' being only 2 per cent below the future 'gainers'. In their first term in the transfer school levels of motivation remain virtually unchanged overall, and the 'gainers' and 'losers' were virtually identical. However, after a year in the transfer school the pupils who have lost ground on the tests of basic skills are about 10 per cent lower on their motivation scores than they were at the beginning of the year. In contrast the pupils who have made progress have very similar levels of motivation at the beginning and end of the year. When groups are compared over time the only substantial differences in the motivation scores were that one year after transfer the 'losers' had dropped from their previous levels of motivation and that there was now a difference between the 'losers' and 'gainers'. These differences were the only scores to reach statistical significance.

The fact that the difference in motivation is apparent at the end of the year but not in the middle of the first term suggests that the decline in motivation is a result of, or has accompanied, the lost ground in basic skills rather than preceding it in a possibly causal fashion. In the analysis of the relationship between teaching styles, pupil motivation and progress in the basic skills in 'Progress and Performance in the Primary Classroom' it was shown that although motivation was correlated with progress in the basic skills this correlation only held in classrooms where work tended to be individualized and was not present in classrooms where a higher proportion of work was based on class or group instruction. The classrooms in the transfer schools more closely resembled the latter type of classroom in the primary school in that there was much more class teaching and group instruction than in the average primary class. This finding is consistent with the suggestion that lower levels of motivation cannot be held accountable for reduced levels of achievement. Although expressed levels of motivation are still fairly high, pupils in the 'losers' group were less motivated by the end of their first year in the primary school than they were at the beginning of that year compared to the other pupils. But this process seems to have accompanied rather than preceded the fall in academic achievement.

PUPILS' ENJOYMENT OF SCHOOL AFTER TRANSFER

Two items on the attitude to school questionnaires were designed to measure children's overall positive or negative feelings towards school. These were 'I am happy when I am at school' and 'I enjoy school'. Using the scores from these two items combined in the same fashion as the motivation scores and also expressed as percentages of a possible maximum, it is possible to trace this overall attitude towards school over time as pupils transfer to their new schools and to compare these results for different groups of pupils. These findings are presented in the bottom half of Table 5.8 and show that, in general, just as pupils were fairly highly motivated towards school achievement they were also likely to express enjoyment in being at school. In the term before the transfer overall level of enjoyment of school was 70 per cent; in the middle of their first term in their new school this had increased slightly to 75 per cent and at the end of their first year in the new school it was only very slightly below 70 per cent. Before transfer the future 'gainers' and the future 'losers' were virtually identical in expressed levels of enjoyment. After the first few weeks in the new school both groups had slightly higher levels of expressed enjoyment, although now the future 'gainers' were about 4 per cent higher than the future 'losers'. By the end of the first year this gap had increased considerably. 'Gainers' were still well over 70 per cent while the 'losers' dropped to just above the 60 per cent level. There is now a gap of almost 12 per cent between the two groups in their expressed levels of enjoyment of school.

As well as dropping behind in their academic progress, the group of 'losers' could also be differentiated from other pupils in terms of attitude to school. They had lower levels of motivation and of enjoyment of school compared both to other pupils and to their own previously expressed levels of enjoyment. While these results are hardly surprising, it should, however, be noted that these attitudinal changes appear to accompany losses on the tests of basic skills rather than to precede them.

SOME CHARACTERISTICS OF SUCCESSFUL PUPILS IN THE TRANSFER SCHOOLS

Despite the overall pattern of poor academic progress in the first year in the transfer school, there were pupils for whom a change of school was associated with increased levels of progress in the basic skills. While most pupils made very little gain in test scores compared with their levels of progress in the primary school, and some pupils actually fell back in their scores on the basic skills, there is a small sub-group in the sample who made greater progress during their first year in the transfer school than they had in their last year in primary school. In most of these cases the differences in rates of progress in the two years were quite substantial. For the sample of pupils overall the average gain during a year in the feeder primary school was in the region of twelve marks on the tests, while the average gain in the first year in the transfer school was about three marks (out of a total of 90 marks). For the sub-sample of pupils making greater progress in the transfer school this pattern is reversed; their average gain in their last year in primary school was 2.9 marks on the tests while their average gain in their first year in the transfer school was 12.8 marks. This suggests that these 18 pupils differ quite dramatically from most of the other pupils in the sample and are not simply one end of a relatively even distribution.

The conclusion that this is a rather separate group of pupils is reinforced by their sex distribution. For the sample as a whole girls were very much more likely to have made progress in the transfer school than were boys. However, in this sub-sample boys slightly predominate. The 18 pupils consist of 10 boys and 8 girls. The phenomenon of children who made greater progress in their transfer school, the *accelerators*, does not seem to be associated with particular schools or classes. All of the six schools in the study had at least one pupil in this group and all but three of the twelve classrooms studied had at least one pupil.

Table 5.9 Attitudes and involvement in work before and after transfer of accelerator pupils (%)

		Accelerators	All pupils
Motivation			
	Summer before transfer	73.7	72.7
	1st term after transfer	78.8	73.4
	End of first year after transfer	80.8	69.2
Enjoyment			
	Summer before transfer	62.6	70.3
	1st term after transfer	73.4	75.4
	End of first year after transfer	77.0	69.8
Time on task			
	Mean score before transfer	50.8	58.1
	Mean score after transfer	69.7	68.2
	N =	18	81

An analysis of some of the behavioural and attitudinal charac-teristics of this group of pupils is presented in Table 5.9. In the final section of the table the amount of time spent by the accelerators on work during lessons is compared with the total sample both before and after transfer. In their first year at the transfer school the accelerators spent the same amount of time involved in work as did their fellow pupils. However, in the year before transfer they spent considerably less of the time involved in work than the average pupil. In the transfer school the average level of involvement in work goes up 10 per cent, but for the accelerators it goes up nearly 20 per cent.

Levels of motivation and of enjoyment of school are also presented in Table 5.9. Before transfer the accelerators had very similar levels of motivation to the sample as a whole. Soon after transfer their level of motivation had increased slightly, while the other pupils had remained fairly constant, but by the end of their transfer year the accelerators expressed levels of motivation were considerably higher than that of the total sample. A similar pattern of change occurred in the levels of enjoyment of school although here the changes were from different relative bases. Before transfer the accelerators were enjoying school less than the average pupil, immediately after transfer their levels of enjoyment were fairly similar and by the end of the transfer year their levels of enjoyment of school had increased to a point where they were considerably higher than that of the average pupil.

The accelerators are a group who have clearly benefited from their transfer to secondary education. In the primary school they did less work than the average child, enjoyed school less but expressed similar levels of motivation to succeed. As the transfer year proceeded they caught up with the other pupils in terms of their involvement in work and by the end of the year expressed higher levels of motivation and of enjoyment of school than the average pupil.

It is of interest to look at the origin of the accelerators. Thirteen of these pupils (72 per cent) belonged either to the intermittent workers or the attention seekers during the first year of the study in the primary school. Nine of these children were among those of whom it was estimated that they spent at least one day a week off task. The overall data from the time in the primary classroom would suggest that they did not improve on this during the second year in which some of them were observed. In the essays that children wrote before transfer one or two pupils recorded that they had made a bad start in this school but were determined 'to do better in the new one'. It would seem that these pupils were motivated in similar ways and responded to the new styles of teaching they received after transfer. However, they form a small minority of the sample of pupils who were observed in the transfer schools. For the majority, it would appear that the trends which were beginning to develop prior to the change of school had by the end of the first year after transfer become more established. In the primary classroom different children were engaged for different amounts of time on their set tasks but this did not have a dramatic effect on their levels of achievement. In the transfer schools, although levels of task work were higher because of the shift away from individualized working, the gap had widened between those who

continued to improve in their performance and those who did
not. Presumably these differences continue to increase so that
by the time the children reach the age of 13 years and beyond,
when important subject choices are being made in the secondary
school, the die has already been cast and the processes of
differentiation reported in a whole range of sociological studies
have become a permanent feature of these children's lives.

PROGRESS IN THE FIRST YEAR AFTER TRANSFER

The results presented in this chapter make it clear that for most
pupils in the sample the transfer into the six secondary schools
is marked by something of an hiatus in their progress on the
basic skills as measured by the three tests of mathematics,
language skills and reading. This is a characteristic that extends
across all the schools in our study (both those of a primary
type and of a secondary type), and at all three ages of transfer.
For the great majority of pupils levels of progress were reduced
and for many children actual losses were made. Girls, however,
did considerably better than boys in terms of progress in their
first year in the transfer school.

Perhaps surprisingly other aspects of pupils' behaviour in and
attitudes to school do not seem to change in parallel fashion to
the decline in rates of progress. Levels of involvement in work
increased from the primary school and levels of motivation and
of enjoyment of school remained relatively high. However, levels
of motivation and of enjoyment in school among pupils who have
continued to make progress, albeit in most cases less progress
than before, are higher than among those pupils who made losses
in their scores on the basic skills.

There is also a small group of pupils, under a fifth of the
sample, who have made progress in their transfer schools in a
way they were never able to achieve in the primary school.
These are pupils who have made considerable gains on the basic
skills and who in their last year in primary school made very
little progress. These pupils are characterized by having
increased their levels of involvement in work to the average level
from their relatively low level in the feeder school and by having
higher levels of motivation and enjoyment of school after transfer
than the average pupil.

This and the preceding chapters have dwelt on the frequency
and the type of interactions taking place in the classroom both
before and after transfer and the relationship of this process
with the progress that the children make over this period. The
instruments used, the Teacher and Pupil Record, were not
primarily designed to monitor the quality of such interactions,
so that although, for example, children spent different amounts
of time at their tasks, there has been no discussion about the
nature and the difficulty of the tasks which were set. This, and
other issues, are the subject of the following section. There,

however, the main research technique is participant observation, where the observer tries to record in some detail just what it was like to be a pupil and a teacher in the classrooms that were visited. When the children wrote their essays before transfer they were concerned with three kinds of question. First, what will the work be like? Will I be able to cope with it? Second, what will my teachers be like? Will they be like my present one? Third, what will the other pupils be like? Will I make friends easily or will I find it more difficult to make relationships in the new school? It is these three issues, the curriculum, the teachers and the other pupils, which are the subject of the following chapters.

Part IV
THE ETHNOGRAPHY OF TRANSFER

Sara Delamont

INTRODUCTION

The following three chapters deal with data collected by means
of participant observation in the six schools, especially during
the first month of the autumn term when the sample pupils
arrived there. This introduction locates the three chapters
which follow in relation to the preceding ones, and explains how
they are organized and focused. The three chapters focus on
the curriculum of the six schools, the teachers in them, and
then the pupils' adaptation to these two features of their new
schools. Despite the geographical spread between local authorities
A, B and C, and the age differences of the pupils (9, 11 and
12), and despite the schools' own programmes and policies, the
ORACLE sample's classroom experiences varied according to the
teachers' styles and the subjects taught rather than being
systematically related to the location, age-range or educational
policies of the schools they attended. In other words, in the
first year after transfer, school 'ethos' did not have the impact
which has been reported for it from London (Rutter et al.,
1979) or Mid-Glamorgan (Reynolds, 1976). There are no data on
older, long-established pupils in these schools, where systematic
between-school variations may be apparent. Indeed we are
explicitly arguing that, faced with pupils starting a new school
en masse, all teachers behave in very similar ways to establish
order and social control: ways which could change later. Our
data show very clearly that across three local authorities, three
ages, and six schools, the *content of* schooling is remarkably
similar. The next two chapters give an account of just how
similar the curriculum was in the six schools, and how alike the
teachers were within their disciplines across the schools. Then
there is a chapter on how pupils in the six schools adapted to,
or rebelled against, this.

PARTICIPANT OBSERVATION IN THE ORACLE PROJECT

Throughout the ORACLE projects classroom observation with pre-
specified schedules has been the major method of the data
collection. In the transfer studies the two schedules designed
originally by Deanne Boydell were used extensively, but there
was also a substantial commitment to participant observation or
ethnography. Essentially the difference between the two in terms
of methodology turns on pre-specification and standardization.
The ORACLE observer using the Pupil Record and the Teacher

Record (Boydell, 1974, 1975) is using a standardized research instrument, which consists of pre-specified codings, and must be used in the same way across different classrooms, teachers and schools. The participant observer, or ethnographer, does not have detailed schedules or coding systems, but focuses *first* on the idiosyncrasies of each classroom and school, and is flexible about what is recorded. The theoretical bases of the two kinds of method are very different, reflecting as they do the contrast between 'normative' and 'interpretive' approaches to the human sciences. As this contrast in orientation to classroom research has been widely discussed for the previous fifteen years, it will not be expanded on here. Cohen and Manion (1980) provide an excellent introductory discussion of the strengths and weaknesses of both approaches.

The concern here is to stress the unusual combination of methods used in the ORACLE transfer studies, and to explain how the ethnographic work was done. The large literature on classrooms has not been reviewed because a special issue of 'Educational Analysis' (vol. 2, no. 2, 1980) did this more thoroughly than could be done in a short introduction. Throughout the fifteen years in which classroom research has become acceptable in Britain there have been recurrent calls for a *rapprochement* between 'systematic' and ethnographic observation, McIntyre (1980) being a recent example. In the ORACLE project an attempt has been made to combine the two traditions of classroom research in the transfer studies. There were three good reasons for using participant observation in the first month of our sample's time at middle or secondary school. First, it offered an opportunity of combining ethnographic research methods with data from the Teacher and Pupil Records to discover how far both sets of findings were compatible. Second, it was felt that the initial encounters between teachers and new pupils were peculiarly susceptible to ethnographic observation (Ball, 1980). Third, unlike many other participant observation studies, a team effort in ethnographic research, where different observers studied the same classes, could be mounted and this was thought likely to produce some interesting methodological issues. This applied, in particular, to the problem of triangulation.

In two ways, the ORACLE project was engaged in *triangulation*. Cohen and Manion (1980) distinguish between three kinds of triangulation:

(1)   between-method triangulation;
(2)   within-method triangulation;
(3)   investigator triangulation.

Between-method triangulation, as its name implies, means using three different methods to surround (triangulate) the same problem. Within-method triangulation means testing a finding from several different angles to confirm or refute it. Investigator triangulation means using several different researchers to

approach the same topic. In the ORACLE ethnography both
between-method triangulation and investigator triangulation
have been carried out. The between-method triangulation came
from using two kinds of observation, plus interviews, pupils'
essays and tests and questionnaires. The use of several
observers during the transfer studies gave us triangulation
between researchers. Throughout this volume conclusions,
findings and arguments are based on events observed and
remarked on by at least two different researchers, and extracts
from fieldnotes taken by at least three separate ethnographers
in each school have been used. (Individual researchers, like the
schools, teachers and pupils, are not identified in the text.)
Within the ethnographic work, however, no attempt was made to
devise ways of triangulating of the kind proposed by Denzin
(1970).

With these general points in mind, a description of the observations undertaken for the ORACLE project transfer studies will
now be given.

OBSERVATION IN THE TRANSFER STUDIES

As described below, the transfer studies described in this volume
were based on two different kinds of observation, with a pre-
specified schedule and using field notes. The use of systematic
observation systems in the ORACLE project has been exhaustively
described in 'Inside the Primary Classroom' and the two schedules
are reprinted in the Appendix. Here a brief account of the
ethnographic work which had not been used in ORACLE before
the transfer studies is given. While ethnographic studies of
schools and classrooms have become quite common in Britain in
the last ten years (Hammersley, 1980), most of them have been
case studies of single schools done by an individual researcher.
Many of these observers have spent much longer in their schools
than the ORACLE team, and the findings generated from this
transfer study cannot claim to reflect the same depth of experience as those of either Stephen Ball (1980) or Peter Woods (1979).
However, two kinds of comparative data have been obtained.
Six schools have been studied for the ways in which they social-
ize new entrants, and three observers have been placed in each
school, with each observer working in at least two of the six.
Indeed one observer worked full-time in the two 9-13 schools in
1977, and in the two 12-18 schools in 1978. Team-based ethnographic observation is unusual in Britain, and ORACLE provided
a rare chance to do such research.

Since there are many standard texts on ethnography, no
attempt will be made here to describe the research techniques in
any detail, except in so far as the ORACLE research is concerned.
Briefly, there is a myth that the ethnographic researchers believe
that they have an open mind when they enter the field. No ethnographer believes this. Ethnographers do not have immensely

detailed checklists like the researchers armed with the Pupil
Record, but do have certain ideas (whether consciously or unconsciously) in their heads. Good ethnographic researchers have
to be both self-conscious and reflexive, bringing their preconceptions to the fore for the findings to be rigorously tested
against these preconceptions. In the ORACLE project the
observers had a list of points to which they had to pay attention.
These were foreshadowed problems or 'sensitizing' concepts, or
'high-inference' issues, very different from the low inference
items on the Pupil and Teacher Records. Thus, for example,
observers were asked to look at the schools using Bernstein's
(1971) 'classification and framing' dichotomies as sensitizing
concepts, as well as 'sibling labelling' and 'the use of rules'.
Each observer was to compare *practice* in the two schools in
major areas such as the curriculum, the adjustment of pupils,
the staffroom relationships, and responses to bullying.

In each town there were regular meetings between the observers to discuss their findings, but the very nature of ethnography means that the different observers are bound to 'find'
different things. There can be no inter-observer reliability of
the kind essential to 'systematic' observation. However, turning
a team of ethnographers loose without any common queries can
produce a series of incompatible and unrelated accounts leading
to idiosyncratic ethnographies which provide fragmentary
portraits of different schools and school districts from which
it is difficult to uncover any generalisations. One of the main
aims in the ORACLE transfer studies was to make the ethnographic accounts compatible, by discussion and by using the
shared list of 'foreshadowed problems', as well as by making
sure each school had more than one observer, and each observer
more than one school to study.

Once the fieldnotes were gathered, all of those taken by five
of the six observers were handed over to Delamont, who has
analysed them and written up the material. This was considered
to be the only practical course, but also has the effect of giving
a coherence and common focus to the resulting account. It must
be stressed, however, that all the points made are based on
events seen by more than one researcher, and that fieldnotes,
or commentary written outside the field, by all six observers
have been used in this book.

The analysis and writing up of ethnography has been less
discussed in the literature on research methods than data collection or the negotiation of access to the research setting. The
analysis of the ethnographic material from the six transfer
schools was based on Delamont reading all the observers' notes
and diaries several times, indexing them to locate examples of
significant events, and then discussing the themes which arose
with the rest of the research team. The analysis and the writing
are somewhat unusual, in that the themes and arguments high-
lighted from the fieldwork are a mixture of ethnographic findings
(generated solely from the fieldwork) and illustrative material to

accompany the data generated by the Teacher and Pupil Records and the test results. That is, this book presents the results of both between research triangulation and between method triangulation, as it was hoped, back in 1975, the ORACLE transfer studies would do.

The ethnographic data presented here match the pupils' own perspectives. Before transfer they talked and wrote about their hopes and fears in connection with changing schools. Hopes and fears about transfer focused on four topics: the architecture of the new building ('getting lost'), the new subjects, the new teachers and the new pupils. These concerns are considered because they are of clear significance to the pupils as well as emerging from the data.

6 A VERY COMMON CURRICULUM

Before transfer pupils were concerned about the curriculum in their new schools. Many were looking forward to doing new subjects, while many were anxious that they might be unable to understand the work in their new schools. This chapter examines the curriculum in the six schools, and gives an account of how the subjects were taught. Four main aspects of the curriculum will be considered; the shift from a generalist to a specialist system, the similarities across schools in the overall curriculum, the differences between subject teachers, and the similarities in each subject across schools.

TOWARDS A COLLECTION CODE

All the pupils in the sample had experienced, in their feeder schools, a *general* curriculum. That is, they spent most of their time with one teacher, in one room, doing a restricted range of subjects. Once they moved up to the transfer school they faced a much more specialized, differentiated curriculum. At APT and BPT the pupils stayed in one area for much of the time, while in the other schools they moved between teachers; but in all six they began to be taught by specialist teachers. That is, they met for the first time what Bernstein (1971) calls the collection code, a curriculum made up of subjects taught by specialists in a rigidly segregated way. Indeed during the ORACLE fieldwork, the new head of BPT decided that for the following year he would reorganize the teaching in such a way that pupils moved from one specialist area to another, rather than staying put in one area all the time. The existence of a series of specialist teachers and separate subjects was made visibly clear to the pupils before transfer, when they visited their next school, and was equally apparent when they joined the schools in the autumn term. Even APT, in which the system came closest to that of the feeder schools, had some specialist facilities and rooms.

The six schools were deliberately selected because they were rather different in organization. For example, AST, BST and CST had homogeneous ability groups, while the other three had mixed-ability teaching. However, after intensive ethnographic observation in the six schools our conclusion was that *at class-room level* the curriculum was very similar at all six schools, and almost identical in the classes for the same age-group in each pair of schools. In other words, the content of the teaching for

pupils of the same age was likely to be the same, whether the
school was streamed, banded or had mixed ability teaching. Our
examples of 9-13 schools, APT and AST, were apparently very
different, yet showed great similarities inside the classroom.
They are used here to demonstrate this point, although the other
two pairs of schools could equally well be used.

When the two schools were sampled, the research team expected
to find that curriculum form and content at APT would be of the
kind labelled by Basil Bernstein as an invisible pedagogy, while
AST would have what Bernstein (1975) terms the visible
pedagogy. These terms are discussed in more depth in Delamont
(1976), but briefly they are a development from Bernstein's
earlier notions of classification and framing. By classification
Bernstein meant the degree to which subjects are kept separate:
strong classification implies subjects kept in watertight compart-
ments, while weak classification means integrated subjects such
as 'general science' or 'integrated humanities'. Framing is the
term used by Bernstein to distinguish curricula where the pupil
controls the pace and direction of his or her own learning from
those where external authority controls the level, pace and
direction of the pupils' effort. Thus programmed learning is an
example of very strong framing. Bernstein argued that where
both the classification and the framing of knowledge in the
school are weak, the pedagogy is invisible, that is the control
is implicit, although it is still there. In the visible pedagogy, the
classification and framing are strong, and the social control is
explicit. In Bernstein's theory, this should mean that the subjects are rigidly separated at AST (strong classification) and
integrated at APT (weak classification), while the teacher is
in control of the pace and direction of work at AST (strong
framing) and the pupil in charge of the pace and direction at
APT (weak framing); The history and architecture of the two
schools encourage an expectation of different pedagogies.

The two schools, AST and APT, had been deliberately chosen
for their different histories, buildings, staffings, organization,
and ideologies, to permit a close study of the ways in which
different middle schools handle children between 9 and 13, an
age at which two different educational philosophies meet. The
two schools served similar catchment areas with council and
owner-occupied housing, but were otherwise very dissimilar.
AST had a staff of specialists who had secondary teaching
experience, while the staff of APT came from both junior and
secondary backgrounds and most of them taught a wide range
of subjects to their forms. AST operated with two ability bands,
each containing three forms (and a remedial class in some years)
while APT had mixed ability groups (although there was setting
for maths in the later years). The former put the children into
houses which competed in sport, work and conduct, while the
latter stressed the individual, was non-competitive and had no
vertical groupings at all. AST had an intrinsic system of rewards,
based on merit points and demerits, while APT stressed self-

control, and an intrinsic system of responsibility, self-discipline
and individuality. AST was explicitly Christian, with hymn
practices on the timetable, the houses named after saints, and
assemblies that stressed Christ concerning himself with children's misdeeds. At APT assembly might include a Greek myth,
or an Indian fable, and the emphasis was on morality rather than
religion.

APT was in purpose-built premises which had opened in 1974
as a 9-13 middle school, in contrast with AST which had been a
girls' secondary school, and before that an elementary school.
Indeed it became a mixed middle school only in the three years
preceding the research, and had been through a transition stage
when girls taking 'O' levels shared the building with the new
mixed intake. The staff had not changed substantially, although
one or two men had been appointed. There were, for example,
no male PE teachers, and only one woodwork and metalwork
master compared to five home economics staff. APT started with
a mixed staff, mixed pupils and a headmaster. Both schools were
in reasonably modern buildings for AST had been re-housed in
1966. However, the school was architecturally very different
from APT. It had two storeys, with private self-contained classrooms joined by long corridors, and many specialized features.
There were two cookery kitchens, and a model flat, sewing
rooms and art rooms, three science laboratories, a fully equipped
gym, and a large hall with a proper stage. In contrast APT was
built on a wheel plan, with a 'hub' and 'spokes'. The new
facilities which were shared by all pupils were in the hub, with
the set of classrooms protruding as spokes from this centre. The
hub contained a library, a cookery room, an art and needlework
room, the hall/gym, and the dining/music room. However, all
these were also corridors through which pupils had to move to
get from one classroom area to another. The school had no stage,
the gym facilities were far less lavish than at AST, and music
lessons in the afternoon had to wait for the kitchen staff to
remove the crumbs and custard from the floor.

In the light of all these differences one would expect APT to
have an invisible pedagogy, and AST a visible one. Certainly at
AST pupils moved from one specialist teacher to another, thus
shifting visibly from a science laboratory to a geography room,
while at APT nearly all subjects were taught by the class
teacher in the same form room (strong versus weak classification).
As the weeks went by it became clear that pupils at APT saw
just as many teachers as those in the two bands at AST. In an
ordinary week pupils at APT were taught by *all three* first year
teachers, the music master, the French master, and the deputy
head. Many of them would also be taught by the remedial
teacher, a PE master, the art teacher and the home economics
teacher. At AST many staff 'doubled up', teaching maths and
science, English and geography or history and PE, so pupils did
not see nearly as many teachers as they had subjects. Classification was fairly similar as far as teacher supply was concerned.

The pattern of work at AST was class work, with all pupils doing the same task at the same time (strong framing), while at APT the pupils were on different individual tasks at their own pace (weak framing).

However, the reality was not so simple. The field diary for the second week records:

> AST has much stronger classification and framing – *but* those at APT are not weak – Maths is Maths – there is not a sense of integration *across* subjects. The classifications are equally strong but the framing is weaker at APT.

Such suspicions were increasingly confirmed as the fieldwork progressed.

At APT there was a strong boundary between maths and English signalled by different text and exercise books, and exhortations to 'finish your maths', or 'get on with your English.' Then the whole class would be stopped to go to music, or games, or because the French teacher had arrived. APT paid great attention to French, starting the 9-year-olds with three periods a week, which were class-taught and involved a change of teacher. Thus, the field diary records that:

> Miss B said today that she thought PE and Music were over-emphasised. In some schools 'everything stops for music' but at APT 'everything stops for French'.

The way in which French was clearly separated from other subjects was also clear from the fieldnotes. It may be argued that there was clear classification at APT even if it was not as strong or as visible to casual outsiders as that at AST.

While framing was certainly much more visible and explicit at AST, nevertheless there was a good deal of control over the pupils' pacing of their work at APT too. For the slower pupils the results were probably not very different. The reader can compare fieldnote extracts from the two schools.

> Mrs A says 'Will you finish the sentence you're writing and then close your books.' (A few seconds silence ensues.) 'Right, I think you've had time now. Stop writing. Put your pen top on and any felt tip top you are using. . . . Close all your books please. *Essential Science* and your own books please. . . . Are they all closed at the back? No they're not . . . .'
>
> A science lesson at AST school

Here we see strong framing. The pupils are being taught as a group, and moved forward together. But the pacing and teacher control of work is also apparent at APT, as the following field notes show:

As break approaches Miss B tells those who have not started
their Schonell work to read their library books because Miss
C is coming for French. I hear groans . . . 10.55 Miss C
starts French.
    Miss C gives back some work – marked and says they don't
read the questions. She reminds them of the rules; they must
get each piece of work as they go. Kenneth's book is held up.
    She tells whole class, 'No excuse, ever, for things like
this' . . . Kenneth has miscopied from the board – eleven
copying mistakes . . . (A reprimand, given publicly for some
seconds.) 'Can you imagine what it'll look like in ink?'
    She explains that the headmaster wants the whole first year
to be writing in ink. She sets the whole class some work, on
work sheets, which is later to be in the book. The work is on
measuring. She goes over the work on the board for the whole
class.

Here was relatively strong framing, in which the pupils were not
given control over the direction and pacing of their work, but
forced to listen to a general teacher instruction.
    At AST motivation was explicit, in that pupils were given letter
grades or marks for their work, and 'credits' for good work and
behaviour, with demerits for misbehaviour. These were credited
for the pupil's house. Promises of credits, and threats for
demerits were used to gain quiet, attention, co-operation and so
forth in class. In the top band credits were mainly for good work,
but in the lower band a credit would be given to a whole class
for going down to assembly in a straight line, or getting one
more mark for spelling than last week. This was an obviously
explicit way of motivating pupils, and APT had nothing like it.
Nevertheless, at APT extrinsic sanctions were used to regulate
pupils' work. A pupil who had not completed the work for the
week by Friday afternoon was kept in and missed games. Others
who had not learnt their tables well enough to pass the test on
them had to miss football or netball. One boy was observed in
tears as Friday afternoon approached because he had failed his
tables test. This does not seem any less explicit a sanction than
the demerit awards at AST.
    In another way too, there were similarities in the curricular
content at the two schools. The content of the English was very
similar, and both schools demanded that the pupils learn spelling
lists, and then tested the pupils; both expected correct spelling
and grammar, demanded that corrections were done, and wanted
sentences that began with capital letters and ended with full
stops. At AST, children read aloud round the class more often,
and copied extensively from the board, but what they read and
copied was very similar to what was offered at APT. The pupils
at APT did 'Oxford Middle School Maths', but also conventional
sums and like the pupils of AST, they were expected to learn
their tables off by heart. Perhaps the most noticeable overlap
was in the area of 'social studies'. At AST pupils did history and

geography in separate rooms with different teachers. However, the *content* of history, the changing style of the home - from cave through Roman villa to Anglo-Saxon great hall - looked very like the topic chosen for 'integrated studies' at APT, which was 'shelter'. Overall the curricular differences were largely stylistic, involving such matters as copying from the board rather than doing worksheets, and centred on three subjects, science, French and religion. The 9-year-olds at APT got no science, and no explicit religion in lessons, but did get French from a specialist teacher and an *assistant*. At AST the children did not get French, but did start a general science course; and they did get a large amount of explicit religion in the week. Otherwise the knowledge being offered to the children was very similar.

It could be argued that the similarities between APT and AST were coincidental, or that they were related to age of the pupils. However, similar 'coincidences' were found at both 11-14 and the 12-18 schools. Perhaps more surprisingly, the lessons taught to all new pupils irrespective of age were remarkably similar. That is, introductory science lessons are apparently 'the same' whether a pupil is 9 or 12. The project team found that the older the pupils the more similar the curriculum became, and the less the individual schools differed in what was taught.

Although BPT and CPT were in some important ways more 'progressive' than BST and CST, at classroom level the teaching was very similar. BPT and CPT both had mixed ability groups, while BST had bands and CST used subject setting to produce more homogeneous ability grouping. However, lesson content was often similar and sometimes identical. This showed up particularly clearly in science. At CPT the pupils had general science in mixed ability groups, and in the first weeks they learnt about the bunsen burner and measurement. At CST pupils did the three sciences separately, but their first chemistry involved the bunsen burner while the physics was all about measurement. Similar parallels were found between the teaching at BPT and BST. Compare, for example, English at the two schools:

> Miss D went on to remind the children of work they had been doing on nouns, verbs and adjectives. She then told them to get out 'English through Experience' and open it at page 14.
> She asked them to list nouns, verbs and adjectives to do with the poems they had been doing. . . .
> She then told all the children to write three sentences underlining verbs, adjectives and nouns.
>
> BST (11-14) school

This can be compared with the following from BPT (11-14) school:

> Mrs E said today that they should head their paper in the right way and then copy what was on the blackboard. Then

for homework they should do spelling corrections and afterwards take them to her for checking.
The stuff which they had to copy from the blackboard was
as follows:
Punctuation Marks
1) *Full Stop*. A full stop ends a sentence which makes a statement. It simply marks where the sense and the sentence come
to a full stop.
2) *Question Marks*. A question mark is used to mark the end
of a sentence that asks a direct question. E.g. How many
children are in the class?

These extracts show how similar English was for 11-year-olds in
the two schools. One of the observers working in local authority
B had come to doubt the depth and pervasiveness of the apparent
differences both between BST and BPT, and between either and
the feeder schools from which their pupils came. Towards the
end of the first month she wrote:

> However, I am beginning to wonder just how different the
> environment at BST is from the schools they were in before.
> Although the school atmosphere may seem disciplined and
> orderly, inside the classroom there is very little difference
> between what they were used to at their feeder schools and
> what they get now . . . . I also begin to wonder just how
> different the classroom atmospheres of BST and BPT are.
> Certainly in terms of curriculum content they strike me as
> remarkably similar and in the operation of lessons . . . .
>   Both schools have tests at the end of each section of work
> completed in, for example, maths and science.
>   One major difference which affects the children is obviously
> the system of remuneration for work done. . . . BST of course
> uses house points whereas BPT doesn't . . . .
>   At BPT initiative is praised, at BST obedience is.

This observer decided that the main differences between BST
and BPT lay in motivational and disciplinary issues rather than
curriculum content. Exactly the same point has been made about
AST and APT, and can be made about CST and CPT. With pupils
of 12, the two schools offered very similar lessons in most areas
of the curriculum.
    English at the two schools in local authority C looks very
similar. For example, at CPT in the middle of September an
English lesson consisted of writing essays on 'homecomings' as a
way of checking that pupils could use quotation marks. At CST
at about the same time the pupils wrote an account of a story
they had read, with an emphasis on learning to use paragraphs.
A detailed examination of lessons in the general area of social
studies (history, geography and religion) shows similar parallels
and similarities to those found in science, maths and English.
There was far more unanimity across the schools than might have

been predicted. Overall the pupil entering any one of the six
schools would find that the new work was similar wherever he or
she went, as Tables 6.1 and 6.2 show.

This pervasive similarity encompassed not only the timetables
of the six schools but also the contents of lessons. Table 6.1
shows the timetables of APT (Miss B's class) and AST (Mrs A's
A Band form); and Table 6.2 shows the timetables of classes
studied at CPT and CST. The similarities between them are
unmistakable. (Times have been omitted to simplify the tables.)

Table 6.1 Timetables at two 9-13 schools

A	*AST -*	*Mrs A's class*
	Day	*Subjects*
	Monday	Arts & crafts, maths, games, English
	Tuesday	Singing, RE, library, English, maths
	Wednesday	Art & Crafts, PE, 'topics'
	Thursday	PE, maths, English, music, history, English geography
	Friday	Maths, English, science, history, singing, geography
B	*APT -*	*Miss B's class*
	Day	*Subjects*
	Monday	Class studies, French
	Tuesday	Class studies
	Wednesday	Music, class studies
	Thursday	Swimming, class studies, French, class studies
	Friday	PE, French, games, class studies

While Miss B's class may look as if it is doing something rather
different, once one realizes that 'class studies' equals maths,
English, library, social studies and art, the only clear difference
between the two schools is French at APT and science at AST.
The tables look different but the content, as we show below, is
very similar. CST and CPT do not even differ in appearance, as
Table 6.2 shows:

Table 6.2 Timetables at two 12-18 schools

A	*CST -*	*(Class E4)*
	Day	*Subjects*
	Monday	English, maths (German),* physics, games

Tuesday	Needlework or woodwork, home economics or metalwork, geography, German, French, music
Wednesday	Biology, games, French, RE, history
Thursday	Geography, French, English (German), chemistry, maths
Friday	Art, technical drawing, French, RE, English

*Only a select group of high-ability pupils did German, leaving maths and English halfway through a double lesson.

B   CPT -   *(Mrs F's class)***

Day	*Subjects*
Monday 1	PE, music, French, crafts
Tuesday 1	Maths, science, history, English
Wednesday 1	Crafts, maths, English
Thursday 1	French, music, science, swimming, RE, geography
Friday 1	Maths, French, English, RE
Monday 2	PE, maths, French, English
Tuesday 2	Maths, science, French, geography, English
Wednesday 2	Art, music, French, crafts
Thursday 2	History, geography, swimming, French, music
Friday 2	English, RE, French, maths, art

**This school had a two-week timetable cycle.

Table 6.2 shows a common pattern to the two schools although there are some differences, such as German at CST, where the craft subjects are also sex-segregated. Music figures more prominently at CPT, and science appears as a generic category. However, the similarities in the timetables are much greater than the differences. The same is true of the actual syllabus content. In the first lessons observed in the autumn term, the following patterns emerged:

English

School	*Work/topic*
APT	Punctuation
AST	Autobiographical essay Sentence construction
BPT	Essay on the holidays Punctuation
BST	Autobiographical essay 'English Now' Book 1
CPT	Essay/story 'Homecomings' (writing conversations)

Maths

APT	Tables
	Simple addition and subtraction
	'Oxford Middle School Maths'
AST	Tables,
	Addition, Subtraction
	Factors, Products
BPT	Geometric shapes
BST	Tables, Addition, Subtraction
CP	Basic addition and subtraction
CST	Worksheets of addition and
	Subtraction
	Algebra

Science

APT	None
AST	Cereals
	Autumn
	Migration
BPT	The bunsen burner
	Salt crystals (Purification/dissolving things)
	Ink (solutions)
BST	The bunsen burner
	Thermometers (e.g. measurement of heat)
	Fire
CPT	The bunsen burner
	Measurement
CST	The bunsen burner
	Salt crystals/ink
	Measurement of length, heat
	Motion and time
	Living things

Social studies (e.g. history/geography)

APT	UK towns and mountains
	'Shelter'
AST	History - shelter
	Geography - Australia
BPT	Evolution (Atlases and Maps)
BST	History - The Bronze Age/'Homes through the ages'
	Geography - local geography
CPT	History - spread of Christianity in UK - The Romans
	Geography - Africa, maps/atlas - the Nile valley

Home Economics/Needlework

APT	Soft toy
	Cheese loaf
AST	Chocolate crunchies
	Soft toy
BPT	Hot snack and drink (e.g. Poached egg and tea)
	Soft toy

BST   No data
CPT   Quick-mix buns
CST   Aprons (girls only)

Wood/Metalwork/Craft
APT   No data
AST   Gluing - wooden design/picture
BPT   Plywood key ring
             Enamelled fish
BST   No data
CPT   Learn tools
CST   Learn tools

These charts show similarities in work, *and* emphasis on basic
skills such as punctuation and tables, across all six schools. In
English, for example, a typical exercise involves making up
sentences around words given by the teacher to learn sentence
construction, punctuation and parts of speech. For example:

> In Miss B's class, pupils are doing sentences, including three
> words from the board: boy, football, window;
> gorilla, cage, keeper;
> monkeys, coconuts, hunters;
> soldier, army, tank.
> Several ask her about the words so she reads through them.
> Says of 'soldier, army, tank' 'That's one for the boys really
> I suppose.'

This comes from APT in the second week of term, but could be
seen in any of the schools. This extract is also typical in that
there is an entirely gratuitous comment by a teacher implying
that only boys are interested in warfare. It adds nothing to the
lesson, and indeed may detract from it. Less stereotyped sets
of words such as 'girl', football, window', 'WRAC, army, tank',
might even be more stimulating for the pupils, who could still
practise inserting verbs, articles and prepositions. The other
class was working on capital letters and punctuation. The
following sentences were on the board for correction by the
pupils:

(1)   george is between edward and arthur
(2)   peter was ten last saturday he invited john david and
      gary to tea with him (Again there seems no reason why
      Peter should not have Mary to tea instead of Gary!)

It is clear then that the curriculum was very similar in all six
schools, and within each pair decidedly so, despite the different
ideologies espoused by the schools. The next section concerns
the common feature of the curriculum, its division into specialist
subject categories.

TRANSFER MEANS GOING SPECIALIST

All the pupils in the transfer studies knew that there would be
new subjects at their new schools by the time they had reached
them in the autumn. Many had seen the new building on a pre-
transfer visit, and there the specialist curriculum was physically
present: laid out before them in the architecture of the school.
The physical plant of the schools, and the range of staff,
featured in all the pre-transfer visits, as is illustrated below.
At CPT (9-13) school the pupils heard a French lesson and saw
the language lab, the science lab, the art room, and the library.
They were told that they would learn a good deal of French but
'don't think the work is all French - just four periods a week -
a tenth of your time'. There was a similar tour at AST and at
the schools taking in older children. For example, at BST (11-
14) school in the June before transfer:

> The first room we entered was the laboratory. The teacher told
> the children that it was full of dangerous things but that it had
> 'quite good facilities: gas taps and things like that'. She said
> they would have two lessons a week in the lab; and another
> lesson in a different lab where there were animals. . . .
>   From the dining room the group went on to the biology
> laboratory where she repeated that they would have one lesson
> a week . . .
>   She said, 'There are all different animals that you will
> probably study. Locusts and things. Fish. Have a quick look
> and I must whizz you on somewhere else.'

This tour also included visits to the rooms used for French,
history, Latin, cookery, needlework, music, woodwork and
metalwork. Later in the day the children visited Mr G, the
Metalwork master, who demonstrated some of the tools. Such a
demonstration was unusual, but a glimpse of the range of facilities
available was not. At CPT children were shown craft facilities,
and at CST the language laboratory.
  Among these specialist facilities which were pointed out as new
to the children were those pertaining to sport and games. For
example at CST the sixth-former took her tour to 'the main hall
where assemblies etc., are held', where 'a class of badminton
and table tennis was in progress'. Later outside the tour passed
'tennis courts and the extensive field'. When Mr H, the head of
the year, addressed them he included the sports teams in his
talk. At CPT (12-18) school, fourth-formers escorted the pupil
tours. These did not include the sports hall, and afterwards the
newcomers asked Mrs I if they 'could have a look in the Sports
Hall under the plastic balloon'. They were told that they could
not, because there was no one to operate the airlock. When
another group were told that they could play football in the
lunch hour the observer heard 'Oh brilliant!' from the row in
front of her.

In these ways pupils were shown specialist rooms and facilities as a visible manifestation of the collection code they would be facing after transfer. They *saw* language labs and woodwork rooms, biology collections and badminton courts, and thus they 'saw' a complex curriculum for the first time. Once they reached the new school in September they were quickly introduced to the 'new' subjects. In discussing how the specialist curriculum was introduced to the pupils, a comparison will be made of the ways in which pupils met strange subjects and the old familiar ones in the new school, before the whole issue of the curriculum is considered in detail.

The pupils at all six schools faced a more specialized and differentiated curriculum than they had previously known. They met some completely strange subjects, some stalwarts (e.g. maths), and some subjects which turned out to be rather differently taught in their new school. Before looking at these three kinds of subject, it seems appropriate to demonstrate a common feature of all subjects, new, old and transformed, namely, the emphasis on *terminology*. All the teachers in all six schools placed great emphasis on establishing the existence of specialist language, and many spent time on teaching it. For example:

> Mathematics with Mr J. The children were working from work-sheets. Mr J. began by reminding the children that every subject has its own language. In games there are terms like 'off-side', 'pass', etc. On the blackboard the children could see, left over from a previous lesson, a few words which are only used in social studies: 'erosion', 'crust', etc. Mathematics also has its own language, we talk about dividing, not sharing.
>
> BPT (11-14) school

Similarly, the same class had an English lesson in which Mr K told them the proper terms 'punctuation' and 'parts of speech'. Many more examples of this emphasis on terminology will be given as this chapter proceeds.

The pupils were expecting new subjects, and familiar ones. They may have been less aware that some subjects would be taught in very different ways in their new schools. Yet this was the case, as these examples show:

> Mr L is the art master. . . . He began by explaining that the children would be approaching this subject in a very different way from the one they had used in the junior school. He said, 'Instead of a bit of splash and fun, we are going to really think about drawing. I'm going to tell you about what we refer to as the basic elements of design: these are line, colour, shape and form.
>
> BPT (11-14) school

Similar redefinitions of the content of a subject were recorded in music in several classes, where pupils were told it was not just

singing, but involved writing, and meant learning about the
orchestra, composers and theory. For example:

> Mr M began by telling the children to take out their music
> literature books, and reminded them that these were the books
> with the lines in them. . . . He played the beginning of a
> record on which a trumpet was later joined by a variety of other
> instruments. . . . The children made several guesses about
> what instrument they had heard. Eventually sombody suggested
> a trumpet. . . . He then produced a trumpet as by magic
> from under his desk.
> (After a demonstration of the trumpet) . . . he wrote the title
> on the blackboard:
> The Instruments of the Orchestra.
>
> BST (11-14) school

When the pupils met new subjects, the teacher introduced them
in a very similar way. For example in their first two days at
CPT the pupils met French and science, which were new subjects
for some of them. In French Mr N told them about *gender*, a new
idea to those who had never done French before. In science,
they met a whole new area of the curriculum.

> I go with one group to science with Miss O. She tells them
> they have three double periods of science a fortnight, two with
> her and one with Mr P. She puts her name on the board. She
> gives out exercise books and gives them instructions for
> labelling them. . . . Then she brings them out round the
> bench at the front and says they are going to do *general*
> science. She then asks what do they think science in school
> might mean. A boy volunteers 'the weather', and is told that
> is part of science. A boy volunteers 'chemistry' – he is told he
> is correct. Then she says there is another science 'one ladies
> perhaps like more than chemistry – I don't know why, but
> girls tend to like it better'. A girl volunteers 'animals' – and
> is told she is partly right. A girl volunteers 'biology' – and
> is told she is correct. She leads them to see that biology
> includes animals and plants and elicits the proper term 'zoology'
> from a boy. Finally she gets a boy to volunteer 'physics' and
> has the trilogy complete. After a discussion and exposition of
> what physics and chemistry 'means', Miss O moves on to the
> bunsen burner.
>
> CPT (12-18) school

Miss O went on through a lively discussion of gas, both coal gas
and North Sea gas, and on to the workings of the bunsen. She
lit hers, and demonstrated the two flames, introducing labels
'yellow' versus 'blue' and 'luminous' versus 'non-luminous', and
the effect of moving the collar.

  This was a typical 'first lesson' in a new subject, involving
mapping out the subject and introducing technical terms at the

intellectual level, and, at a more mundane level, the distribution and labelling of exercise books, and the handling of new
equipment. Lessons such as the one described took place in all
the 'new' subjects.

The pattern in familiar subjects was slightly different. In
maths and English particularly the teacher typically began with
a test, or a more informal investigation, to discover what work
pupils had done, and what level of work they could manage.
At the same time the screening to remove the 'remedial' groups
in these subjects was beginning. For example, at APT in the
first few days all the children were taken outside their classrooms to read aloud to Mrs Q, the remedial teacher, and were
later given a standardized reading test. Then each classroom
teacher gave an informal maths test, and asked for something
written in 'best handwriting'. These assessments allowed
teachers to assign pupils to appropriate work. A similar
pattern was found among the 11- and 12-year-olds. A few
examples show teachers sorting out what the pupils can do:

> In the first three English lessons . . . Mr R had already
> made a mental note of the children's ability in speaking,
> reading and writing. He had also graded them in terms of
> a vocabulary test which he had given. . . . He then told
> the children to form groups . . . each person was to tell
> the others in that group stories about what they had done
> in the holidays and then each group must choose one story
> which would then be told to the class in turn. He then
> began to give out folders in a casual kind of way to the
> groups, but whilst doing this he was carefully listening to
> the stories to discover who could tell them very fluently.
> After one representative from each group had told their
> story they were all asked to write their story . . . he then
> went around the class looking at the children's handwriting.
> . . . In the second lesson he again asked each group to
> collect a set of books (all the same) and read to each other
> in turn. Whilst he was ambling round the room he was again
> carefully listening to find who were fluent readers and who
> had difficulties.
>
> BPT (11-14) school

This is an accomplished and relatively informal form of assessment. Other teachers used a more formal procedure:

> The maths master is doing a test. He tells them it is not
> for grouping but to see what they know. He also says that
> the sums are probably easy and stresses that he doesn't
> want any copying. The test is on a duplicated sheet and
> the first two questions are badly reproduced (and hence
> unreadable). He puts them on the board. Class turn over
> the sheets and begin. They are quiet. . . . Mr S watches
> them . . .

'Don't look at your neighbour's: Look at your own, lad!'
Goes round and moves some people away from their
neighbours. . . .
By 9.40 most pupils have finished. Mr S said a few
minutes ago they have another five minutes.

CPT (12-18) school

So the new pupils may well begin their familiar subjects with
a test. However, this does not mean that the new teacher can
begin fresh work. All the schools except APT wanted the
pupils to work as a class, and this caused problems in all
those five schools. For example:

The children got on with their work and Mrs T . . . went
around the room helping with various problems and marking
children's work. Quite often Mrs T remonstrated with the
children for being a bit noisy. . . . There was one item
(involving minus quantities) which many children could not
do. They were told to say it was impossible. Miles, Lester,
and Earl, were all rather at sea throughout the whole of
the lesson, finding the work much too difficult for them. . . .
Mrs T said (to me) that it was quite hopeless and ridiculous
having them in the class.

BPT (11-14) school

Thus an ability gap was opening up by the second week of
term. However, even when there were not large ability ranges
(and AST, BST and CST grouped by ability to avoid them)
the pupils had always come from a number of different feeder
schools each with its own syllabus. All the teachers had to
start work in basic subjects at a point which was repetitive
and too easy for some pupils, while for others it was too
hard, too advanced or simply strange. Some examples from
AST will make the point. Even in the 'A' band, where ability
should have been relatively homogeneous, some children were
finishing work in twenty minutes which others were struggling
to finish in forty. For example:

Mrs A moves round the room going to pupils who have a
problem. Some have maths problems, but Sonia has a query
about her pen. . . . 'Lawrence and Gavin you don't look
as though you're working very hard. I know they're not
very hard, Gavin, but you have to do them - and get them
all right.'

AST (9-13) school

Here was explicit recognition that the work is too easy for
Gavin. This boy was frequently a problem for the teachers
who had to try and keep the whole class together because he
found the work too easy. For example:

In English with Mr U they are to do a comprehension
exercise. He tells them about not starting till he has gone
over the setting out. He does so: ruling off, not wasting
the space . . . he stresses headings, capital letters, etc.
He finds Gavin has started. Tells him he's done it wrong
and that he must rule it off and do it over again. . . . He
tells them it is not a race - the first to finish may be the
worst work. . . . Gavin is obviously a very fast worker.
He asked if they were to go on to question 3, and was told
there was probably not time. He might have time, but
mustn't forget to answer the questions (i.e. not just copy
incomplete ones off board).

> AST (9-13) school

Here the English master was trying to stop Gavin getting too
far ahead. The strategy of telling him that his work was too
untidy or careless, and getting him to repeat it, was used
frequently to keep him 'slowed' down. On a single day he was
kept back in science, in maths and in both his English lessons.
However, in the English lesson at the end of the day he was
the first person to complete the work, fifteen minutes before
the end of the period, while three children had not finished
when the bell went. When interviewed Gavin said that English
was his best subject and maths his worst. Some of the time
the maths was too easy for him because it covered ground he
had already covered at his previous school, while most of the
time it was too hard.

In their interviews all the pupils drew similar distinctions
between work that was new and old, between subjects they
liked and those they did not, and between those they were
good at and those in which they were poor. For example, Rex,
a good pupil at CST, told us that the boys in his middle
school did some science so these subjects are not entirely new
to him. He liked biology and chemistry, but not physics,
because, he said, the teacher was boring. . . . He was in the
group which did German 'the best ones do German, Miss'. He
thought it was 'all right' and he quite liked French. In comparison, Selwyn, a lower-ability pupil at CPT told us that he
very much liked woodwork, was not keen on maths and he
detested French. . . . This had nothing to do with the subject
as taught at the school because he had done French at his
middle school and he had hated it there.

In these ways the pupils met new subjects, the teachers
tried to sort out the pupils and their abilities, and the pupils
began to judge the subjects and their reactions to them. It
was possible to see how pairs of schools organized similar kinds
of pupils, and, as has been argued earlier in the chapter, the
curriculum offered in all six schools was very similar. In the
next chapter we highlight the ways in which teachers of each
subject or subject group were alike in the different schools,
and different from teachers in other subjects in their own school.

7 TEACHERS AND THEIR SPECIALIST SUBJECTS

Throughout this volume, and also in the earlier books, it has been argued that teachers tend to influence pupil behaviour and not vice versa. That is, pupils change their classroom behaviour to suit the regime desired, established and controlled by the teacher. A second argument is that as pupils get older, the teaching they receive in any subject is similar whatever school they attend. These conclusions are, in part, based on the analysis of data obtained using the Teacher Record. The main focus of this instrument, however, is the teacher's cognitive style. This concerns the intellectual and managerial transactions used by the teacher to ensure the set task is carried out to her satisfaction.

To create this workmanlike atmosphere the teacher needs to impose order and discipline, so that whenever pupils move to a new teacher there is a settling-in period while each tries the other out. The teacher will make rules governing the manner of working and the way in which she expects pupils to behave. The pupils will seek to discover the limits of the teacher's tolerance so that they begin to learn what is acceptable behaviour and what is not. This process of adjustment is captured in a comment by a teacher, an infrequent changer, who began each year with very strict rules until the pupils had acquired 'correct learning habits' ('Inside the Primary Classroom', p. 125). The systematic observation, using the Teacher Record, collected little information about the ways that teachers established these 'correct habits' in the classroom. However, the issue is an important one, and the participant observation provided many examples of the way in which pupils learned to adjust to their new regime.

This process of adjustment can be seen more dramatically when children transfer to new schools where they meet many new teachers. This chapter begins by looking at how the teachers in the six transfer schools established order and gained control over the pupils. Stephen Ball (1980) has written perceptively about how initial pupil encounters can be analysed and the data here are broadly supportive of his arguments. This chapter shows first how the teachers in the six schools laid down the rules about the new pupils' behaviour. Second, it examines the differences between teachers in three specialist subject areas, science, mathematics and English. Within the first few weeks in the new schools the pupils begin to experience very different styles of teaching associated with particular

subjects. These experiences are common to pupils who are
about to enter 9-13 middle schools or 12-18 secondary ones
and the evidence presented here strongly supports the conclusions of Chapter 3 of the book, based on the analysis of
the systematic observation data.

Ethnographic data is used here to describe the period of
adjustment to the new schools. Central to this are the ways in
which the rules governing pupil behaviour and academic work
are introduced to the new intake. The establishment of order
is a central task for a school faced with new pupils, and this
chapter is concerned with how order is brought about. The
ORACLE researchers were able to enter five of the six schools
on the first day of the school year, and all six were visited
regularly from the first week onwards. The data collected show
considerable uniformity across the six schools although the
pupils were of three different ages (9, 11 and 12) in three
different towns. All the points made apply to all six schools
unless otherwise specified, although the illustrative extracts
from fieldnotes and diaries are drawn from only one or two of
the schools for reasons of space.

Typically the first day began with all the new pupils
marshalled into a large space (hall, gym, playground), organized into classes, and despatched to their formroom with their
new form teacher. Then the new pupils faced a substantial
period of time (from half the morning up to the whole day)
with their form teacher, who began the process of fitting them
into the school and its rules, routines and procedures. The
class teacher, and later the other staff, spent a good deal of
time *locating* the pupils in time and in space; giving them the
rules for using both new and familiar objects; and explaining
how the authority structure and the curricular system func-
tioned. In this chapter data are presented on how pupils were
oriented to the school's time and space, to the use of objects
and to authority. The following chapter will focus on the
pupils' view of these experiences. Particular stress is laid here
on rules, because the overwhelming impression observers
received was that the schools had rules about all aspects of
their organization, about use of time, space, and objects, and
about authority.

CONCERNS ABOUT TIME

All six schools placed considerable emphasis on organizing the
pupils in time. There were two aspects here; time usage inside
the school and the relationships between school time and the
external world. All the schools but APT gave the pupils a
clear, written timetable to organize their school time, and all
six placed stress on the importance of school time *vis-à-vis*
the wider society. For example, schools stressed that pupils
should attend regularly, come punctually, and send in notes if

they were ill. Pupils were also given to understand that their
time outside school was partly a concern of the school. All
children received some homework, and some teachers in every
school worried about late bedtimes. The following extracts from
the fieldnotes show this concern with external time:

> Assembly on the first day of term. Mr H (the head of the
> year) welcomed the children briefly and then got down to
> information on school rules etc. . . . He said it was very
> important to be on time and that everyone who was late
> got a detention. Anyone thinking of playing truant should
> know that there were two attendance officers who were
> sent to visit their homes if anything was suspected – so
> in case of genuine absence parents should phone or send
> a letter.
>
> > CST (12-18) school

> Miss V reminded all the children to come promptly in the
> mornings.
>
> > BPT (11-14) school

> The pupil who hadn't done any homework is yawning. Mrs
> A finds out that she went to bed at 10.0. Says this is
> 'obviously' too late, because her 'yawn was so big I could
> have jumped down your throat.'
>
> > AST (9-13) school

As the term advanced attendance and punctuality were
stressed and rules enforced, as in the following extract:

> (Registration with Mrs W)
> One boy comes in a few minutes late. The teacher makes
> him go and give his name to the people on duty, and get
> a detention.
>
> > CST (12-18) school

The schools attempted to get pupils to do homework, and
CST provided a room where it could be done at lunchtime.
Typical comments about pupils' use of the evenings were:

> (English with Mr U)
> This . . . comprehension lesson consisted of Mr U reading
> the paragraph about a boy, living on a farm, who had
> endless hobbies and watched TV only occasionally (on wet
> evenings). He then used this to lecture to the class on the
> virtues of reading a good book or indulging in other
> hobbies rather than watching TV.
>
> > AST (9-13) school

> Mr X (the physics master) says that they have a week in
> which to do their homework. It will take about 10 minutes

and if they can't do it they should come and see him
before the next week.

CST (12-18) school

The children filled in their homework timetable and Miss Y
told them that she would sign it when she knew that their
parents had seen it.

BST (11-14) school

The school could do little more than attempt to control
pupils' attendance and leisure time. It did, however, have
total control over what pupils' schedules inside the building
looked like, and organizing pupils' school day was given the
highest priority. It was the first task of the year in all the
schools but APT. The importance of the timetable is shown in
the following extracts.

In Class 2.1 Mrs F is doing the timetable. The class have
the first two periods with her, then music. . . . She puts
up the timetable on the blackboard for them to copy down
while she sorts out the register.

CPT (12-18) school

Miss Y worked through the timetable which she had written
on the board and asked the children to copy all the details
in their own book. She managed to bring the timetable to
life by discussing various subjects and saying such things
as 'Tuesday is a good day for you. You have games in the
morning and design in the afternoon'. . . . She gave the
children about 20 minutes to copy out their new timetable.

BST (11-14) school

On the first morning when they went into their form rooms
to meet their form teachers for the first time, the first
hour was devoted to handing out timetables.

BPT (11-14) school

Organizing the pupils' time continued during the first
month at least, with teachers checking that pupils had kept,
understood and followed their timetables. For example:

I go to 2.1 for registration, now all done with Christian
names except where there is an ambiguity. Mrs F reminds
them that today they have maths, science or art, history
and then English.

CPT (12-18) school

While the pupils were sometimes confused about what lessons
were coming next, this did not last, and they very soon
internalized school time. For example, at CPT on the second
day of term Wayne turned to one of the observers and asked

'Miss - what do we have next?'. By the third or fourth week
of term this would have produced derision among his classmates. The interviews with target pupils nearly all revealed
the short-lived nature of such confusion. For example, Rowena
at BPT said that the first week was 'ever so confusing'.
When she went home at night everything seemed to be swirling
around in her head and she could not sleep. It was because
there was so much to get used to and so many things to try
to remember. However, she did not seem to think that this
period had lasted very long; she mentioned only the first few
days as being bewildering.

Organizing the children's time in school was an important
task for the first morning. The second task, in all the schools,
was to locate the pupils in space (both inside and outside the
classroom).

CONCERNS ABOUT SPACE

In all six schools an important part of socializing the new
pupils was showing them the layout of the school campus and
organizing the room(s) in which they would be taught. The
class teacher had to organize their home base, other staff had
to show them how to use the specialist subject rooms, and all
pupils had to learn how to find their next lesson, the lava-
tories and the way home. Orienting the pupils in space was a
major task in the first weeks of the year, as the fieldnotes
show. Sometimes the teacher used a plan, and sometimes a
tour to familiarize the children with the school.

Mrs F does the geography of the school. She draws a map
of the school on the board, and shows that the main building is in the shape of a cross. She shows them where their
formroom is, where the dining room, the hall and offices
are. She explains that if they are ever lost, they should go
to the central point of the cross, recognise the Hall, and
then they should be able to discover where they are.
Failing that, they should come to this room and find her.
. . . After describing the structure and layout in some
detail she asks who has seen round the school. Nearly all
the pupils have - one girl hasn't. Then she does a
'navigation' test: asks how to get to new building . . .
second year yard . . . dining room . . . maths area.
                                    CPT (12-18) school

At 10.15 Mrs Q brings all the girls out of Mr Z's class and
shows them the laboratory and the place to hang coats, etc.
Shows them Miss B's and Miss C's classrooms, and intro-
duces them to Miss C. . . . She then takes the girls on a
guided tour of the school. I follow the guided tour and we
see other areas: music, hall, gym, library, staffroom,

office, domestic science, art and craft, science, and the
language lab.

APT (9-13) school

Miss Y said she would take them out to show them where
their pegs were. I went with her while she took one group
of girls to their cloakroom. In the afternoon I went into
form 1 B1. . . . Mr McA asked the children what they
should do if they didn't know where a room was, and
various children suggested that they should ask a child,
a teacher, or a monitor; he agreed with the suggestions.

BST (11-14) school

In these extracts teachers can be seen locating pupils in
the school, and thus helping with their anxieties about the
size and complexities of the buildings. At the same time, the
curriculcum was also being located as the pupils heard of maths
'areas', science labs and cookery rooms.
    Within the formroom, the teachers also had arrangements to
make. The pupils had to have a seat, a storage space, and
possibly some rules about the use of 'their' room. These
arrangements are apparent in the following extracts from the
notes. On room use, typical rules are given in the following
extracts.

Miss C tells her class that if they haven't got any soft
shoes already she would like them to get some to wear in
the classroom because there is a carpet there. The care-
taker does not like them to come onto the carpet in outdoor
shoes because of the mud. But they are lucky not to have
all carpets so that they can paint in the classroom.

APT (9-13) school

Mrs F tells them the room was cleaned and painted last
year and so she would like it kept nice. All pupils will be
given lockers for their books. They must not leave any
litter, and bubble and chewing gum are *absolutely* forbidden
because of the messy remains.

CPT (12-18) school

Miss V said to one child 'If I gave you a stool with two legs
you'd complain'. This was after he'd been tipping it up.
. . . 'Don't just whip out of the room, you must always ask
first,' this was said when a child had raced off to his
locker to fetch a pen in order to write something down in
his rough book.

BPT (11-14) school

In these ways teachers controlled the cleanliness of their
floors, furniture and overall surrounding, by focusing on how
pupils ate and what they wore. They also laid down rules for

the proper use of furniture, and how and when pupils might
move. Most class teachers spent some time organizing their
rooms, as the following extracts show:

> In Miss B's class after break I find a spare chair and take
> it into a space by the window. Miss B settles them and has
> a discussion of storage drawers. During the rest of the
> morning she allocates each child a storage drawer, and the
> wherewithal to label it with his name.
>
> APT (9-13) school

> In 1.5. Sonia asks if 'Gabrielle and me' can swop desks.
> She is told they can but only after she has rephrased her
> request to 'Gabrielle and I'. Mrs A says that people can
> change desks to be with new friends because new friends
> come with being in new schools.
>
> AST (9-13) school

Once class teachers had organized the pupils' home bases
they would continually remind pupils of the rules until they
were internalized. A similar process went on in each subject,
and a prominent feature of the new pupils' encounters with
each teacher in the opening weeks of term was that *all* the
teachers gave rules about the use of space. A few examples
will illustrate this:

> Down in the annexe for craft.
> The metalwork master gives them the rules for the use of
> the metalwork room. If copied down correctly the rules
> should spell RATS down the margin in capitals. The rules
> are:
> Running, messing about and shouting are not allowed.
> All accidents must be reported to the teacher.
> Tidiness is most necessary in the workshop.
> Switches and machines.
>
> CST (12-18) school

> Cookery with Mrs McB. Once they are all here Mrs McB
> gives the following 'rules' for using the kitchen safely:
> Don't run.
> Don't hold knives carelessly.
> Don't be a Fred (this means stupid behaviour) and the
> example is leaving pan handles sticking out dangerously!. . .
> Then they learn to light gas ovens, practising lighting
> both the burners and the ovens. . . . Then they are
> gathered round an electric stove and told how it works.
> Mrs McB gives them sensible reasons for the rules. For
> example they are told never to touch the burners on the
> stoves because they may be hot.
>
> AST (9-13) school

The foregoing examples both involved specialist areas with many potential hazards. However even ordinary rooms had rules:

> After break Mr U . . . takes them for English. He begins 'All you have got to do is to sit down quietly. It is not a club where you come in and talk. All you have got to do is sit still and listen to me. . . . Now I don't like a lot of noise and I don't like a lot of fuss. I never will as long as I teach you.'
>
> He then follows with a set of rules about what to do when pupils arrive at his class. First, wait outside on the left-hand side of the door, side by side; second don't do to the other side of the door because Mrs A lives there and you can't STEAL her space.
>
> AST (9-13) school

One interesting difference between teachers was the way in which they presented their rules to the new pupils. Some gave apparently genuine reasons (such as 'Change your shoes so we do not get mud on the carpet') while others gave highly improbable ones (such as Mr U in the extract above talking of 'stealing space'). A similar range of credibility of ostensible reasons can be seen in the use of objects in the classrooms.

CONCERNS ABOUT OBJECT USE

All school work in the six schools involved using objects – textbooks, rulers, pottery kilns or hockey sticks – and all the teachers had their own ideas about how these objects should be used. Sometimes the rules were concerned with familiar things such as exercise books or pencils, and sometimes with things which were new to the children, such as bunsen burners or microscopes. The following extracts show how both kinds of objects were introduced.

> Mr G the metalwork master gave the children some account of design subjects. . . . He told the children that they would each be given a design folder. These folders were very expensive (in fact they were simple manilla folders and cannot possibly have cost more than a few pence each). He asked the children what they should do with the folders, and accepted as correct that they should not rip them and that they should put their names on them. He emphasized that if they lost or seriously damaged a folder they would have to buy a replacement. He told the children to take their folders home tonight and do their best to cover them. He said some children had a bad habit of doodling and the teachers did not want pictures of the Incredible Hulk on

the front of people's folders. Furthermore they must not
stick their folders into their pockets or into a carrier bag
because that would make the corners dog-eared. The folders
must be kept flat and must be looked after.

BST (11-14) school

Here is a wide range of rules about using a familiar object
which mark it out as 'special'. In a similar vein Mr McC at
AST required the children to draw a book, with labels showing
the spine, the pages and so on. In particular, every teacher
gave some rules on how pupils should use pens, pencils,
rulers and paper when setting out work. This matter will be
considered in more detail later, but one example will do here:

The entire lesson was concerned with the drawing of the
diagram of the bunsen burner in their exercise books. . . .
Mr McD told the children to write the date on the first
page of their books. They should also do a margin which
should be either the width of a ruler to the nearest square
or three squares wide. He told the children that they
should write in ink not ballpoint. They should draw in
pencil and label in ink. . . . Form 1B2 has exercise books
made up of squared paper. . . . He spent some time telling
the children how to draw a curve. . . . He emphasised
that he did not allow felt pens.

BST (11-14) school

Here we see Mr McD's rules about using a whole series of
familiar objects in his own special ways in science lessons.
Felt tip pens and ballpoints were not allowed, and pencils were
to be used for drawing. This extract also shows pupils' first
meeting with the bunsen burner, and this had its own rules,
and named parts, and was treated as a central part of introductory science, as will be seen later in this section. Mr McD's
lesson also shows the importance attached to the way in which
work was set out on the paper. Learning how to present work
for each teacher and subject occupied an enormous amount of
time in the first weeks of the new school experience. For
example, a class from CST was observed spending a whole day
at the craft annexe in the pupils' first month in the school.
They had technical drawing with Mr McE who emphasised
throughout a lesson on the angle and the protractor how work
should be set out and equipment handled. Then, after break,
pupils had art with Mr McF who spent much of the lesson
giving them rules about labelling their work and the use of
the paints. Finally, after lunch they had either cookery or
woodwork or metalwork. The observer went to metalwork where
the lesson quickly fell into a familiar pattern.

Mr McG tells them to pick up their pencils in their right
hand (unless they are left handed) and draw a margin in

pencil. He then says: 'Each teacher you come across will
have their own way of setting out work, and this is my
way. You've heard the song *My Way* but I won't sing it
because there's a lady present' (the observer).

His way is neat. In the fifth year the pupils can choose
their own way of setting out their work. In the fifth year
they can think that Mr McG's way is OK for this work and
not for that work, and choose how to set out what they do.
For now, though, they should do it his way. This involves
a margin a rule wide down the left-hand side of the page
plus a margin across the top of the page. Then they are to
put the date in the square in the top left-hand corner.
Then he shows them how he likes lettering done in metalwork, and throws chalk at Neville because he is not watch-
ing. Mr McG tells them he is lucky it was not a board
rubber.

CST (12-18) school

Here pupils were meeting a unique way of setting work out,
which they had to learn to use immediately if they were not to
fall out with the metalwork master.

All the foregoing extracts on presentation were also concerned with meeting strange objects. Typical of these new
objects was the bunsen burner. At four of the transfer schools
the observers sat through many lessons in which new pupils
met the bunsen. Similarly in design at BST an observer saw
Mr McH remind pupils about the use of rolling pins in pottery,
demonstrate the damp cupboards, plaster of paris, the whirler,
the paper towels, and the clay props, and take them on a
visit to the kiln room. He also warned them not to throw clay
about, and explained how they could pay for their models if
they wished to keep them.

In these ways the teachers introduced their new pupils to
the rules of the school and of their classrooms and the unfamiliar objects therein. As well as focusing on the ways in which
order was established, the observers were interested in the
reasons offered for them, and it is to these we now turn.

The new pupils had to learn about using time, space and
objects correctly, and to recognize the school authority and
its concerns. The six schools varied in the extent to which
they offered the pupils reasons for their rules as well as in
the nature of the reasons offered. Some schools and teachers
offered apparently genuine reasons for their rules (e.g. 'if
you make a noise in here it disturbs the office') while others
offered such implausible ones as the following:

Miss McI talks about new work. This week they are to stick
some pictures of Spain into their folders. (They are supposed to have found a picture of an hotel, a Spanish
dancer, the sea and a map of Spain.) Miss McI says she
likes pictures cut into the shapes of circles, triangles,

diamonds or rectangles. Not squares. She says this is
because this is 'healthier' and because she is an art and
craft teacher.

AST (9-13) school

   Underlying all these rules about the use of spaces and
objects was a concept of *authority*. Establishing who was who
in the authority system and how that system worked was a key
task for teachers in the first few weeks. Teachers also gave
rules about the way children should set about their tasks in
each subject area so that within a short time the well-
motivated children had grasped what the teacher expected of
a 'good' pupil. In this highly controlled environment it was
very difficult for individual pupils to initiate their own learning strategies, and the most successful children were those
who adapted quickly to the subject subcultures which have
been revealed earlier in the book from the systematic data.
Thus right from the beginning of the new school year pupils
began to learn what secondary science, mathematics and
English were going to be like.

SCIENCE TEACHING: MEETING THE BUNSEN BURNER

Chapter 3 has shown some ways in which teachers of any
particular subject are alike across schools. Chapter 6 has
already covered the similarities of curriculum content and the
data on classroom processes illustrate how this curriculum is
made manifest. The similarities across all the earlier lessons
was most dramatic in science. All the science teachers told
pupils that labs were special, dangerous places, and then
taught 'measurement', or simple biological taxonomies, or the
bunsen burner, followed by work on crystals. The following
extract is typical, both of the 'bunsen' lessons, and of those
on unfamiliar objects and their uses in the science lab.

   In a chemistry lesson, Mrs McJ takes the register . . .
   gives out exercise books and briefly goes through the work
   done in the previous week - the rules of labs and also the
   diagram of the bunsen burner. 'Get out one bunsen burner
   and mat per table'. . . . She tells them to unscrew the
   chimney of the burner, and describes the various parts.
   She asks various questions . . . and goes round lighting
   burners, then asks them to describe the different flames as
   the collar is rotated. . . . The burners are turned off and
   the class move around the front bench to watch the teacher
   demonstrate the difference between luminous and non-
   luminous flames. . . .
   When I'm not using a bunsen I must always turn it to a luminous flame. Why?' A boy answers, 'So that people can see it.'

CST (12-18) school

Here we see pupils being taught about one piece of apparatus, and the rules associated with it, in a typical 'scientific'
lesson. All the 11-year-old pupils in the schools in local
authority B met the same basic lesson.

> Science with Mrs McK where again presentation was the key
> purpose of the lesson. They were reminded that they were
> to draw a diagram (of the bunsen burner) not a picture.
> Mrs McK told them that margins had to be 2 cm wide and
> the title had to be written in ink. The diagram was to take
> up all the page and was to be drawn in pencil. The labelling
> was to be done on the right of the diagram in ink, and the
> lines showing which part of the bunsen they were labelling
> had to be drawn in pencil. Never on any account were
> diagrams in science to be coloured, the pupils should just
> leave a beautiful clear pencil drawing.
>
> BPT (11-14) school

Science with Mr McL was again the same lesson with another
class.

> Mr McL told them that in science drawings were not meant
> to be works of art, neither were they scruffy. They were
> to do 'neat diagrams, which is what we call pictures in
> science'. He told the children to draw in pencil because
> 'you can't rub out a mistake in Biro'. The pencil must be
> very sharp. They must always draw a margin in pencil 2
> cm wide and give a heading.
>
> BPT (11-14) school

Once the basic equipment had been catalogued the pupils
at BPT did experiments on salt and ink. Thus, in the second
week of term Mr McL's class

> . . . were evaporating a salt solution to obtain the salt
> which had been dissolved in it. Mr McL warned the children
> in rather a casual way not to lean too close over the
> evaporating basin, because it might spit and he did not
> want them to get splashed with boiling salt solution. At
> the end of the practical part of the lesson he said that he
> did not want the children to taste the salt. . . .
> The children put the apparatus away and then their task
> was to write up the experiment. . . . Mr McL said 'At the
> end of each experiment we write down what we have dis-
> covered.' In this case the conclusion of the experiment was
> that rock salt can be purified if we grind, dissolve, filter
> and evaporate. He told the children to write down a con-
> clusion at the end. This was another science word, and the
> conclusion was the most important part of the experiment. . . .
>
> BPT (11-14) school

In the parallel lessons taught by Mrs McK the same experiment was set up by going over the list of terms: tripod, pestle and mortar, dissolve, filter, funnel, evaporate, evaporating basin, clamp and stand, solution.

In these lessons we see common concerns of all science teaching, which were found in the five schools which did science. Teachers wanted pupils to experience experimental work early on, to learn not to taste anything in the lab, to heat things in safety, to draw diagrams, to write up experiments and to learn specialist vocabulary. These are aims which many science teachers would endorse. Another such aim was teaching accurate measurement, and this also was tackled in all the five science-teaching schools. For example, at BST Mr McD:

> explained that he was going to show them a thermometer, describe it to them, get them to practise actually using it and taking each others' temperatures and show them how to read the scale on the thermometer.

MATHEMATICS TEACHING

At CST Mr X went through a series of lessons on measuring different things; first length (with a metre rule), then area, then time (with a pendulum). Similarly at CPT Miss O was taking a group through measurement of length and area. The work pattern was similar in all the science lessons, too, with practical work being done in pairs or small groups rather than individuals. This was in clear contrast with maths, where the common pattern was solitary work from worksheets or a textbook. In maths too, the teachers were very similar across the schools. The early lessons were mainly assessment, while teachers found out what the pupils knew, and the later ones consisted of brief expositions and then individual work. However, there were some similarities between science and maths lessons, in that accuracy and precision was valued in both, as the following extracts from BPT school show:

> Maths with Mrs T who explained that the purpose of the lesson was to get used to using squared paper, to learn to copy diagrams clearly, and make 'a neat beginning to your book'.
>
> Presentation was obviously very important. She continued by saying: 'We work in pen and underline in Biro. We make a small margin, we underline the date, we write in ink and draw in pencil.'
>
> The pupils were given a sheet of geometric shapes to copy. Drawing these geometric shapes took at least two lessons. . . .
>
> Again presentation was the main thing that the children were supposed to learn.

Maths with Mr J was the same lesson with another form.
He said 'What is the first thing to do?'
The children put up their hands and said: 'Write down
the date, draw the narrow margin.' Mr J replied, 'How
narrow?' 'Two centimetres' was the answer. Mr J then
reminded the children always to use a sharp pencil.

Throughout the first month, actual maths teaching was inter-
woven with reiteration of rules about presentation. For example,
at BST in the first week of term Mr McM (using 'Modern
Mathematics for Schools Book 1')

. . . began by asking whether everyone had finished their
previous work as far as No 20. He said that those who had
not must go on until they reach No 20, and those who had
reached No 20 could go on to exercise Two. . . . He moved
around the room from one child to another, going to children
who had their hands up.

Mr McM stopped the lesson to explain how the next subtraction sums were to be set out. Individual work continued until
nearly the end of the lesson when . . .

. . . at five to ten he announced what homework would
be. They were to do Exercise three, page 3, numbers 1 to
10. . . . He reminded the children that they must do no
lines in Biro or pen; all lines must be done in pencil and
the work must be set out in two columns.

Alongside basic work in addition and subtraction, all the
maths teachers laid great stress on terminology. At BPT one
of the observers noted:

Week two could perhaps be called terminology week. Again
and again . . . the children were being introduced to the
specialist language of the different subjects. In fact in
mathematics the second printed sheet which the children
were given was entitled 'The language of Mathematics'. . . .
After that they had worksheets which included many of the
symbols of mathematics moving from the simple addition and
subtraction signs to signs meaning 'more than', 'less than',
and 'belong to'. Much of the work consisted of explaining
what mathematical sentences meant. . . .

Maths lessons very quickly fall into a pattern; so that after
only a few days in the 'B' band at BST . . .

Mrs McN told the children to rule a line under their last
piece of work, put the date and continue with the sums on
page 14. This was subtraction. They should make sure that
they had copied it down right either from the book or from

her blackboard. They must be careful to put the two figures underneath each other so that they could subtract more easily. They could put the letter H, T and U above the sums if that was a help, but they could leave it out if they could do without it.

Throughout the rest of the lesson she went around the classroom and sat beside children helping them.

Similarly at AST by the third week of term:

Mrs A announced that everyone should turn to page 24 in their maths book, Exercise 14. She wants everyone to be on this page today – the longer take-aways and the problems. Dominico has finished both. Mrs A tells them to leave their other work – rule it off and start a new exercise . . . rest of the lesson consists of silent individual work.

Similar lessons were recorded at CPT and CST and at APT. Indeed all the observers commented on the monotonous character of maths.

One of the most lively lessons took place at CPT. It contained more explicit teaching directed to the class, than is ususal. Yet it reveals the 'typical' features of maths teaching. Mrs McO was going to take 2.1 as their regular maths teacher was ill. She began by sorting out what work the class was doing. The observer wrote:

The class fuss a bit, Petula is miles ahead of everyone else, Melvyn is miles behind, and a girl who is absent has to be helped to catch up. Mrs McO gathers round her desk the three who have been away – they all sound quite competent (the work is on fractions, and reducing them so that $\frac{5}{15}$ becomes $\frac{1}{3}$)

Thus even at the beginning of the lesson there were pupils whose performance is widely different. Because maths is a cumulative subject, the pupil who had been absent *had* to be helped back into the fold, Petula had to be kept within reach of the rest of the class so she did not get too far ahead, and Melvyn had to be prevented from falling too far behind. The notes continue:

Mrs McO says aloud:
'If you are conversing because you are working, that's all right – but if like these ladies at the front you are just conversing. . . .'

She says they can talk about work – but if it is a big difficulty they should go to her. . . .

She moves to mark Petula's work, then Norman's, then his neighbour's. Then she bases herself at her desk and is marking rapidly. . . .

There is a constant buzz in the room, but it sounds
tolerable . . .
Mrs McO says aloud:
'If I have marked your book and I have put an equals sign
this means the answer is not taken to the last stage.'

This was a typical maths lesson comment, in that public, class-
oriented statements in maths very frequently dealt with errors
common to all the books recently marked for individuals. This
lesson continued with individual work, and Mrs McO looked at
each pupil's work in turn. Only two boys – Lloyd and Glen –
seemed to be getting most of the sums wrong, and she spent
more time with them than with the other pupils. At the start of
the second period of the double lesson she stopped the work,
telling the pupils to finish what they are doing and turn to what
they were doing on algebra. The notes continue:

Mrs McO checks that they have met the word equation, and
says that today they will do substitution. She gives the whole
class an explanation of substitution using the football analogy.
Glen gives a bad explanation of substitution in football. Mrs
McO then uses a good analogy from cooking. She demonstrates
how you do substitution, replace one thing by another. . . .
Doing $2 \times a = 2a$
$2 \times y \times x = 2xy$
$a \times a = a^2$ etc.
Class are to rule off fractions and put page 73 Algebra and
copy what she has put on the board.

The class then settled down to work on substitution problems
from the book, until the bell went for break. The lesson was run
very competently and bore all the hallmarks of maths classes in
the six schools. The teacher called for quiet, occasionally demonstrated a new technique on the board, and tried to mark all the
pupils' books. The pupils must have experienced maths as an
essentially solitary, and endless, activity. The systematic data
in Chapter 3 reveal that this pattern is repeated throughout the
year.

ENGLISH TEACHING

English lessons were, as Chapter 3 also shows, rather different
from maths and science. There was more oral work and more
discussion, and yet solitary writing still filled a major part of
the time. For example:

Miss McP gives out the books and the pupils have to pass them
back. Pupils call out 'Are we going to finish that story?' and
'What page?' She goes over what has happened in the story so
far. The story is about a boy with TB, a trolley, and a 'secret

love', who does not go to school. She starts them reading round the room.

CST (12-18) school

This is one typical kind of English lesson. A story is read out by pupils or the teacher, with frequent stops for explanation, recapitulation and vocabulary checks.

> Most of the answers come from boys. She stops Peggy reading because she hasn't paid attention to the punctuation. She makes her examine a question mark and read it like a question. . . . Stops for some time to go over 'optimistic' and 'pessimistic'. . . . The boys are doing most of the reading . . .

When the class reach the end of the story they have to write their own account of it.

> Miss McP gives out a paper, and tells the class to put name, date and title 'Spit Nolan'. A boy asks whether he should put a margin, and is told not to fuss. 'Do we have a margin?' Pupil says 'yes', but there is a lot of fussing about the margin. . . .
> Miss McP puts headings on the board for them to recreate the story. Pupil asks:
> 'Miss, can you draw pictures?'
> 'Not until you've done the writing'.

This was a very characteristic piece of lesson organization in English. Maths and science had essential diagrams, while English teachers used drawing as a reward for completing written work and a way of filling up time for fast workers while the slow-coaches caught up. Another common concern was the spelling:

> A girl asks how to spell 'tuberculosis'. Miss McP writes it on the board. When a boy asks for the spelling of 'quite' she hands him a dictionary. . . .

Also important to all the English teachers in the study were punctuation, paragraphs and handwriting. Thus:

> Miss McP reminds them that if she has mentioned their writing before they should try to improve it. She tells a boy near me to try to make his writing smaller now he's at secondary school. . . . At 10.25 she stops everyone to go over how to do paragraphs.

When pupils had written what they thought was enough they took their work to Miss McP. If it was long enough they could draw, if not they had to write more. At the end of the lesson all the papers were handed in for marking.

The English lessons at the other schools were essentially similar.

In the same week at BST (11-14) school class 1A1 spent one lesson reading a play, and another on nouns, verbs and adjectives. At BPT (11-14) school that week form 1S had a similar lesson from Miss E:

Today they should head their paper in the right way and then copy what was on the blackboard.

On the blackboard were notes on punctuation. Once these were done the class had to do spelling exercises from a book, working alone. Great attention was paid to correct spelling.

Children who had made spelling mistakes in their homework had to write the corrections three times each. Josh wrote the word 'holiday' six times because he got it wrong twice.

The age of the pupils made little difference to English teaching. At AST (9-13) school, Mr U gave the following lesson:

This morning's task is to read through a small piece of comprehension. They are then asked to complete the following sentence orally and are told that they are wrong if they don't use the right format.
Teacher: What colour are Sally's eyes?
Pupil: Blue.
Teacher: Wrong.
Pupil: Sally Brown's eyes are blue.
Teacher: Good, why didn't you say it that way in the first place.

Mr U then went over his rules for the presentation of work, and moved around the room looking at individual pupil's work.

'Very nice, Gabrielle, that's good writing.' In this way he goes round looking at books and correcting mistakes. 'That's very nice', he says to one girl, 'it's a pleasure to see, unlike one or two we are not going to mention; are we, Gavin?'
For the final part of the exercise the pupils have to write an account of their own family. Some of the children protest they have already done this, but Mr U silences them by saying:
'Well you had breakfast yesterday, you've had breakfast today, and I expect you will have it tomorrow, won't you.'

Mr U's last comment might almost be taken as a paradigm of the English lessons observed. The pupils read something and wrote about it yesterday, they are doing the same thing today, and they will be doing it again tomorrow. Certainly the data from the teacher and pupil records lend strong support to this impression gained during many hours of participant observation, and goes some way towards an explanation why teaching style was such a dominant influence on pupils' performance.

8 THROUGH THE EYES OF THE PUPIL

The two previous chapters have described the curriculum in the six schools, and the teachers' strategies for establishing control and imposing their teaching styles on the pupils. The theme of this chapter is the pupils' adaptation to their new schools and the teachers, beginning with data on their fears about their new classmates and schoolfellows, and then moving on to comparisons between specific pupils who reacted very differently to their first weeks in a new school.

PUPIL - PUPIL RELATIONSHIPS

The new pupils had two worries about the other children in their new schools. They were concerned in case they were separated from old friends and unable to make new ones. Some pupils were also anxious about bullying. In this section data are presented first on these two anxieties, and whether they were resolved, and then on how pupil-pupil relationships were used and developed in the six schools.

Many pupils expressed the fears that they had had before transfer about lacking friendship. For example Stephanie (APT) said in her interview that she did not know how she would get friendly with children from other schools and she worried about that. Similarly among the children going to BPT, Karena and Fida felt worried that they would not meet new friends there and would be left on their own. Not only girls worried about this, for Josh and Luke (also transferring to BPT) said that:

> they had been very worried about finding new friends here and were very scared that they would not make friends easily and get very left out....They both admitted that once they arrived here they did in fact make friends very quickly.
> (Interview with researcher)

These pupils can be contrasted with those like Nathan (BPT). He knew he was coming up with his particular friend, Amos, who was in the same class, and felt no worries of any kind. Certainly, once people had made some friends, their whole attitude to the school improved. For example, Kirsty, a target at APT, was not 'all that keen' on the school at the very beginning...however, once she had met new friends she found things were 'not too bad'. This sentiment was echoed by most of the children.

New friends *were* found, and school became more bearable.
Friends and siblings were useful for helping to get through the
school day, especially at first when things were strange, as
can be seen from the following interviews.

> Brendan (AST). When he first came to the school he got
> worried about dinners because he didn't know when to go
> in. A girl told him and then he felt much better about it.
> He wanted to join the gym club but didn't know how to. His
> sister took him so that was all right.

> Terence (AST) sometimes gets confused about what dinner
> sitting he is in, but his friend seems to be very alert and
> helps him out.

Most of the pupils at all six schools had transferred with other
pupils from the same feeder schools. Few children who had lived
in the area for any length of time were strangers to all their
new classmates. On the other hand, some children had only
recently come to the neighbourhood and were likely to be 'alone'
in the new school at first. Some of the schools deliberately mixed
up children from different feeder schools, while others consciously put new pupils into classes with their friends. Where the
latter course was adopted, it did reassure pupils, although it
may have had negative consequences later.

The first way in which pupils associated was through seating,
and in most schools the pupils began by staying close to old
friends. For example:

> As the children came into the room for the first day they
> were allowed to sit wherever they chose. This in fact meant
> that the children from a particular feeder school sat together
> and children from another also sat together etc. Not only did
> they sit together school by school; they also sat together
> class by class.
>
> BPT (11-14) school

Gradually new patterns formed, and it was possible to watch this
happening in lessons. Nearly all teachers in all schools allowed
pupils to sit where, and with whom, they liked. However, the
opportunities for 'socializing' in lessons varied considerably
across schools and teachers, as did the extent to which the staff
were likely to direct one pupil to look after another, socially or
academically. For example on the first day at APT (9-13) school
the following incident was recorded.

> The school secretary brings a West Indian girl - Marcia -
> down to the first year area to join Miss C's class. Miss C
> finds that 'you know Stacey' and lets Stacey show Marcia
> where to put her coat, etc.

This was not an isolated incident for the next day a similar one was recorded in Miss B's class:

> There is a new girl in the class today – Rebecca. She has a friend, who is showing her what to do.

APT expected pupils to help each other with slightly more academic things also, as the following incident shows:

> In Miss B's class.
> There is also another 'progressive' feature of this class. Early on this afternoon Miss B took Charles to the 3-dimensional shapes set out on a table in Miss C's classroom. Now she tells each pupil reaching that particular exercise (in 'Oxford Middle School Maths') to ask Charles to show them the shapes.
> ...Dominic and Phillip are sent to Charles to be taken to the shapes.

However, pupils were not usually expected to help each other with their work, or do it for each other. Indeed, sometimes a claim from a pupil that he was only helping a neighbour would be dismissed.

> In Miss B's class.
> Rebecca is told off; she says she was telling Sue what no. 7 is. Miss B says Sue should go to her, or get up and look at the board herself.

At AST (9-13) school pupil talk was not allowed in the majority of lessons (cookery and art being exceptions). Not only were pupils not allowed to help each other, but competition was actively fostered between children. The procedure in oral tests exemplified the different spirits of the two school regimes. At AST in tests children all stood up, and as they got a wrong answer they sat down. This eliminated pupils until one or two were left on their feet in desperate competition to be last one standing. At APT children sat down as soon as they had one correct answer, and pupils left on their feet were given easier questions until they could answer correctly and flop down in their places.

Because there was no legitimate way in which pupils could chat in classes at AST, it was not possible to gather the same evidence about how pupils exchanged information about themselves when they were new to each other. There this process went on outside the classroom, while at APT it was a simple matter to watch it happening because there the children sat round tables, and a good deal of quiet conversation was allowed. Much 'conversation' consisted of borrowing rubbers, rules, coloured pens or felt pens, and much was not work-related at all.

Quite a lot of the conversation I overhear is not work-
related: comics, food and mum.
Some is: what colour crayon to use, etc.
There are mixed and single-sex tables in both Miss B's and
Miss C's rooms.
I overhear two girls.
'Do you watch Coronation Street?'
'No. My mum and dad do, but I'm not allowed.'
'Is Liz?'
'No.'
The first girl is obviously puzzled by this parental censor-
ship.

In the early days the pupils were quickly getting to know
things about one another. Later that lesson in Miss C's room a
boy was overheard saying firmly, 'Every car you see in "Bugsy
Malone" is American'; so it was not only girls who began new
relationships via discussions of the mass media. Pupils also
began to find out about each other's families: 'My sister's 23.
She's got a baby and a husband', and beginning to establish
their own academic reputations: 'Polly's a better reader than
me'. Of course pupils who had come together from the same
lower school were aware of each other's reputations. Some did
not hesitate to communicate the reputations more publicly. For
example:

In Miss C's class.
Dean is threatened with being moved. Tom says Dean behaved
like that at his old school. Miss C says Dean is not going to
be like that here. He is moved and put on his own. Told to
concentrate on work, not clowning.

Where conversations were related to the school, they frequently dealt with the rules and mores of the new school. For
example:

In Mr Z's class.
They all seem to have brought games kit but no one has a
towel. So there is an earnest discussion of showers and
towels among two lots of girls near me. They are worried
about having showers, being forced to have them without a
towel, and generally the whole advent of a new experience.

Later that day a group of girls were discussing, in a somewhat
anxious way, the reading tests. Mrs Q was removing every child
in the first year one at a time to read to her, in order to find
the ones who needed remedial reading. This meant a child's
going out into the area between the classrooms, then reading
to Mrs Q, and then, on return, sending out the next child. This
process was apparently mysterious to some pupils for the observer overheard the following exchange:

Girl on Table 4 asks, 'Polly, where is it you have to go to read?'
Told just outside in area.
'And is it Mrs Q?'
Told yes, but it's *Miss* Q, and they have an argument about that.

In these extracts pupils can be seen meeting each other, sizing each other up, and helping each other through the school day. Similar acquaintance processes were going on in the other schools, as can be seen in the next extract:

In the craft area they are able to talk while they work. Dominico is talking about his father, and says he has been a waiter, a bus-driver and a wrestler before he got the chip shop. Mentioning the wrestling causes disbelief for Barny.

AST (9-13) school

In fact, the father told the observer during an interview that Dominico was called 'chippy' by the other children because of the chip shop. He reported that he had told Dominico not to be upset by this; on the contrary he must think himself fortunate that whenever he wanted a bag of chips he could have one without having to pay out any of his pocket money. Whether Dominico took this advice we cannot know, but he certainly survived better than his classmate Gavin Radice, who ended up changing his name, to avoid being called 'Radish'.

The pupils quickly started expecting certain kinds of behaviour from each other, as Colin Lacey (1970) reported in 'Hightown Grammar'. For example by the third week of term the following was recorded:

In science with Miss O. She returns their homework. When she says one boy got 'rubbish' written on his work several people near me say 'Wayne Douglas' with total confidence that he was the one.

CPT (12-18) school

Certainly it was clear to the observer that such a comment could have been made only about Wayne or his neighbour and collaborator Alan. In these ways reputations were established in the peer group.

BULLYING, FIGHTING AND SCRAPPING

Fears of bullying were more widespread, because even those children who knew they were transferring with lots of friends from the same school could worry about strange, dangerous children. In the summer term before transfer two of the schools

explicitly tried to calm pupil fears about bullying by arguing
that the new school was not dangerous, and that trouble was
quickly stopped. Thus in June the head of the first year at
CPT told prospective pupils not to worry about bullying:

> Mrs I then attempts to reassure them about stories of bully-
> ing by saying that she knows they will have heard that new
> boys get rolled off banks and get their heads pushed down
> the toilets but it is not true...'You have got a year tutor
> and he will be there to look after you.'

When the BPT staff visited one feeder school the head of the
first year, Mr McQ, raised the issue of bullying.

> Mr McQ began by saying that another topic which usually
> came up but hadn't on this occasion was bullying. He assured
> all the children that stories they had heard or were bound
> to hear about all the bullying and baitings that go on were
> quite unfounded and that there was no bullying of any kind
> at all.
>   He then appealed to the two exhibits (a boy and girl pupil
> from BPT) who had come along. They nodded their heads
> vigorously in agreement. Mr McR (another BPT teacher) then
> said behind his hand so that all could hear 'I'll give you your
> 50p afterwards for saying that.'
>   There was general laughter.

When the sample pupils were interviewed during the autumn term
bullying did come up as a fear pupils had, at all six schools.
From the accounts of interviews written up by the researchers,
it is clear that both the primary and secondary types of transfer school had scared pupils. For example at APT (9-13) school,
Stacey 'sometimes hides from the big children on the way home
and waits until they are gone so that they will not annoy her',
while Louisa 'was a bit scared of the bigger children' when she
came but had 'got over that' when interviewed. Roy says he does
not like 'the big children fighting in the playground'. Boys and
girls at AST (9-13) school also reported some playground trouble.
Dominico said that at first he was worried about what he described as bully boys, but his brother sorted that out for him.
Joel told us that the bigger boys 'knock you off the apparatus
sometimes', but 'you get used to it'. A very small boy, Randal,
mentioned bullying, but what he described sounded less like a
vicious campaign of intimidation, than the sort of rough and
tumble which a boy of his size could find distressing. During
the first few days Crispin got bullied by someone who took his
tennis ball and then hit him, but a teacher came around and
soon put a stop to that. The most serious case of continued
bullying involved Gavin Radice, worried in his early days in the
school about the fourth-year children who took his crisps. This
was the boy whose parents had his name finally changed from

Radice to Radley, because all the other children had been making fun of him by calling him Radish.

Some of the sample reported schools tackling bullies, as at CPT (12-18) school, where Lucinda had a 17-year-old sister who had been a pupil at the school and who said she had liked it, but that there was a lot of bullying. According to Lucinda, 'There isn't any bullying now' because 'you get caned if you do'.

However, at BPT (11-14) school, two girls clearly believed there was a reign of terror at their school. The observer interviewed Jasmine and Lavinia and reported that:

> The main information which these two girls had got from their siblings was to expect bullying. They had been told that the third years often pick on you. When I asked them if in fact this had happened to them they said no it had not. They have been very careful to avoid it, and they very rarely went out at break time or lunch time so that they would not have any trouble. They said they had seen some of the boys being bullied. Jasmine explained that some of the big lads came up and half strangled them. Nobody came to help, 'They daren't.'

None of the big boys in the BPT sample reported bullying, and it is possible that these two girls were cowering indoors for no reason. However, it does suggest that control of the playground was not all it might have been. Some of the children reported less bullying than they had known at their former schools; for example, Camilla (AST) said that she had been bullied a bit at her feeder school but that she had not had much trouble here. Similarly Oliver emphatically said that he liked APT school, and would certainly much rather stay there than go back to his old one where there had been a great deal of bullying.

The ORACLE observers witnessed few examples of bullying in the schools, and perhaps it is rather unlikely that it would occur in their presence. Indeed, they were sometimes called in to stop pupil-pupil violence or intimidation if it occurred in their vicinity. For example, one observer was at AST waiting for a PE lesson to begin when a boy emerged from the male changing room and asked the (female) observer to come in and stop a fight that had broken out. The observer did so. The fact, then, that bullying did not happen in front of the observer should not be taken as evidence that it did not occur at all.

Given that the pupils were scared of being bullied, it is important to see what the schools did to allay their fears and stop bullying. It is widely believed that secondary schools are violent, even riotous, places, where teachers do not even attempt to prevent bullies operating. Thus, for example, 'Woman's Realm' (19.4.80) carried an article called 'School bullying: can it be beaten?' This article claimed that:

If you look into reports of school bullying - and they are very common occurrences - you'll find that the school's reaction is disappointingly negative.

In the six schools studied in the ORACLE project teachers did try to prevent bullying. For example, CPT kept the second years in a separate playground. At CST the headmaster did a regular playground duty by the second year annexe where he could watch over the children. AST staff clamped down on all fighting, regardless of the willingness or otherwise of the participants. An idea of the attempts made by the schools to deal with bullying can be gained from the following extracts:

> One particular group of children in 1S has been causing a lot of difficulty in all their lessons, this includes Jacky, Dickon, Greg and Sinclair. They are often quarrelling among themselves and sometimes involved in punch-ups, not only in the playground but in the classroom as well....
>   However in every single lesson they have caused trouble, and it ended with a real punch-up between Jacky and Dickon in an English class with Miss E. She therefore sent all four of them to see Mr McS, the head of the first year, first thing the next morning and he apparently gave them a severe talking to. From now on they are to be split; not put into different classes, but split within their class.
>
> BPT (11-14) school

Here the staff at the school separated a group of boys who fought frequently, so that the habitual losers could be protected. By the end of that week, Greg and Sinclair had been detached from the other two even at playtime and were no longer suffering.
CPT had a special yard for the new second years. The following comments were recorded at the school:

> In assembly (held just for the second years in the drama hall) Mr McT gave them a lecture till Miss McU (the senior mistress) came to take the assembly. It would usually be Mrs I (the head of the second year) but she was off sick. Mr McT gave them a homily based on Everest, about the importance of team work. Hillary and Tensing depended on a team to make their individual achievement. There was a hymn 'Jesus I have promised' and then three prayers. Then Miss McU gave them another homily, and this was followed by quite a few notices from other staff about the bookshop, the tuckshop, football and boys' cross country. Mr McT talked about the tuckshop. He told them that if the second years lingered in the larger yard after visiting the tuckshop it would be closed. Bullying - which I think was the main reason for not wanting second years in the main yard - was not mentioned. No phoney reason is given for the edict either; they were just told not to linger.

The following day this contribution was recorded:

> Break is in a special yard and there is a teacher on yard
> duty. So there is reasonable order and little fighting.

CPT was not alone in using assembly to preach against pupil-
pupil violence. For example:

> Assembly for the whole school in the main hall. A senior male
> teacher was in charge until the headmistress, Miss McV,
> arrives. Then there is a hymn 'Jesu good above all other',
> followed by a reading from the two third-year girls. Then
> prayers. Then Miss McV gives a lecture about not fighting
> and there is an announcement of football results.
>
> AST (9-13) school

It was not only the more formal schools which tried to stop pupil-
pupil violence as can be seen from the APT data:

> Dudley informed me today that he beat up Robin last even-
> ing. He told me that Robin went to Mr McW (the head of the
> lower school) who ran him home. Dudley said, 'I wish I'd
> been beat up', meaning then he could have had a lift home
> in a car.
>   Miss C later told me that Robin had been brought to her
> and that he had had a very large lump. (I assume it was she
> who got Mr McW to take him home.)
>   In first-year assembly Miss C says that she wants to see
> Dudley and ticks him off very sharply in front of the whole
> assembly for his 'abominable behaviour'. She also keeps him
> behind after assembly and bawls him out for some time in the
> area outside the classrooms. I am inside a classroom but I
> can hear her clearly although Dudley's replies, if any, are
> inaudible.
>   Tuesday lunchtime means gym club and cross country
> which seem to appeal to a lot of the first years. I go down
> to the first-year area and some girls come into the area to
> tell the playground aides that there are boys fighting in
> the yard, including Kenneth, Oliver and Nigel. The dinner
> ladies go out to intervene and bring the culprits inside. I
> put some Savlon on Oliver's leg which is badly grazed. He
> is tearful and resentful about his attackers. The bell goes
> for the end of the dinner hour.
>   During afternoon school Miss C is called to the office to
> talk to Robin's mother on the phone. When she returns she
> tells me she dislikes Dudley, but Robin provoked him.
>
> APT (9-13) school

This long extract from one day's notes at APT shows the staff
trying to prevent a repetition of fighting that has already occurred as well as intervening to stop a fight that had been spotted.

The 'dinner ladies' were quick to stop the boys' fight, and when Miss C appeared she was quick to reprimand all the participants. However, reprimands do not necessarily work, for only three days later Dudley was in trouble again!

> After break I am in Miss C's class. She goes out, and comes back with Khalid from Mr Z's class. She then bawls out Alan who together with Dudley has apparently been stamping on Khalid's feet, which are in plaster and bandages after an operation. Miss C tells Alan that he is to stay right away from Khalid and 'then it can only be Dudley'.
> Alan is reduced to tears. Miss C tells him to stop crying and stay away from Dudley. He returns to his table and sits there sobbing noisily.

The six schools in the sample, therefore, attempted to stop pupil-pupil violence. Overall the data suggest that there was not extensive bullying in school, and that most new pupils quickly made some friends. The two commonest pupil fears ahead of transfer were not, therefore, sustained once the children had made the change.

In addition to concern about the other pupils, the children in the sample had worries about the teachers. The following section takes up the matter of pupil-teacher relationships, in the light of the evidence from the systematic observation that pupils change their behaviour to suit their teacher's style.

PUPILS AND TEACHERS

Throughout the ORACLE books it has been argued that as pupils get older and move up the school the successful ones spend more time working on their own, while the unsuccessful ones either have not learnt how to keep their heads down or choose not to behave in this way. The following section illustrates ways in which some of the pupils display these patterns of interaction with their teachers. Rex Mackie from CST has been chosen as an example of an attention-seeking fusspot who was impressing teachers as keen and alert, in contrast with Wayne Douglas, an extreme easy rider from CPT who was a disruptive pupil causing 'trouble'. Both boys can be contrasted with Davina, an 'ideal' pupil, from Miss C's class at APT, who was a group toiler or a hard grinder as the occasion demanded.

Rex, as was mentioned in the previous chapter, was following an older brother who had been anti-school and disliked by teachers. Rex himself said he had been 'scared to come to CST' because his brother said 'it was rubbish here'. However, he 'quite liked' it at the school by mid-autumn. He played a lot of football and was in the class team which was doing well in the lunchtime league. His manner can be gauged from his interview comment on his class football team:

'He's brilliant, our Captain, Miss'.
'Oh, who's that?'
'Me, Miss.'

He had, apparently, set out to be different from his brother, and his classroom behaviour gave him high visibility, but a positive image. His behaviour across a range of subjects shows how he set about building his reputation.

Biology with Mr McX.
In this lesson Rex asks several questions, about what he should do next, as the class are led through the classification of living things....Mr McX has a half-completed diagram on the board and Rex asks if Mr McX is going to complete it!
Another boy asks about lugworms....Mr McX begins to describe vertebrates, ticks Rex off for putting up his hand before the question has been asked, but then allows him to call out an answer (correct).
Another boy is told off for the same kind of behaviour: 'Don't shout out! I like a little politeness!'....
Rex answers several questions, and puts his hand up several times and is not called on. They are asked to copy the five classes of vertebrate into their books, and Rex points out that Mr McX has not listed 'lays eggs' under 'birds' - and Mr McX is already calling him by his name.

During this lesson Rex had made himself known, but he had contributed several correct answers, and appeared keen on the subject and had stayed alert. This very clearly contrasts with Wayne Douglas at CPT. In the third week of term he appeared in the wrong science class:

Miss O calls the register - and there are some wrong pupils - boys are here who should not be, including Wayne Douglas ... Wayne is sent to Mr P (head of science) because Miss O doesn't think he is in this group - he hasn't got a book in the pile she is returning....
Wayne returns - he is in Group B (not this one) - so Miss O asks him where Group B are. Wayne says he does not know. Miss O asks him loudly why he didn't ask while he was with Mr P and sends him back to find where Group B are.

By this time Wayne had 'wasted' some twenty minutes of his double-period of science, and impressed himself on Miss O as a nuisance. His behaviour in an English lesson with Mrs F was similarly calculated to annoy:

Mrs F tells them they need books, writing equipment, because they are going to continue writing a story called 'Homecom-

ings'. She wants to hear some first paragraphs....Mrs F
asks for some ideas about how to end the story....Wayne
is told off for muttering....Mrs F moves round the room
reading the stories....Wayne has done the wrong story and
is told off.

Again here Wayne can be seen behaving in a way calculated to
annoy any teacher: doing the wrong task. This can be compared
with Rex's behaviour in French, for which he was in a top set
of children who also did German.

Mr McY's group are in the language lab. He goes round the
class, in French, asking questions....He starts with Rex
who answers readily....the questioning proceeds rapidly in
French with very occasional English words or phrases. Rex
seems to be a star – he usually has his hand up first, and
when asked he is usually right. There is one point where he
and another boy give good answers and Mr McY says that
they had a good teacher last year....
  Rex's hand is the first to go up, and he is told that he
always has plenty to say, and must put his hand down....
  They now play Fizz Buzz in French and at first they play
sitting down, but Rex is keen to try standing up so success
(or failure) is visible.

This was a typical performance from Rex, in that he was visible
in a positive way and eager to participate. In a biology lesson
that day he said to Mr McX: 'Sir, I read in a book that if all
the birds flew away the insects would take over'. This kind of
addition to a lesson served to impress him on staff as a pupil
worth taking seriously. Again this can be compared with Wayne's
behaviour – which was equally noticeable but completely different. In art with Mrs McZ, who

  ...is very strict, they are not only to be silent, but are also
not allowed to fidget or pick up pencils....
  They are to get three things and draw a pattern using their
shapes....
  Wayne is reprimanded twice for slouching and he and his
neighbour are told they are planning wrongly....
  Wayne is told off for slouching again....
  Wayne is reprimanded again, and made to stand up....
  Wayne is persisting in doing what he was told not to do –
he is drawing freehand rather than around the things....
  Wayne's drawing is rejected as too fiddly and he is set to
work again on the reverse side (of his sheet) to use two books
and a ruler and start the whole exercise again.

In this lesson Wayne persistently slouched and was repeatedly
made to sit up straight, and managed to do the wrong task for
most of the double lesson, ignoring all the instructions Mrs McZ

had given. Within two or three weeks Wayne's reputation was
fixed. One day he was due in a science lesson straight after
break, but did not arrive. The observer could actually see him
and a friend outside in the playground, where they wandered
for some twenty minutes before someone brought them to the
lesson. Miss O returned some homework, and said that one boy
had had 'rubbish' written on his work; and all the pupils near
the observer immediately said 'Douglas'. When Wayne and his
friend arrived at the lesson:

> Miss O gives out small pieces of graph paper, and asks 'Who
> hasn't got a ruler?' Needless to say Wayne and his friend
> haven't. Miss O points this out and asks 'have you forgotten
> your brains?'

Later in this lesson Wayne took another boy's stool, had to borrow a pencil from the observer, had forgotten to bring his
exercise book to the class, and eventually got Miss O to draw
his diagram for him. Such behaviour made him very unpopular
with teachers and notorious among other pupils.

The contrast between Rex or Wayne and Davina, originally
a quiet collaborator and now a very industrious pupil at APT is
as great as the difference between the two boys. It is hard to
write about such children because they keep such low profiles
in the classroom, so that unless the observer consciously decides
to observe them, they can easily remain invisible in the fieldnotes for long periods. Delamont (1976) has already written
about the difficulty of producing vivid accounts of conformist
pupils without making them appear prigs - bad pupils make
exciting reading, solitary workers do not. Davina was Miss C's
favourite pupil in her class at APT. She worked quietly alone
or with Nanette, and it is very difficult not to give an impression of smug complacency.

Just as Rex had come to CST with a label because his elder
brother had already been there, Davina had a brother who had
attended APT. However, Rex's brother had had a reputation
for bad behaviour and low ability, which Rex had decided to
counteract. Davina's brother had been one of Miss C's favourite
pupils, and she told the observer how she had deliberately put
Davina into her own class because she liked the family. Miss C
said that the family produced children who were participators
and that was what she liked in pupils. Davina and her brother
worked hard, swam, played instruments, sang, acted, read
widely and had lots of hobbies. That is what Miss C wanted in
her pupils and so she wanted Davina in her class. It is interesting to speculate whether Davina would have been a favourite
if her classroom style had been disruptive or attention seeking.
However, she lived up to Miss C's expectations, as will be
shown.

As it happened, she was the first pupil to become visible to
the observer. At 9.20 on the first day of term when all the

pupils were strangers to the school Miss C asked Davina if she
could find her way to the office to take the dinner numbers to
the secretary. Davina could, and did. When she returned Miss
C sent her into Miss B's and Mr Z's classes to take their dinner
numbers to the office. At 9.50 Davina went to the office with the
form's dinner money, and on her return was again sent to Miss
B and Mr Z to see if they wanted her services again. Miss B
then asked her to take Candy to the office with her, so that
Candy could be Miss B's register monitor in future. When Candy
came back, Davina told the observer 'We're doing nothing - it's
rather boring.'

When work began after lunch, Davina settled alongside
Nanette to the first real task - copying with apparent enthusiasm A.A. Milne's 'Four Friends' from the board in best handwriting. Nanette recognized the poem, and the two girls, seated
in the centre of the room, were already 'visible' as co-operative
hard workers. During that first afternoon the pupils had individual reading tests with the remedial teacher, did a spelling
test, experienced their first French lesson, and began drawing
a pattern to decorate the walls. Davina and Nanette took part
in all these activities, and were not in any trouble. A week
later Davina was still the class's 'official runner' fetching and
carrying registers, dinner money and other documents around
the school for Miss C. One day Davina and her three table-
mates managed to miss going for their school photographs when
the other girls in the class went, but Miss C did not reprimand
them at all. She comforted them and arranged for them to be
taken at the end of the fourth-year pupils' session. Davina
was swimming in Miss C's special training group, playing an
instrument, and spending her lunch hours in Miss C's room
doing craftwork of various kinds. She had become the kind of
pupil Miss C liked. Within a couple of weeks her academic
achievements were becoming obvious, as a French lesson showed.

> Pupils can now say their own name, answer 'Comment
> s'appelle-t-elle?' and count. They do competitive count-
> ing - all stand up and go round saying numbers - if wrong
> they sit down. When about half are down - class goes over
> to French version of Fizz Buzz - where they must say
> 'Cuckoo' instead of multiples of two. Davina is the last one
> on her feet.

In this extract Davina is shown both as successful - she can
manage to play Fizz Buzz in French - but also as a participator.
Pupils who are unenthusiastic about schoolwork make mistakes
or fail to answer early in such competitions and 'escape', that
is, they sit down and relax as early as possible. Similar commitment was shown when the class were writing house agents'
blurb for unlikely properties. The idea was to choose an
unusual 'home' - such as a rabbit burrow or a bird's nest - and
then write an advertisement for it which both disguised what

it was, and painted it in glowing terms. The class settled to
work:

> Miss C is moving around the room – looking over some
> pupils' shoulders – and pupils wanting help get up and go
> to her, waving jotters if they want a spelling....Nanette
> has finished – but has mis-spelled scenery....Dean keeps
> going up for spellings; Miss C asks 'Who's writing this,
> you or me?' Davina brings her essay for me to read – I can't
> guess what kind of home it describes but I give her two
> spellings....she tells me her 'home' is a teabag box with
> wallpaper lining – I suggest she says 'the ceiling can be
> raised for ventilation'. Miss C sends everyone back to their
> seats and says it is time to hear some of the completed
> advertisements. Nanette reads her – a bird's nest; Roy his
> (a football stadium); Duncan his (a bus), and then Davina.

While Nanette, Roy and Duncan all read out descriptions which
enabled someone in the class to guess what was being offered,
Davina's foxed everyone:

> After many guesses, Miss C asks me if I can guess. I say I
> know, but would never have guessed it. Davina tells the
> class. Rosalie is next....

Rosalie was followed by Daniel (a doll's house) and Dean (a
telephone box), and subsequent children offered a stable, a
rabbit burrow, a tree house, a wardrobe and a church steeple.
The class were praised, and then Miss C moved on to discuss
some words that could be used in such advertisements such as
'compact' when something is very cramped.
   Davina did not figure very much in the observer's notes
compared, for example, with Dean who was attention seeking.
She and Nanette worked hard, and rarely misbehaved, and consequently attracted little teacher attention or notice from observers. Davina had learnt, within a few days, how to succeed at
APT and serves as a nice contrast to Wayne Douglas. There
were, of course, pupils like Davina at the other schools: in
Rex's class at CST there were two girls – Ellen and Dawn – who
were very similar in behaviour, and at CPT boys called Vincent
and Norman were equally conformist. Good behaviour and adaptation to the teachers' desire for co-operation and hard work
was not limited to girls, just as messing about and causing trouble was not peculiar to boys.

LINKING THE ETHNOGRAPHIC AND SYSTEMATIC OBSERVATION

The descriptions of pupils such as Davina and Wayne in the
previous paragraphs support and extend the profiles of pupil
personae from Chapter 3 and demonstrate in convincing fashion

the value of combining both systematic and participant observation in a single study. There are also other examples which emphasize the usefulness of these ethnographic accounts when seeking to explain the findings reported in earlier parts of the book. In English lessons nearly 60 per cent of the boys were easy riders compared to just over 44 per cent of the girls. This sex difference was reflected on the scores obtained on the language skills test. Fifty-six per cent of boys failed to make progress after transfer compared to 44 per cent of the girls. For reading this disparity was even more marked: 57.5 per cent of boys failed to make further progress compared to 27 per cent of girls. The accounts presented in the previous chapters show just why some children reacted to English lessons in the way that they did. Apart from the occasional discussion pupils were given exercises to do or were told to read something and then write about it. Messy writers, like Wayne, were at an obvious disadvantage compared to neat workers like Davina and were likely to lose interest in the subject, faced with constant criticism from the teacher about the quality of their work.

Mathematics appears to present similar problems to even more children. Over 80 per cent of the sample studied using systematic observation adopted the easy rider persona in this subject. Accompanying this fact 45 per cent of boys and 35 per cent of the girls performed less well on the tests after transfer than they did before. There was also considerable overlap between the teaching style used in the primary feeder schools and that used by mathematics teachers in the transfer schools.

In 'Inside the Primary Classroom' it was shown that teachers made much use of straightforward computation exercises involving the four mathematical rules, place value, fractions, etc. Often pupils would begin with the same addition sums at the start of each year in the junior schools so the teacher could discover for herself just where the class was at. In the typical primary classroom about a third of the time was devoted to mathematics and it was estimated that two-thirds of it consisted of the above kind of activities.

After transfer the amount of time given to computation increased. Pupils spent most of the period in mathematics doing worksheets and textbook exercises involving sums they were first taught to do at the start of their time in the junior school. The teacher would do one or two examples on the board and then leave the class to get on with the rest by themselves. The observers were unanimous in the opinion that mathematics lessons in all the transfer schools were among the least stimulating seen. Clearly this was the view of some pupils too, judging by the large number of easy riders and the drop in the levels of motivation and enjoyment reported in Chapter 5. It is difficult to equate this emphasis on repetitive drills and tests with the high educational ideals often voiced by the heads and staff of the transfer schools in conversation with members of the research team.

It could be argued that mathematics teachers found themselves in a more difficult situation than their colleagues from
other disciplines. The science teachers had all the paraphernalia
of a brand-new subject with which to grab the interest of their
pupils at the beginning of the school year; and the English
teachers could, if they chose, offer both novelty and variety in
a subject whose enormous range encompasses the informality
and creativity of improvised drama, the austere discipline of
grammatical analysis, the excitement and hilarity of stories and
word play. The mathematics teachers, however, faced a considerable initial problem in offering a cumulative subject to groups
of pupils of mixed and unknown achievement levels coming from
a variety of previous feeder schools each with its own traditions
of mathematics teaching. Their decision to begin the year with
a rather simple, very repetitive practice of the four rules in
principle offered them a means by which they could quickly
assess the skills and weaknesses of their new pupils.

In practice it offered a kind of treadmill from which neither
teachers nor pupils could easily escape. The initial strategy of
giving everybody in the class work which presupposed little
or no previous mathematical achievement proved a very ineffective means of assessing individual pupils' competence. The few
pupils who could do virtually nothing were instantly identified
and then had to be kept occupied while the process crept slowly
up the ability range. Meanwhile the pupils for whom the mathematics presented no problems had to mark time almost indefinitely.
Those whose inadequacy had been identified in the first week
of the school year nevertheless had to go along with the exercise because of the teachers' reluctance to make public their
low position within the class by prescribing a special treatment
so early on in the term. Consequently within a few weeks the
competent pupils had become bored and the less competent
demoralised. Thus for different reasons most pupils were eventually driven towards the adoption of the easy rider persona.

Part V
TEACHING AND LEARNING IN THE CLASSROOM
Maurice Galton

9 THE PRIMARY CLASSROOM REVISITED

The data presented in the previous section served to reinforce
the findings obtained from the use of systematic observation.
Although the schools claimed to operate within different educational philosophies concerning the social and academic development of their pupils, in practice they all sought to impose very
similar patterns of behaviour. Immediately they enter a new
school pupils are confronted with all sorts of rules concerning
behaviour both inside and outside the classroom. Directions
that are issued for the purpose of maintaining discipline and
control also include instructions about 'correct' ways of working
and learning. During this transition period problems arise
because a child may not immediately realize that although science
and English lessons are different the behaviour expected from
a 'good' pupil is the same in each case. For most children, however, this period of adjustment is very short, so that six weeks
into the term the pattern of schooling is well established and
the only decision left for individual pupils is whether to go
along with it.

Despite the deliberate choice of contrasting pairs of transfer
schools no significant differences between schools were established with respect to pupil achievement, motivation or pupil
attitudes. The differences that did occur involved individual
pupils' adjustment to particular teachers over matters of teaching and learning rather than being specifically concerned with
transition to new school. Many of the problems that arose seemed
to have similar origins to the ones already fully documented in
earlier ORACLE books reporting on data collected in the feeder
primary schools. This final section of the book is not therefore
concerned with further analysis of the data but is an attempt
to link the main findings presented in this volume with those
described in the previous three publications arising out of the
research. It marks the conclusion of the first stage of the
ORACLE project in which pupils have been observed during
the final two years of primary education and in the first year
of the transfer school.

The present book, however, has not only attempted to provide
detailed descriptions of the ways in which the new pupils adjust
to various aspects of their new school, to its rules, its buildings
and its new and varied curriculum. We have also chosen to
explore at some length one particular issue, the ways in which
pupils react to new teachers, both in their feeder schools and
when they move on to the more complex environment of the

transfer school. We have shown that one of the more important issues of transfer concerns the ease with which pupils adjust to their new classrooms. In this respect the 'transfer problem' is of a similar nature to that which confronts the pupil when moving from one teacher to another in the primary school, except that it may require more adjustment because more teachers are involved. Transfer is therefore bound up with the more general problems associated with teaching and learning which cut across school differences. In this study, although we chose to work in pairs of contrasting transfer schools, differences in teaching methods were shown to be associated with differences between curriculum subjects, irrespective of the type of school chosen.

RECENT RESEARCH ON TEACHING

If this view is correct, it is important to go beyond the process of mere description and to seek explanations as to why certain teachers and pupils behave in the way that they do and the effects such behaviours have on pupil learning. The search for such explanations requires a somewhat different approach to that used for the analysis of much previous empirical research on teaching. These researches, most of which have been conducted in the United States, have sought to isolate clusters of behaviours which differentiate between effective and ineffective teachers without attempting to explain how different behaviours achieved their particular effect. Such studies appear to aim at identifying a 'master teacher' whose characteristics can be prescribed to future generations of student-teachers during the course of training. At the primary stage in Britain these characteristics have concerned the decisions that teachers make before actively engaging in teaching, relating to matters such as classroom organization, curriculum planning and opinions about various teaching methods. The resulting analysis of teacher responses enables individuals to be placed at some point along a formal-informal continuum and the performance of each teacher's class is then evaluated.

The evaluation of this research is, however, by no means unanimous (Anthony, 1979; Gray and Satterly, 1981); and a reanalysis of Bennett's (1976) Lancaster study has cast doubts on some of the main findings (Aitkin et al., 1981). In the United States similar controversies (Rosenshine, 1976; Flanders, 1976) have led researchers to pay greater attention to pupil rather than teacher behaviour since pupil behaviour is now regarded as a better predictor of progress. The task of the teacher is to organize the classroom and structure the curriculum in ways which enable as many pupils in the class as possible to exhibit these 'successful' behaviours and the teacher's major role is now deemed to be an 'executive' one, as an efficient manager (Berliner, 1980). Given these disagreements, it is not surprising that research into teaching has largely failed to engage the interests of practitioners. Those who do make the effort too often find that the conclusions of the study are either difficult to relate to their own classrooms or appear to be so obvious that they hardly seem worth the research effort involved. For example, one interpretation of Aitkin's reanalysis of the Lancaster data on teaching style is that teachers who 'have discipline problems' are less likely to be successful than those who have few difficulties with classroom control. This would seem an obvious, and not altogether unexpected, finding although the more sophisticated reader might question whether 'having discipline problems' was a characteristic of a teacher's style or a consequence of it. For those unfortunate teachers who found discipline difficult it is important to know which classroom events caused the pupils to behave badly, but the analysis has little to offer on this point. Indeed, some of these poor disciplinarians favoured the formal end of the continuum and some the informal. There is thus little motivation for teachers to attempt to locate the point along the continuum which they occupy, and one can concur with the authors of the report that such descriptions may have now perhaps outlived their usefulness ('Times Educational Supplement', 24.7.81).

THE ORACLE RESEARCH PERSPECTIVE

Studies like ORACLE, which base their descriptions of teaching style on different patterns of teacher-pupil interaction, try to offer an alternative perspective. At the outset it was recognized that the complex nature of these exchanges was such that the analysis was unlikely to yield a single 'best buy' with respect to different styles. It seemed safest to assume that different teachers would achieve similar ends by different means so that the main purpose of the analysis is to explore how different kinds of pupil react to specific patterns of teacher behaviour. At the same time it has to be recognized that each teaching situation is to some extent unique so that teachers who wish to make use of these results must re-evaluate the research findings in the light of the particular circumstances in which they find themselves. This is in itself a difficult task but the researcher can simplify matters if the descriptions which he offers teachers can readily be applied to individual pupils within the context of a particular class. Thus descriptions of pupils as intermittent or solitary workers are of use only if a teacher can easily put names to such pupils in her own classroom. Only when this happens will it be possible for the teacher to plan her own teaching in ways which strike a reasonable balance between the advantages and disadvantages of certain practices which appear to affect the distribution of such pupils.

To illustrate this point consider, for example, the findings presented in the first two volumes, 'Inside the Primary Classroom' and 'Progress and Performance in the Primary Classroom', showing that individual attention is associated with progress in reading while class teaching helps children to acquire mathematical skills. But the more individual attention offered the more likely it is that a higher proportion of pupils will spend up to one hour a day talking to each other on matters unrelated to their work. Although the extent of this intermittent working will decrease when the teacher engages the whole class, many of these pupils remain silent throughout any discussion so that now nearly two-thirds of the class are solitary workers, some of whom must lack understanding but who remain reluctant to voice their difficulties. The fact that these intermittent workers make similar progress to the solitary ones suggests that the former do not consist solely of slow pupils who have a problem in concentrating for any length of time. There may be some who do not find the task sufficiently stimulating to engage their attention for continuous periods.

A teacher seeking to use these findings will first need to identify the potential intermittent workers within the class. Any decision to shift the emphasis away from individual attention then clearly depends on the particular pupils involved. If the pupils come from socially deprived backgrounds then the teacher might be happy to accept four days' work and one day's conversation each week as a reasonable compromise between the need for such pupils both to acquire social skills and to make reasonable academic progress. Others might judge that the need for such conversation was less important and would therefore seek ways to cut down the amount of intermittent working within the class and devote the time gained to other neglected areas of the curriculum. Most teachers, however, would be unhappy simply to modify the pupils' behaviour by changing existing practice unless they were afforded some explanation which accounted for the change in behaviour. Thus the researcher's task is not only to describe the characteristics of intermittent working but to attempt some partial explanation as to why some pupils engage in these practices while others do not. What to do about intermittent working will depend on whether it is seen as an attempt by pupils to draw the teacher's attention to the somewhat monotonous nature of the work being set or whether it simply reflects a tendency of some children in the class to get away with as little effort as possible.

In searching for explanations of this kind it has to be admitted that systematic observation by itself is of limited value. While the analysis of frequency counts enables links to be made between certain courses of action by the teacher and certain responses by the pupils it is necessary to 'flesh out' such findings by describing the context under which the behaviours occur. This was one reason why the observers in the ORACLE study were required to record their impressions of each particular classroom at the end of every visit. These descriptive accounts placed particular emphasis on the behaviour of the

teacher and of the eight target pupils. In the present study
once the systematic data had been used to group the teachers
and pupils then it became possible to inspect these descriptive
accounts and look for similarities between the comments of different observers not only as a way of establishing the validity
of the particular typology but also of extending our understanding of how certain practices achieve their effects.

THE PRIMARY CLASSROOM REVISITED

In seeking explanations which can account for the main findings
of the ORACLE study it may be useful for the reader to revisit
the 'typical primary classroom' which was described in Chapters
4 and 5 of the first volume, 'Inside the Primary Classroom'.
Unlike the earlier description, however, which was based solely
on analysis of the systematic data, it now becomes possible not
only to include more detailed descriptions based on the observers' impressions but also to incorporate some of the explanations
offered by teachers as to why they favour certain practices.
This latter information was obtained during interviews conducted
as part of Phase II of the ORACLE project.* A comparison of
the two descriptions will indicate how the ideas of those associated with the project have been modified and extended over
the five-year period.
    A visitor to one of the ORACLE classrooms is likely to find
about thirty children seated at tables (or desks pushed together) in groups of four or five with the teacher's desk situ-
ated at some point along the edge of the room. This will be true
even in open-plan areas where the desk is often placed outside
the line of vision of the other teachers working in the area.
The groups will normally be mixed in ability and sex, apart
from mathematics where children are likely to be re-grouped
so that they are working on either the same or very similar
tasks. The walls will be covered with displays of children's
work, much of it written, based on particular themes or topics.
The visitor will at once be struck by the air of 'busyness',
particularly with respect to the teacher. For 70 per cent of
the time spent interacting with pupils in the classroom she
will be involved with individual children rather than with groups
or the whole class. Either she will move rapidly round the
tables, checking work, clarifying instructions and giving information or she will remain seated at her desk while the pupils
form a queue.
    It is a constant and exhausting battle to keep the queue of

*Group Work in the Primary School, SSRC project no. HR 7212,
University of Leicester, School of Education. This project
sampled the opinions of over 700 teachers in local authorities
A, B and C concerning their use of different ORACLE teaching styles.

pupils as small as possible. In her efforts to achieve this the teacher has very little time for detailed discussion about the work itself. Often if a sum is right the pupil gets a tick and if not, a cross, and the instruction to try again. Most of the exchanges between the teacher and the pupil therefore consist either of marking work without giving detailed feedback, providing information which helps the pupil complete his given task or giving a fresh set of instructions about what to do next. In extreme form these patterns of interaction give rise to a teaching style termed individual monitors. All teachers, to some extent, behave in this manner but those who are identified by this style are the ones who make more consistent use of the approach. A small proportion of teachers manage to overcome the difficulty which individual monitors have of not having time to talk with the children about their ideas and their work. These are the infrequent changers, the busiest of all in the ORACLE study, interacting with children for over 90 per cent of the time they spend in the classroom.* This extra time is used for probing challenging questioning and for providing detailed feedback on the work which has been done.

PUPIL BEHAVIOUR IN THE PRIMARY CLASSROOM

If our visitor now switches his attention from the teacher to the pupils, and in particular, if he picks pupils at random and observes them over a five-minute period, then some interesting contrasts between the 'busyness' of the teacher and of the children will begin to emerge. One consequence of the teacher's decision to interact mainly with individual pupils is that a child in a primary classroom must inevitably spend much of his time working on his own. Pupils concentrate on their set tasks for nearly two-thirds of the time they are in the classroom but nearly 80 per cent of this work time will be spent in relative isolation. When pupils do talk it is largely about matters unrelated to work. While much of this isolation is a consequence of the teacher's wish that for certain activities, particularly mathematics and English, pupils 'keep themselves to themselves' there seems a marked reluctance on the part of some pupils to collaborate even when they are requested to do so. For example, in one observer's account, a group of pupils were given a worksheet in which there were rows of words. Pairs of pupils were told to discuss together the meaning of the words and to work

*The observation data were collected only for activities which took place in the classroom or base area. Music, cooking, games and PE, etc. were not observed. However, a detailed timetable was kept by each observer and from these returns it is estimated that classroom activities occupied, on average, 84 per cent of total teaching time available (see Appendix 4, 'Inside the Primary Classroom').

out for themselves which word in each row was the odd one
out. One dictionary was supplied for each pair of pupils in
case they had difficulty in working out the meanings. The
observer noted, however, that the pupils worked through the
sheet by themselves, borrowing the dictionary from each other
whenever they needed to look up a word. Only when they had
completed the exercise did they look at each other's solutions to
check that they were in agreement. Such behaviour is typical
of a group of pupils identified in the study as quiet collaborators
who, although instructed in groups, nevertheless work individually, preferring to call on the teacher for help rather than
the other children at their table.

By the time the visitor has spent a couple of days in the classroom he will begin to form the impression that some of the work
which the children engage in is repetitive and fairly low level.
During topic work there is much copying from books and making
fair copies of corrected work for display. In mathematics there
are numerous exercises concerned with straightforward computation, basic numeracy, place values, fractions, decimals and
so on. Often these exercises consist of parallel worksheets so
that when the pupil has done one set of examples he is asked
to do another which is slightly more difficult. In this way the
pupil is given something to do while the remainder of his group
catch up and are ready for the teacher to introduce some new
idea. Under this system a possible reason for the marking of
work without giving detailed feedback begins to emerge. Once
the pupil has completed the first set of examples, then, if he
makes a mistake on the second sheet, the teacher is at first
likely to assume that it is due to carelessness. She will therefore indicate with a cross that it is wrong and hand it back
with the instructions to 'do it again'. Only if the pupil returns
to her desk on more than one occasion with the wrong answer
will she begin to work through the example with him.

In English too there appears to be a need to contain the range
of activities taking place. Thus the most essential equipment
after a pen is a good set of 'felt tips' because, when a story is
written, pupils will usually be told to draw a picture and 'colour
it in'. Writing appears to be an excellent way of keeping individual children busy while the harassed teacher deals with pupils
who have a particular need for her attention. Much of the writing is not concerned with creative aspects but is to do with
completing comprehension exercises, correcting sentences so
that they are grammatically sound and filling in missing words in
paragraphs.

ATTENTION SEEKING IN THE PRIMARY CLASSROOM

For a teacher who wishes to make individual attention her main
organizational strategy there appear to be two dominant issues;
first, how to divide her limited time in the most effective way

and second, how to keep the remaining children occupied when dealing with a particular child. This situation is exacerbated by the needs of one group of pupils in the class who came to be called attention seekers, some of whom seem to need regular reassurance about their work. Some are children who come back after the teacher has read over their composition and said how good it was because 'there isn't a tick on it'. Others are rarely seen to move on to the next sum without coming out to the teacher's desk and asking 'I've finished this one. Should I now go on to the next?'

However it is another kind of attention seeker who causes more problems. Whenever there is a disturbance or excessive noise and the teacher looks up there will usually be at least one of these pupils present. When asked 'What are you doing?' he will invariably reply, 'Nothing, Miss', and when the teacher tells him to bring the book out for inspection this will prove to be the truth since the page is often blank! Everywhere these pupils go there will be little pockets of conversation. When questioned by the teacher, they have no difficulty in providing an excuse, whether it be collecting data for a bar chart describing the type of housing that the class lives in or measuring the area of the room. When such a pupil joins the queue waiting for the teacher he has a habit of taking one step backwards to allow newcomers to go ahead of him so that he spends more time waiting for the teacher than other pupils in the class. Dealing with these attention seekers can become a full-time occupation so that unless their activities disturb too many other children they are allowed to get away with it on occasions. If there are more than one or two such pupils in the class then the teacher is likely to fight shy of activities which allow pupils to move around freely and work together, preferring to set more routine tasks which require children to remain in their place and work on their own. Hence the preference will be for worked examples in mathematics rather than data gathering for practical problem-solving.

SOLITARY AND INTERMITTENT WORKING IN THE PRIMARY CLASSROOM

Dealing with such pupils is also made easier by the presence of a sizeable proportion of dedicated solitary workers. These are pupils who simply get on with what they are asked to do and require the minimum amount of individual attention. They listen carefully to instructions and watch what the teacher says or does when talking to other pupils. They tend to avoid contact with other children on the table, preferring to work on their own. Not so another sizeable group in such classes. These are the children who do some work and then chat and then return to work, the intermittent workers. These children are always interested in what the teacher is doing if only because

when the teacher is looking in their direction they give the
appearance of working hard but as soon as she turns away
they go back to their conversation, which is usually unrelated
to the work in hand.

On occasions in order to involve more pupils the teacher will
talk with the whole class. This has the effect of reducing considerably the number of pupils behaving as intermittent workers
since all pupils are now within the teacher's line of vision almost
continuously. These class exchanges are usually strongly
teacher directed; she may begin with certain notions about the
best solution to the problem under discussion. Although welcom-
ing the children's ideas, she will be careful to see that the
discussion does not stray in too many directions lest some of the
class become confused. In an attempt to steer the discussion
in the right direction she will perhaps unconsciously tend to
repeat acceptable answers from pupils and rephrase others
which are a little off the point. In some cases she may even
ignore certain answers which do not seem to lead anywhere.
Once a pattern of this kind is established, then some of the
children will refrain from attempting to answer the question
unless they can guess the answer they think the teacher is
looking for. Eventually within the class only a small proportion
of children are prepared to engage in these conversations with
any regularity, the majority realizing that if they look as if
they are thinking for an answer but remain silent the teacher
will eventually pass on to someone else. Thus class teaching,
although generally more stimulating than the individualized
approach, seems to turn more and more pupils into solitary
workers even though the teacher may worry that some of these
children do not fully understand all that is being talked about.

TIME AND ORGANIZATION IN THE PRIMARY CLASSROOM

Time and organization are key issues. Children seem to be
reluctant to work together co-operatively in groups and often
when the teacher tries to use this strategy she finds that the
talk is dominated by one or two children. 'I think that children
of this age are just not capable of working usefully together,'
one teacher told the observer when discussing the problems of
children working in groups. In certain situations, open-plan
areas and vertically grouped classes, whole class teaching is
difficult and sometimes impossible to operate effectively. An
individualized approach appears to offer the only satisfactory
solution for dealing with the varying needs of the children,
with the teacher trying to divide her time so that certain children receive extra help but others are not deprived of opportunities for contact. 'At the end of the day', said one of the
ORACLE teachers, 'I am very conscious of the fact of having
spent a lot of time with certain children and being forced to
neglect others so I make a mental note to compensate for this

next day.' Just how successful such teachers are in attempts to balance the distribution of their time is shown by the data presented in 'Inside the Primary Classroom' where the charge by the media that bright children receive less attention in the modern primary classroom was shown to be unfounded, at least as far as the ORACLE sample was concerned. Pupils in both the top and bottom achievement quartiles received similar amounts of the teacher's time.

Satisfying the requirements of about thirty children means that the teacher is under continuous pressure throughout the day and this is often increased by the demands emanating from outside agencies. There are visiting advisers, for example, reminding teachers that more time should be given to communication and study skills and to helping pupils to explore ways of scientific thinking. Transfer schools now call for detailed record-keeping and some local authorities have recently introduced 'guidelines' listing the precise skills and content which must be covered before a child leaves the primary school. One teacher reflected these additional pressures and no doubt spoke for many others with her remark, quoted in 'Inside the Primary Classroom', that there was 'only time to teach basics' and that she used work cards and books to present ideas she herself was too busy to discuss with her pupils.

The publication of the previous ORACLE books has given rise to considerable comment on the contrast between this typical classroom and the idealized Plowden one. The research has pointed out the gaps which exist between theory and practice but it would be wrong if, in so doing, the books convey to the reader that teachers and pupils in the classes studied accomplished very little. In spite of all the problems and difficulties outlined in the previous paragraphs children in the ORACLE classrooms were, for the most part, well behaved, highly motivated and contented. All primary classes in our study made considerable progress in mathematics and reading during the first two years of the study. When this is set alongside the evidence from other sources (Whitehead et al., 1977) that children at primary school read more widely and more often compared to those at the early stage of secondary education, it adds up to a considerable list of achievements. Even if the claims made about primary teaching in England during the late 1960s by American visitors now seem to have been exaggerated for propaganda purposes,* all our observers commented favourably on the contrast between the atmosphere in today's classrooms and those where they were pupils.

*See B. Simon, The Primary School Revolution: Myth or Reality? in 'Research and Practice in the Primary Classroom', ch. 1, pp. 11-12.

MOVING FROM THE PRIMARY CLASSROOM

To achieve this success, however, the teacher, using an individual approach, is forced to rely on more solitary working
to find the time in which to deal with difficult pupils or those
with special needs. As is shown in this volume by both Willcocks
and Delamont this isolation of pupils increases after transfer.
The extent of such practices is rarely evaluated in secondary
schools, as no single teacher is able to monitor the whole curriculum. Children draw maps and take notes in history and
geography, draw diagrams and make notes in science, cookery
and craft and continue to fill in worksheets for mathematics.
Only in some English lessons does it become legitimate to be
busy while talking so that the practices learned in the junior
classroom are reinforced by the pupils' later experience in the
secondary one. Writing, in particular, becomes in the child's
view, and the parents' too, the main way in which to learn
things. One teacher told the observer, 'If I spend some time
on an activity with no writing a child is sure to come up and
ask "When are we going to do some work, Miss?" '
  With the increase in class teaching after transfer the possibilities for intermittent working decrease. The teacher's eye
now falls more frequently upon such pupils, cutting down
opportunities for casual conversation. Thus in the transfer
school the overall proportion of time in which children were
engaged on their tasks was higher than in the feeder schools,
but apart from some of the English lessons, the nature of this
work was very similar across subjects and across schools.
Chapter 6, in this volume, describes the pattern of this work
in the first few weeks after transfer. There was much note
taking, copying diagrams and doing written work. With greater
amounts of class teaching, it was necessary for teachers to
restrict the range of children's activities. Delamont explains
how this was done by slowing down the faster pupils and making
the slower ones speed up. It could be argued that one of her
principal examples, an introductory science lesson on using the
bunsen burner, was a special case. Strict instructions about
using this essential part of laboratory equipment are necessary
if experiments are to be carried out in safety. However, the
fieldnotes taken at other times of the year show that drawing
diagrams and copying notes from books or worksheets formed a
substantial component of most science lessons. In geography,
too, drawing maps and making notes was also a regular task.
In one lesson the pupils were provided with a worksheet with
an outline map of Egypt. They were told to turn to page 132
in their books and to copy the names of the towns, rivers and
other features which were displayed on the map. Some of the
pupils seemed to have very little idea of the exact location of the
country. When one pupil asked the teacher, 'Where is Chicago,
Sir?' he was told 'Cairo not Chicago. Don't worry we'll get to
Chicago later.' In this lesson when some pupils had finished the

task before time they were instructed to turn over to the next page where they found a picture of an ancient Egyptian water-wheel. They were told to draw a picture of the wheel and colour it in with a promise by the teacher that 'Next time I'll tell you why it isn't used any more.'

Faced with experiences of this kind many pupils appeared to adopt a strategy whereby they did the minimum work required. Whereas the intermittent worker in the primary school worked hard for short periods, breaking off for a conversation when the teacher was engaged elsewhere, this is no longer possible when there is more whole-class teaching. The pupils now work for longer periods but accomplish less during that time. This pattern of behaviour describes the easy rider persona, and if a large number of pupils within a class adopt this persona, it creates difficult problems of management for the teacher. As the amount of work produced by the children falls, the gap between the easy riders and pupils like the hard grinders and group toilers who work harder increases. If the class or the set is to move along together, then these latter children have to be slowed down by supplying them with additional tasks like drawing pictures of ancient Egyptian water-wheels. Such practices were not confined to classes based on mixed-ability grouping. Exactly the same phenomena were observed in streamed and banded classes.

As in the primary feeder schools, teaching style appeared to exert a dominant influence on the pupil's behaviour. In the feeder schools the majority of pupils changed their type when they changed their teacher and in the transfer schools children changed their personae when they moved to different specialist subject teachers. Easy riders or hard grinders in one subject were not necessarily the same pupils in another. This was especially the case in English and science lessons. In the former subject the majority of easy riders were boys while in the latter they were girls. Thus the sex bias in respect of subject specialization is already in evidence among children of only 9 years old. Mathematics teaching appeared to create the greatest number of easy riders and this was the subject where the teaching style showed the closest correspondence to that used in the feeder schools. This finding, reported in Chapter 3, is supported by the participant accounts of some typical mathematics lessons in Chapter 7. Across all three subjects studied the similarities between each group of specialist teachers appeared to be unaffected by the age at transfer. Science was taught to 9-year-olds in the same way that it was taught to children of 11 and 12. Each subject style produced in turn its own particular pattern of pupil behaviour. In the primary feeder schools the pupils learned to adjust to different teaching styles. In the transfer schools they learned to adjust to different subject specialisms.

PUPIL PERFORMANCE IN THE TRANSFER SCHOOLS

For the first time in the study these differences in pupil
behaviour appeared to affect performance. Although, in a longitudinal study of such complexity, stretching over three years,
complete pre- and post-test data was only available on a small
proportion of the original sample, the findings are in substantial
agreement with earlier research. In particular, Nisbet and
Entwistle's (1969) conclusion that the academic performance of
some pupils deteriorates in the year after transfer received
striking confirmation. Most pupils in the primary feeder schools
made progress in absolute terms, but nearly 40 per cent of
pupils scored less on the same tests of basic skills in the June
following transfer than they did in the final term in the old
schools. The observation data suggests a possible reason for
this deterioration in performance. Pupils made above-average
gains in their final year before transfer because many teachers
'topped up' their classes in basics in preparation for the new
school. However, as the evidence in Chapter 6 shows, teachers
in the transfer schools started from scratch with addition in
mathematics and then worked through the four rules towards
fractions and decimals. Some teachers told the observers that
they made it a practice 'not to look at the record cards of the
children until after Christmas' because, according to one of
their number, 'I like to make my own mind up about each child.'
In the transfer schools failure to make progress was correlated
with the time that the pupils spent working at their task,
although the overall amounts of attention were higher than in
the feeder schools. Motivation remained remarkably high during
the first part of the transfer year, but by June it had declined
among pupils who were falling behind.

As in Youngman and Lunzer's study, pupil progress was
largely determined by earlier performance in the feeder school
(Youngman, 1980). However, whereas in Youngman and
Lunzer's case this comparison was obtained from an analysis
of each individual score before and after transfer the method
used here provides a more dramatic result. In picking children
for observation during the first year of the study, pupils were
randomly selected from each of four quartiles covering the
range of scores in a given class. When these pupils were looked
at again two years later in a new school in completely different
classes and sets containing children from different feeder
schools, then the analysis showed that pupils who were originally in a top quartile in a feeder school were still likely to be
in the top quartile of a set in a transfer school. Although this
result is in agreement with a large number of previous studies
demonstrating that a pupil's score on the pre-test is the single
most important factor in accounting for the variation in the
post-test scores, the evidence provided by the ORACLE transfer study suggests that the main reason for this pattern lies in
the behaviour of the pupils after transfer and not before. In

Chapter 4 it was shown that there was very little variation in
post-test scores across pupil types in the feeder schools. Intermittent workers, who work less hard, nevertheless made the
same amounts of progress as solitary workers. After transfer
the amount of effort that a pupil puts into his work appears to
be more crucial. The small differences in attainment observed
in the feeder schools become magnified after transfer when some
pupils began to take life easy.

In another respect the ORACLE study also replicates the work
of Youngman and Lunzer (Youngman, 1978). They discovered a
small group of pupils who performed badly in the primary schools
but did well after transfer. Such pupils are very similar to the
accelerators reported on in Chapter 5 of this present volume.
These were pupils who turned negative gain scores before
transfer into positive ones afterwards. The majority of these
pupils were originally intermittent workers but after transfer
they are characterized by high rates of working and high levels
of motivation. Accelerators came from no particular age-range
or particular type of school. They appear to be like the pupil
who told an observer, 'I have not done very well at this school
and got on the wrong side of my teacher. Now I am excited
about moving and am looking forward to a fresh start.' Such
pupils eventually learned the lesson that the way to achieve
success at secondary school was to get on with the work and
not attract the teacher's attention unless she asked the class a
question.

PROBLEMS OF MIDDLE-SCHOOL TRANSITION

These findings would appear to question the transition model
of the middle school as an effective bridge between the primary
and secondary stages of education (Hargreaves and Tickle,
1980). Despite the efforts of some schools to organize the lives
of the pupils in ways which preserved as much of the primary
atmosphere as possible, the curriculum and the teaching were
remarkably similar to that which existed in schools which offered
a secondary type atmosphere from the beginning. These secondary influences extended even into the first year of a purpose-
built 9-13 school.

This 9-13 school was in marked contrast to the 8-12 schools
of local authority C. As these 8-12 schools were the feeders for
the 12+ transfer study, children were not observed when
moving up to them at the age of 8. It is therefore impossible
to say whether pupils experienced many problems when moving
to them from their first schools. However a majority of these
8-12 middle schools had the first school in the same or an
adjacent building so any transition problems should be similar
to those of a more conventional infant and junior 5-11 primary
school.

For these 8-12 schools there was no participant observation

data other than the narrative accounts compiled by the observers at the end of each session of systematic observation. Nevertheless, the impression remained that they were much less like
secondary schools than the 9-13 or 11-14 schools described in
the transfer study. Both the curriculum and the teaching were
similar to the feeder schools in local authorities A and B. When
the teachers from the feeder schools were clustered with those
from the transfer ones, only the odd teacher from the 8-12
school transferred to the secondary-style cluster. The vast
majority of the teaching was done by a class teacher or organized
on a team basis. The kind of arrangement whereby other year-
group teachers took over the first-year classes, as at the APT
school, was not observed in the 8-12 school. All the children
in the 8-12 feeder schools made progress in absolute terms during the two-year period over which they were observed.

This evidence lends support to the Plowden recommendation
that 8-12 was the most suitable age-range for a middle school.
It must be emphasized, however, that this conclusion is an
extremely tentative one, given the small size of the sample and
the fact that it is restricted to only one local authority. It could
be that the practice in the 8-12 schools in local authority C was
attributable to the leadership of that authority in particular
rather than to the characteristics of this type of middle school
in general. Certainly the authority's advisers pursued an active
programme of in-service education within the middle schools and
used these occasions to groom selected teachers for rapid
promotion. As a whole, however, the results do suggest that
such schools are more likely to exhibit a distinct identity than
those with a transfer age of 13 or 14.

There would seem an important reason why this should be so.
Transfer from both the 11-14 and the 9-13 schools takes place
at a time when crucial decisions have to be made about subject
choices and courses for the GCE and the CSE. Inevitably there
will be pressure from the secondary school to prepare children
for these choices when they reach the top end of the middle
school. The 8-12 school comes under less pressure because
teachers in the transfer schools still have a year after transfer
to 'sort things out'.

The most dramatic illustration of these pressures concerned
the purpose-built 9-13 middle school, APT. The headmaster
of this school was not unaware of the advantaged position of
pupils at secondary level who opt to do two second languages.
Children who do French and German or two physical sciences
may find themselves favourably treated in other areas of the
curriculum with regard to size and composition of sets. In this
9-13 school the head, although not happy with the secondary
school's policy, wished to give as many of his children as possible a good start. French was therefore taught throughout
the school. This could be done because, beside the one well-
qualified French teacher, others on the staff could also speak
the language. In the first year Miss C had this ability. The

expert French teacher visited the first year three times each
week and took each one of the classes in turn. Miss C then went
round the classes revising and expanding on his lesson so that
the children were ready for his next visit. These lessons, however, were not timetabled rigidly because the expert French
teacher had to provide the same service throughout the school
and it was difficult to build in a rigid timetable for French
within the integrated one for the remaining subject areas. This
special arrangement for French gradually destroyed any sem-
blance of structure within the other areas of the curriculum.
When it became known that the expert teacher wished to visit
Miss B's class next day it was often necessary for Miss C also
to see them before then. The teachers would negotiate the
swop during the lunch-hour and quick decisions would be made
about what Miss B should do with Miss C's class while Miss C
was taking hers. It was obviously easier for Miss B to do
straightforward things, more mathematics exercises or writing,
rather than continue or start topic or art work.

In a similar manner the need to set science at BPT by the
end of the first year, and the concern of the head that all
children should have qualified science teachers, set a pattern
which began to control and determine the nature of the curriculum in other subject areas. Such constraints led to a uniformity in teaching method which was largely dictated by the
nature of the subject matter taught. Teachers working within
these schemes were also less likely to risk more exploratory
styles of teaching. Instead they concentrated on seeing that
pupils got through the syllabus by providing a variety of
teacher-directed activities.

ANXIETY CHANGES AFTER TRANSFER

There is other evidence that 8-12 middle schools come under
less pressure from the secondary schools. During the transfer
year the anxiety of children was measured twice using a modified
form of the questionnaire known as WIDIS. Details of the
administration are given in Chapter 1 and more information
about its construction can be found in Chapter 8 of 'Progress
and Performance in the Primary Classroom'. The data from the
six transfer schools in the three local authorities are shown in
Table 9.1. The questionnaire was administered in the June
before transfer, again in November and again in the following
June after transfer. In the 9-13 and 10-14 secondary-type
transfer schools the pattern of anxiety change was similar to
that found by Nisbet and Entwistle (1969) and Youngman and
Lunzer (1977). Anxiety was highest in June just before transfer, declined in November and again in the following June. Over
the year the mean anxiety dropped by 7.3 per cent at AST and
by 1.9 per cent at BST. Although the trend was not so uniform
in the two comparable primary-type transfer schools the change

Table 9.1 *School mean anxiety scores on WIDIS before and after*
transfer (as % of maximum possible score)

Transfer age and school	9+ APT	9+ AST	11+ BPT	11+ BST	12+ CPT	12+ CST
June before transfer	45.4	57.4*	43.9	47.1	44.5	48.6
November after transfer	48.6	55.4*	41.3	46.9	42.6	45.1
June after transfer	49.2	50.3	46.7	45.2	41.6	47.8
Difference June-Nov.	+3.2	-2.0	-2.6	-0.2	-1.9	-3.5
Difference Nov.-June	+0.6	-5.3	+5.4	-1.7	-1.0	+2.7
Net change June-June	+3.8	-7.3	+2.8	-1.9	-2.9	-0.8
N =	39	38	15	16	15	10

*Difference between 9+ transfer schools significant at the 5 per
cent level (+ve differences indicate increased anxiety).

in anxiety was in the opposite direction. Over the year it rose
by 3.8 per cent at APT and by 2.8 per cent at BPT so that in
the pairs of transfer schools with the same age-range the average level of anxiety was approximately equal one year after the
move to the new school. In the 12+ schools, however, the pattern of change was far more irregular, with CPT showing a
similar trend to AST and BST.

One possible explanation for the differences between the
primary and secondary transfer schools at 9+ and 11+ concerns
a finding reported by Nash (1973). He showed that teachers
in the feeder schools often had false expectations about the
school to which the children transferred and communicated
these to their pupils. The same thing happened in the ORACLE
study. Children transferring to schools with a secondary
atmosphere were continually told by their teacher during the
last term that 'you won't get away with work like this there'.
In fact, the regime after transfer was less extreme. After an
initial effort to speed up slow pupils and slow down quick ones
a pattern developed where teachers tended to accept that
children were working to 'the best of their ability'. Consequently,
as the year wore on the pupils found that things were not as
bad as they had been led to expect. Most pupils were able to
cope with their work. Teachers were, for the most part, as
friendly as their old ones, and once they had mastered the new
rules, the children's anxiety began to disappear.

Before children transferred to primary-type schools, the
teachers told a different story. They reassured their pupils
that the work would be the same, that they would be taught
mainly by one teacher and would stay in a base area 'just like
this one'. These pupils moved to the new school with reasonable
expectations that they could cope with the changes. However,

the reality was different. The teachers were kind but they did
not allow intermittent working and put considerable pressure
on pupils to complete their tasks. The pressure became even
greater towards the end of the year because decisions about
setting and banding in key subjects had to be made for the next
year. As this pressure increased so did the pupils' anxiety.

These trends were not present in the 12-18 transfer schools
of local authority C. In both schools the patterns of anxiety,
as shown in Table 9.1, were typical of secondary types of
transfer school in that they were highest just before transfer,
and declined steadily afterwards. As discussed in Chapter 1,
these schools were less sharply distinguished by the characteristics defining primary or secondary-type atmospheres. Most
teachers in the feeder schools looked upon them as secondary
establishments preparing children for public examinations.
Consequently all the teachers in the feeder schools tended to
emphasize the need to work harder in the final year in order to
take advantage of the transfer.

There was also another factor involved. By the time the
children were rising 12 they were looking forward to their move
with some excitement. Conversations with children before and
after the pre-transfer visits to the new schools brought this
out strongly. Their anxieties were mostly about the size of
the building and possible bullying. Thus the bulk of the children appeared ready for the move in a way which was not so
apparent with children at 9 or 11. When this fact is put alongside the transfer findings about the nature of the curriculum
in the 9-13 schools and the decline in the rate of some pupils'
progress, it appears that there might be advantages in favour
of 8-12 type middle schools compared to the two most common
alternatives.

10 EXPLAINING CLASSROOM PRACTICE

The fact remains, however, that even under the working conditions described in the previous chapter some teachers are more
successful than others. The main arguments presented in the
second volume, 'Progress and Performance in the Primary Classroom', are reinforced by the findings reported in Chapter 4 of
this book. These add strength to the claim that what teachers
do in the classroom, especially the way they interact with
children, is the most important determinant of the pupil's
progress, particularly in basic skills. Any attempt to theorize
about why this should be so must not only take into account
the reality of classroom life as described but must also offer
explanations as to why some teachers did better than others.
In attempting this task several recent theoretical perspectives
will be examined. The first of these explanations arises out of
recent American research. It stresses the importance of classroom organization as a means of keeping the children occupied.
In the words of a newspaper report on a recent American study,
'the way for teachers to succeed is to tell the children what to
do and keep them hard at it' ('Daily Mirror', 10.3.81, p. 6).
The second explanation has developed from studying the sociology of the classroom and concentrates on the difficulties which
teachers have when implementing their ideas and aims while
coping with external pressures from the world of work in the
larger society. In addition the suggestion of a mismatch of the
strategy and tactics of unsuccessful teachers, put forward in
Chapter 6 of 'Inside the Primary Classroom', will be re-
examined and developed in the light of the findings reported
during the second and third years of the study.

EXPLANATIONS BASED UPON 'TIME ON TASK' AND 'DIRECT INSTRUCTION'

A number of explanations of teacher effectiveness use the ideas
developed by Carroll (1963) and Bloom (1971) concerning
teaching for mastery. All hypothesize that successful learning
will take place when a teacher is able to maximize the amount of
time allocated to a specific subject or content area during which
pupils remain actively engaged on their set task (Harnischfeger
and Wiley, 1978; Romberg, 1980). Time on task will be the most
important determinant of pupils' progress providing that the
content and skills assessed by the test are reflected in the

175

learning tasks that are set.

Researchers who subscribe to this model claim that the empirical evidence shows greater progress is made in classrooms where 'direct instruction' is provided (Rosenshine, 1976; Rosenshine and Berliner, 1978; Brophy, 1979a). Direct instruction appears to be a rather nebulous concept, but would include classrooms where more opportunities were given to work, there was a high 'academic' rather than 'affective' orientation and the work was 'academically' focused (an emphasis on mathematics and reading rather than story, art and music). Not surprisingly, such conditions are more often found in traditional settings rather than open ones (Gage, 1978; Peterson, 1979). The teacher's main role is to create and manage this learning environment (Berliner, 1980).

In certain respects the teacher's function is not unlike that of a foreman in a factory who is responsible for the smooth running of an assembly line. Consider, for example, the problems of packing biscuits efficiently in a semi-automated factory. The biscuits come out of the oven on conveyor belts and the packers have to transfer them to tins, arranging them in specified positions. The foreman controls the rate of flow of biscuits on the conveyor belt in order to produce as many completed tins as possible and at the same time avoid time wasting by the packers. If the rate of the conveyor belt is too slow then some packers work below their capacity and, although most of the tins when inspected are packed perfectly, their number is not sufficient to show a profit. If the foreman makes the conveyor belt go too fast the packers begin to make mistakes and many tins have to be returned for re-packing after inspection. Consequently the number of tins produced is still below a profitable level. Eventually the foreman learns to control the conveyor belts so that all the packers work to capacity and sufficient tins are packed successfully on the first occasion to give a profit on the process.

ACADEMIC LEARNING TIME AND THE BISCUIT FACTORY ANALOGY

This biscuit factory model of teaching is the result of recent research in America. With a highly structured curriculum (the biscuits) and direct instruction matched to the level of the pupils' development (the speed of the conveyor belt), it is argued that the time pupils spend on their task is one of the best indicators of successful learning (the number of biscuit tins packed correctly). Not surprisingly, the analogy holds best in traditional rather than informal classrooms. In the former all the conveyor belts contain the same biscuits (single subject teaching) and the foreman is able to put packers with the same level of skill together (ability setting). In the informal situation where, at any one time, more than one kind of biscuit

is being packed (integrated curriculum) the packers are
allowed to choose at which conveyor belt they wish to work
(mixed ability grouping). Time is wasted during these transitions and the foreman finds it much more difficult to control
the conveyor belts with such constantly changing groups and
tasks.

It is obvious that the time that children spend working at
tasks set by the teacher must affect their performance when
tested on these tasks. In the biscuit factory example there is
circularity in the prediction of a relationship between the number of biscuit tins which pass inspection and the amount of
time that the packer spends successfully placing biscuits into
tins. In the same way because the *academic learning time* (ALT)
is defined as the 'time spent by a student engaged on a task in
which few errors are produced, and where the task is directly
relevant to an academic outcome' where 'only tasks measured by
achievement tests are considered relevant' (Romberg, 1980),
it is only to be expected that those who regularly practise
successfully will get good results on a test of the same task in
which they have been coached. Once the goals of teaching are
extended so that they become concerned with understanding
rather than simple retention of knowledge, then the practice
effect of doing the task becomes of dubious value and both
Solomon and Kendall (1979) and Grouws (1981), reporting on
mathematics teaching (Good and Grouws 1977; 1979), question
whether the skills of teaching associated with gains in knowledge
and other lower cognitive outcomes are necessarily associated
with gains in problem-solving, creative thinking and higher-
level cognitive goals. So far much of the evidence from the
United States on academic learning time only concerns fairly
low-level outcomes.

It is claimed that the use of academic learning time as a measure of student success rather than *engaged time* (the time the
pupil spends on the task) is a better predictor of achievement
(Borg, 1980). Borg claims from a review of sixteen studies that
correlations between achievement measures and on-task time
are positive with some as high as 0.87 yielding average values
of around 0.40. Borg argues that academic learning time
(because it attempts to take into account the quality of the
task they are learning successfully) is a better measure than
engaged time and is a useful basis for making decisions regard-
ing time allocation and for shaping policies in areas such as
teacher education. In a review of the findings of the Beginning
Teacher Evaluation Study (BTES), Borg analyses the data to
show that out of the 84 possible comparisons using ALT variables 47 of the relationships with the residual achievement
gains in reading and mathematics were significant. Interest-
ingly, however, he abandons the previous method of comparison
where the size of the correlation coefficient was reported in
favour of giving the proportion of residual variance attributable
to the academic learning time variable. On inspection of the

tables, however, the proportion of variance extracted by ALT is not very different to that accounted for by the more simple 'time on task' variable.

TIME ON TASK AND THE ORACLE RESEARCH

The ORACLE research used the simpler measure of engaged time rather than academic learning time to estimate the contribution of 'time on task' to student achievement. The results presented in 'Progress and Performance in the Primary Classroom' show that the time that pupils spend working on their set tasks in mathematics, reading and language skills account for less than 1 per cent of the variation in residual gain scores. Part of the reason for these findings, in the context of the ORACLE classrooms, lies in the performance of the intermittent workers who, in spite of spending the least time of all on their set tasks, make the same amount of progress each year as the other pupil types. While this result does not totally conflict with the explanation of the American researchers, in that they accept that if the engaged time is to be spent profitably then the quality and relevance of the instruction are of vital importance, it does suggest that keeping children on task should not be singled out for special attention.

In the ORACLE classrooms 'busyness' did not seem to be a major problem for either the teacher or the pupils. None of our classrooms appeared to show the wide variations in engaged time reported in the American literature (Berliner, 1980). The main problems arose from the difficulty teachers had in finding time to assess the level of development of a particular child correctly so that appropriate tasks could be set. Jasman in her contribution to 'Research and Practice in the Primary Classroom' showed that the more successful groups of teachers, the class enquirers and the infrequent changers, were no better than teachers in the unsuccessful styles when making judgments about their pupils' achievements over a wide range of skills. Her evidence suggests that 'time on task' was often used erroneously to predict a child's achievement. Busy pupils were judged to be more creative, for example, and Galton and Delafield report in the same volume that 'busyness' was used to label and then treat pupils of the same initial achievement differently in ways that led to the fulfilment of a 'self-fulfilling prophecy' (Jasman, 1981; Galton and Delafield, 1981).

Difficulties may also arise in obtaining reliable estimates of composite variables such as academic learning time. The observer has to record not only the time allocated to instruction and the time the pupil is engaged on that instruction but he also has to provide an estimate of the student's success rate and the task relevance. There is loss of precision because specific systematic classroom observations are combined with highly subjective global ratings. In order to establish links with other variables, said to be related to time on task, it is usual to carry

out cluster or factor analysis, although the different measures
are very likely to follow very different patterns of distribution
within the population studied and the practice is not usually
recommended. Within such clusters it is by no means certain that
concepts such as direct instruction and structured settings, said
to be prerequisites of high engaged time, have similar meanings,
for example, the word 'structure' is used by Soar and Soar (1972)
to describe 'systematic instructional patterns', by Brophy and
Evertson (1976) to identify 'highly focused learning tasks' and
by McDonald and Elias (1976) to describe 'restricted settings'.

Similar criticisms can be applied to the term 'direct instruction'
which takes place 'in academically orientated classrooms where
tasks are presented in a calm, orderly *structured* manner in a
warm and friendly atmosphere' (Brophy, 1979b; Rosenshine,
1979). Among research listed by Brophy to support the value of
this concept in teaching is that of Solomon and Kendall (1979).
These authors identify a classroom environment cluster which is
'controlled, disciplined, academically orientated and supportive',
which they say resembles Rosenshine's definition of direct instruction (Solomon and Kendall, 1979, p. 135). The cluster is derived
from combining six classroom environment scores, which consist
of second-order factors obtained, in turn, from thirty-three first-
order ones. These first-order factors were themselves obtained
from eight other separate factor analyses of classroom activities.
When the original variables are inspected, one of those with the
highest loadings is a rating by the observer as to whether classroom activities were presented by the teacher in a 'random or an
orderly sequence'.

This conclusion, that pupils will do better if they are first presented with some orderly account of what they are expected to do,
should apply whatever the teaching style used. It is not difficult,
however, to see ways in which an observer might tend to rate
classrooms using a single subject approach with children working
on the same task as 'more orderly' than ones where a number of
different activities were going on and pupils were given an ele-
ment of choice. Terms such as 'direct instruction' and 'structure'
need to be defined with greater clarity (preferably in terms of the
transactions taking place during the lesson) if they are not to be
equated with the traditional rhetoric of children seated in rows,
being taught didactically under strong teacher control. Unless
this is done there is a danger that much of the sterile debate
associated with the 'back to basics' movement of the 1970s will
extend into the whole of the next decade.*

*The same concern is voiced by the co-editors of the 'Beginning
Teacher Evaluation Study' (BTES) in their final summary:
At a time when 'back to basics' is popular, there is a danger that
BTES will be misunderstood. When the casual reader of the report
thinks of ALT, he or she might think of straight rows of desks
and long periods spent in academic drills....It would be unfortunate if policymakers moved too quickly towards mandates based
upon BTES. (Denham and Lieberman, 1980, p. 238).

There is also another reason to be cautious in seeking to apply the results of American research uncritically in British classrooms. Unlike her American counterpart, a teacher in an English primary school enjoys considerable freedom when it comes to planning the curriculum, and this applies, within reason, even to the choice of particular mathematics and reading schemes. In the United States, however, it is the School Board who control the choice of books and work schemes. In some districts goals are specified in terms of pupil learning outcomes and teachers are directed to devote a certain amount of time daily to particular tasks. In this situation it would not be surprising if some teachers felt less responsible for the children's behaviour. Indeed teachers with so called 'progressive' views would have an added incentive not to press the children to work hard since they could regard time-wasting as further evidence that the curriculum forced upon them was inappropriate to their pupils' needs. In this country if a child is not working the teacher must accept that this, in part, may be due to the kind of activities which she has provided. She therefore has an incentive to monitor the work rates of her pupils and take corrective action whenever it is necessary.

EXPLANATIONS BASED UPON A CONFLICT BETWEEN TEACHERS AND SOCIETY

In recent years sociologists have become more interested in classroom interaction. Most of their writings portray schools as agents of a socially divisive, highly stratified society. In them children are taught to respond to various techniques of social control so that those who do less well by the system do not seek to change it, thus enabling society to reproduce itself from one generation to the next. Much of this analysis concerns the structural features of the school system, but some writers are now attempting to relate the pressures which are exerted upon teachers at this structural or 'macro' level to those which occur at a 'micro' level inside the classroom during lessons (Eggleston, 1979; Woods, 1980a, 1980b).

The most detailed analysis of this kind is provided by Andrew Hargreaves (1978; 1979). The teacher is 'a crucial lynch pin in the wheel of causality that connects structural features of the society to interactional patterns in the classroom and back again, thereby reproducing the structural arrangements'. In order to do this the teacher devises 'a set of (coping) teaching strategies which will make life bearable, possible and even rewarding as an educational practitioner' (Hargreaves, 1978, p. 75). Teaching styles are developed 'only insofar as they enable successful coping with experienced constraint', the major ones being the pressures exerted by society through central and local government interference, parental aspirations as well as institutional constraints such as the buildings and the class size. Hargreaves sees the teacher as one who tries, as far as possible, to 'educate and relate to children in the spirit of liberal individualism' while at the same time preparing children for 'the reality of the society in which they will one day live and work'. Hargreaves illustrates the dilemma facing the teacher by examining the process of discovery learning within a middle school. He argues that the eventual decision to use 'guided choice' is an attempt to implement the progressive ideology that children learn best when they actively pursue their own interests while still ensuring that the pupils do not choose something which is beyond them and which will result in a poor assessment.

Explanations of teaching based on the idea that teachers in progressive classrooms use certain coping strategies for survival do not explain some of the findings in the ORACLE study. First, any analysis seeking to distinguish between 'progressive' and 'traditional' practice was shown to do less than justice to the complexity of life in the primary classroom. Our teachers who match the stereotype of a traditional teacher in terms of their organizational and curriculum strategies most closely resemble the progressive model in terms of their teaching tactics, in particular, the use of open-ended discussion and giving feedback to individual children about their work. Teachers who adopted 'progressive strategies' with the emphasis on individualization tended to be much more didactic in their tactical exchanges with pupils. Such differences as exist between teachers had little to do with the fact that the school was said by the staff or advisers to have a progressive outlook.

Second, the findings relating to social class which have been presented in previous ORACLE volumes appear to conflict with explanations offered by sociologists which suggest that teachers, in attempting to implement progressivism, discriminate against working-class children. Although, as in previous studies, there is a positive association between social class and pupil achievement, this was shown in 'Progress and Performance in the Primary Classroom' to be unrelated to teaching style. Teachers using the more successful styles in our study were not successful merely because they had a higher proportion of middle-class pupils in their forms. Further, it was found that both the number and type of interactions which a pupil received from the teacher was not dependent on social class (Croll, 1981) and only in the study by Jasman of teacher ratings of pupils in the same book, 'Research and Practice in the Primary Classroom', was a relationship with social class obtained. In her study teachers tended to rate children better listeners, more creative and better gatherers of information if they come from middle- rather than working-class backgrounds (Jasman, 1981).

Third, the weight of evidence from all the studies undertaken as part of the ORACLE programme points towards the conclusion that it is the interactions which take place between the teacher and pupil which are the most important determinant of a pupil's progress. The analysis carried out in Chapter 5 of 'Progress and Performance in the Primary Classroom' illustrates that a considerable number of external characteristics, said to be important coping factors, do not account for the success of certain teachers in the study. Teaching in a box classroom rather than an open-plan one was not a prerequisite of success. Giving greater emphasis to the basics in the curriculum, time on task, social class, the nature of the catchment areas, and class size were similarly unimportant factors. Thus neither explanations based on time on task nor those which point to a conflict between the aims of progressivism and the teacher's role as an unwilling catalyst in the process of social control and cultural reproduceability satisfactorily explain our research findings.

Teachers are expected by parents and outside authorities to keep pupils busy. Schools do have to cope with considerable external pressures, particularly at the upper secondary level. Teachers complain that examinations force them to do things which, given a completely free choice, they would choose not to do. In their classrooms there will be numerous occasions when notes are dictated and when revision periods are held where pupils work through past papers. There is, however, a danger that a researcher, perhaps with a strong ideological commitment against the examination system, will accept a teacher's explanation for these practices when a more complex set of motives may be the cause. As Delamont shows in this volume, such teaching strategies are by no means confined to examination pupils. They appear to extend right across the curriculum, embracing those subjects with relatively low academic status where such pressures should be reduced. They do not seem to vary across the age-range of pupils studied nor across the different types of transfer school. The unchanging nature of teaching is particularly well documented with respect to science, where the descriptions given by Delamont and Willcocks in this volume parallel those of earlier studies which go right back to the turn of the century (Gordon and Heller, 1903; Tisher, 1970; Eggleston et al., 1976; Stake, 1978).

It may be that classrooms, like living cells, have a life of their own so that teaching styles reproduce themselves from one generation of practitioners to the next. It is possible to alter the characteristics of a living cell by applying sufficient external pressure, but under normal conditions the outer cell membrane acts in such a way as to oppose the direction of the pressure and neutralize its effects. Over the years schools have found ways of neutralizing the pressures brought to bear on their staff by parents, local authorities and the like and, given the truth of this assertion, it is not sufficient to seek explanations of current practice which are based solely on sociological considerations. Teaching must be seen not only as a coping activity but also as a way in which individuals tend to express their own beliefs about teaching and learning. An analysis of the strategies used in the classroom must involve psychological constructs as well as sociological ones.

EXPRESSIVE BEHAVIOUR IN TEACHING

Coping behaviour is not something recently invented by sociologists, but has been used in psychology to describe the way
a person reacts to his immediate environment. Allport (1961)
distinguishes between this *coping* behaviour, an adaptive
activity to overcome the constraints imposed by our surround-
ings, and *expressive* behaviour which concerns 'one's manner
or style of behaving'.* To use one of Allport's examples, an
irritation to the cornea of the eye may be coped with by closing
the eyelid momentarily but the manner of carrying out this
reflex action differs according to the individual. Some people
blink regularly, some intermittently, some close their eyes
completely when blinking while others do not. Coping behaviour
mainly concerns *what* action is taken, while expressive behaviour relates to *how* the action is carried out. An important
point in relation to teaching and learning is that Allport asserts
that coping behaviour is generally conscious, whereas expressive behaviour usually lies below the threshold of our awareness.
    In Chapter 6 of 'Inside the Primary Classroom' a teacher's
cognitive style was defined by the use that was made of a
particular set of teaching tactics. In the ORACLE study these
tactical exchanges are described in terms of teacher-pupil
interaction which may be said to operate mainly at the expressive level since they are concerned with the *how* of the situation. In contrast, teaching strategies, the decisions made prior
to the start of a lesson, are concerned with *what* to do and
reflect a conscious attempt by the teacher to cope with particular classroom situations.
    While some of the pressures exerted on the teacher will
include those identified by Hargreaves, such as the demands
made by society, the physical layout of the classroom, class
size, school policy and ability grouping, the evidence in the
previous chapter suggests that it is the teacher's professional
image, largely determined by the extent of the busyness of
both herself and her pupils which is the more important consideration. This is a direct consequence of the isolation of
the individual teacher within her own classroom so that, apart
from the usual products such as tests and wall displays, there
is little evaluation of the quality of this busyness. It was pointed
out in 'Inside the Primary Classroom' that this isolation was not
confined solely to box classrooms and that many of the open-
plan areas in the study had bookcases strategically placed

*The chapter Expressive Behaviour is reprinted in
B. Semeonoff (ed.) (1966), 'Personality Assessment', Penguin,
Harmondsworth.

across the opening with the teacher's desk pushed away in a
corner outside the direct line of vision of her colleagues in
other parts of the base area. Thus colleagues walking along a
corridor may come to a judgment about the effectiveness of a
particular teacher in terms of what is done rather than how it
is done. One observer noted, for example, that the day after
a visit to the zoo the teacher appeared in the classroom with a
series of cardboard animal templates and that the children used
these to mass-produce a series of animal tableaux in different
colours for the wall display. 'It was', she reported, 'rather like
a factory production line.'

THE COPING CYCLE IN TEACHING

Teachers also bring to the classroom sets of attitudes and
beliefs about what constitutes 'good' educational practice. A
teacher may be encouraged during training to use group discussion to develop in her pupils certain social skills such as
co-operation and tolerance. When using this instructional
strategy she may find that colleagues who prefer silent individual working regard any noise as an indication of indiscipline
among the class. One teacher who had this problem told the
observer that she now only did group work when she could
borrow a mobile hut and was certain that other teachers would
not hear what was going on. Conflicts of this kind create 'cognitive dissonance', a term put forward by Festinger (1962) to
describe the discomfort felt by a person because of the gulf
between their preferred course of action and that which circumstances force them to take. Since this is not a pleasant state to
be in, all individuals try to reduce the amount of dissonance
(Rosenberg, 1960). In the previous example concerning group
discussion one way for the teacher to reduce dissonance would
be to abandon her belief about the value of group work. Such a
change in attitude might be accompanied by expressions of
dissatisfaction about the training received while in college with
the suggestion that the tutors were out of touch or too theoretical. In the ORACLE study teachers when asked about the
use of group work often claimed that it was an unworkable
strategy because 'children of this age are just not capable of
tolerating each other's views'. This kind of justification may
also be a mechanism for removing dissonance.
    The top circle of Figure 10.1 depicts this coping cycle, show-
ing the potential dissonance gap between a teacher's aims and
the need to protect her professional self-image by keeping the
class busy. Such discomfort is more readily reduced by adjust-
ments to curriculum and instructional strategies rather than to
organizational ones. The need to individualize learning is so
much a part of current primary ideology that most teachers
would find it difficult to cope with the resulting dissonance if
they were to abandon the principle completely. They therefore

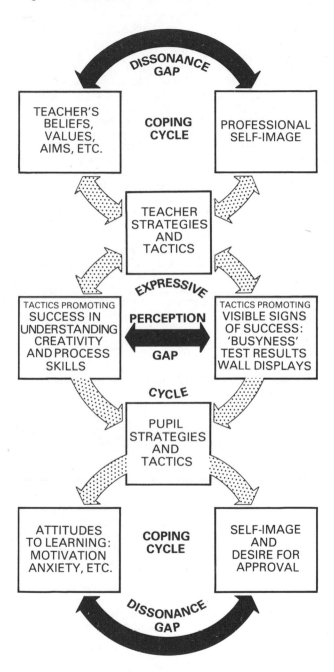

Figure 10.1 Coping and expressive cycles in teaching

continue to give children as much individual attention as possible but use parallel worksheets and writing activities to cope
with the problem of dividing their time among about thirty
children. Teachers who are faced with pupils like Wayne Douglas
(pp. 146-9) will deny him an excuse to move freely around
the round by limiting practical activities and placing a greater
emphasis on getting children to work in their own places. As
described by Delamont in Chapter 6, the range of curriculum
activities will be curtailed to ease management problems. Children will be seated in ability groups for mathematics so that
they work on similar tasks; and brighter children will be asked
to make fair copies of work for display and draw pictures at the
end of stories in order to mark time until the slower ones in the
class catch up. Thus individualization in reality means individual
attention rather than individual tasks matched to the individual
pupil's needs. To control this complex environment it may be
necessary to spend considerable time telling pupils what to do,
particularly in teaching basics where success is judged by the
tangible results of test performance. When questioned by outside researchers, teachers may find it easier to justify such
practices in terms of the pressure exerted by transfer schools
or by parents and local authorities, while giving less emphasis
to their own concerns about their professional self-image.

THE PERCEPTION GAP IN TEACHING

In Allport's example illustrating the difference between coping
and expressive behaviours, coping with a speck of dirt in the
eye by blinking left the person free to express himself by
blinking in any way that he chose. In teaching, however, this
independence between a choice of coping and expressive behaviour cannot be maintained. The ORACLE study has demonstrated
convincingly that the choice of an organizational strategy
restricts the range of tactics a teacher can use. Class teaching
allowed more open-ended discussion, while individual attention
necessitated a large number of managerial and didactic instructional exchanges. The decision to use individual attention as
the main organizational strategy in order to reduce dissonance
at a coping level may result in problems at an expressive level
because there could be a mismatch between *how* the teacher
interacts with the pupil and *how* she would like to respond in
the absence of these organizational constraints.

   According to Allport the motive for most expressive behaviour
lies below the threshold of our awareness. We may not therefore perceive any discomfort caused by the fact that in adopting
certain coping strategies our interactions with pupils in the
classroom conflict with our expressed desires. Instead the sense
of discomfort may be reduced by the mind filtering out any
message which suggests that our expressive needs are not
being met. In the classroom we have a mental picture of the

events we expect to happen and our senses blot out any evidence which conflicts with these expectations. Thus a 'perception gap' opens up between the way the teacher sees the classroom and the way that it actually is.

This perception gap in teaching is shown in the middle circle of Figure 10.1. It appears to be the main way of reducing dissonance between desired expressive behaviour in the classroom and that which actually takes place as a result of choosing certain coping strategies. The existence of the gap helps to explain why teachers in the Ford Teaching Project were convinced that they were engaging in open-ended enquiry-type discussions with pupils when the recorded transcript showed that the discussions were very restricted and strongly teacher directed. Thus 'guided choice' may not, as Hargreaves suggests, be a deliberate attempt to implement a progressive ideology while ensuring that pupils obtain a good assessment at the end of the exercise. More likely it is the result of this unconscious mechanism which attempts to reconcile the teacher's need to guarantee busyness by retaining control of the learning while trying not to appear to tell pupils what to do. To return to a previous example (p. 165), the teacher may fear lest nothing comes out of an open-ended discussion, so she may have in reserve an idea which can be developed in future lessons. Quite unconsciously she may set about making certain that this idea emerges in discussion, repeating pupils' answers which develop this idea, rephrasing other answers to fit in with it and ignoring any replies which take the discussion too far away from the point. At the end of such a discussion the teacher may feel that useful ideas have emerged from the contributions made by the pupils without realizing the extent to which these interactions have been controlled and guided.

AN EXPLANATION FOR EFFECTIVE TEACHING

In 'Progress and Performance in the Primary Classroom' it was shown that certain teaching tactics were used by teachers in the successful styles known as the infrequent changers, the class enquirers and to a lesser extent the group instructors. These teachers cut down the time spent on managerial and disciplinary instructions. They were less didactic, asking more challenging questions, suggesting more ideas and giving pupils more feedback concerning the quality of their work. To summarize, they spent more time talking with pupils rather than talking at them when compared to their less successful colleagues.

These successful teaching tactics are very much a part of the aims of modern primary practice designed to foster creativity, understanding and those process skills that enable pupils to engage in independent study. Yet these successful teachers also had busier classes (fewer intermittent workers) and their pupils did better on the tests of basic skills, outcomes which forced less successful teachers to adopt certain managerial coping strategies. Among the successful teachers there appears to be less need for a wide 'perception gap' to hide the mismatch between desired tactics and those actually taking place in the classroom as a consequence of decisions taken at the strategic level.

One reason for this could be the lack of dissonance at the coping level when choices were made about organizational strategy. Both the class enquirers and the group instructors appeared able to abandon a slavish allegiance to individualization of the learning process without seeming to experience too much discomfort. This in turn gave them more freedom to interact with their pupils in ways that were logically contingent with the aims of modern primary practice concerning processes rather than products.

The infrequent changers were a particularly interesting example because of the contrast with the less effective individual monitors. They both gave pupils the highest amounts of individual attention in comparison to other styles. In use of teaching tactics, however, the two styles differed markedly. The infrequent changers emphasized the enquiry aspects of teaching while the individual monitors emphasized the didactic.

The infrequent changers were far more flexible in their use of individual attention and appeared to monitor its effects closely, not only on the pupil receiving it but also on the rest of the class. Two examples quoted in 'Inside the Primary Classroom' showed one teacher gradually increasing the amount of individualization after the children were observed working in acceptable ways. Another teacher who had discipline problems with a small group of children cut down on the amount of individualization because the other children were not getting their fair share of it. In contrast to the individual monitors these teachers saw individualization as a means to an end and not as an end in itself. The purpose of a particular organizational strategy was to implement a certain set of desired tactics and only in conditions where it did this successfully was it used.

To sum up, the less the teacher experiences dissonance when reconciling her educational aims with the need to maintain control and busyness in the classroom, the less likely she will be to perceive the teaching situation inaccurately. In particular, teachers who are prepared to modify their classroom organization without abandoning their major teaching objectives are likely to be able to evaluate their teaching tactics more effectively and so find ways of increasing the type of interactions which the ORACLE study has shown aids pupil growth.

EXPLANATIONS OF PUPIL BEHAVIOUR AND PROGRESS

Nothing has so far been said about the pupils' coping and expressive behaviour. The research findings in this and the previous volumes provide overwhelming evidence that pupil behaviour is largely a matter of coping with the demands of the teacher. The pupil's coping cycle is presented in the third section of Figure 10.1. Within this cycle dissonance may develop between the pupil's desire to learn interesting things and his anxiety lest teacher and the other children will think him a failure because he cannot cope with these more demanding tasks.

This 'fear of failure' is illustrated by a personal anecdote in John Holt's book 'How Children Fail'. Holt, a teacher in an American public school, recounts how with time on his hands towards the end of a lesson, he asks his pupils what they feel like when he asks them a question. Immediately the relaxed atmosphere in the classroom evaporates. He sees tension creeping into the children's faces. Finally, one boy replies 'We gulp.' Holt (1969, p. 50) attributes this behaviour to the effects of competition which pupils are subjected to in the wider society. However, there may be another simpler explanation.

Holt was obviously well liked by the pupils. The same can be said of the ORACLE teachers on the evidence of the observers' accounts and the comments of the pupils in their transfer essays. It might be that the children's reluctance to be seen to be wrong was based on their fear of losing this approval rather than fear of competition. It is all too easy to see how the kind of 'guided' discussion described earlier, where the teacher repeats and rephrases certain of the pupils' answers, is taken by them to mean that there is only one correct answer. Pupils may be reluctant to risk a reply unless they think they know what that answer is. This kind of behaviour is not unlike that of the solitary worker who listens rather than participates in class discussion. Many of these children were among the most successful in the class. They always paid attention and looked as if they were thinking of an answer, confident that after a few seconds the teacher would repeat the question and try someone else.

One of the interesting results presented in this volume is the high levels of motivation. Only towards the end of the transfer year, when some of the children were no longer making progress, did the levels begin to fall. Yet in order to cope with the problems of individualization teachers set much repetitive work which was undemanding and at times not very stimulating. Given this fear of failure, however, it may be that the children preferred such tasks rather than having to face more challenging ones. Thus for different reasons both pupils and teachers adopt the same coping strategy. The teacher sets such work to keep the children busy and the children agree to keep busy on such tasks because it avoids a risk that their work will

be singled out for comment in front of their peers. Group work
may create most anxiety because the teacher is likely to be more
persistent when smaller numbers are involved and there may
also be challenges from other pupils. Thus quiet collaborators
renegotiate their task so that they avoid having to talk to
anyone when the teacher isn't present. If they have a work
problem they wait for the teacher to return and engage in
private interaction instead.

PUPIL BEHAVIOUR AFTER TRANSFER

The profiles of pupils presented in Chapters 3 and 8 of this
book suggest that there was a degree of polarization taking
place between pupils who continued to work hard (hard grinders
and group toilers) and those who seemed less content and were
reluctant to engage in more than the minimum of work (easy
riders). The descriptions of Wayne Douglas and his friend
(pp. 146-9) appear to indicate the beginnings of the sense of
alienation described by Paul Willis in his study of pupils at the
top half of the secondary school (Willis, 1977).
    There are probably a number of reasons for Wayne's increas-
ingly deviant behaviour. First, as the year progressed he was
expected to work harder and the teachers made more demands
on him to complete his set tasks. Second, there was more class
teaching and therefore less chance for him to discuss work
problems in private interaction with his teacher. But there may
also be another reason to do with the attempt by some teachers
to remove the dissonance between their 'progressive' aims and
the coping strategies they adopted. As described by Delamont
in this volume, some teachers, for example, while forced to have
testing, sought to make it less competitive. An illustration of
this was provided in Chapter 8 (p. 139). In one class in a
secondary-type transfer school mental arithmetic was a competitive activity. The children all stood up and the teacher began
the sequence of computation by saying, 'I am thinking of the
number four, double it, add six, take away two, what is the
result?' Pupils who failed to give the correct answer were told
to sit down but it was permissible for children to sit down at
any time if they were no longer able to follow the sequence.
The pupil left standing at the end was declared the winner and
given a star.
    It was interesting to observe how the pupils coped with this
competitive situation. Some put their hands on their foreheads
and screwed up their faces in a public demonstration of concentration to the rest of the class that they were keeping up
with the calculation. The observer could see that these pupils
watched the teacher surreptitiously and if they thought that
she was about to ask them for the answer they quickly sat down
with an exaggerated gesture of annoyance at having momentarily
lost their concentration. In this classroom it became a fine art

to remain standing for as long as possible without being questioned by the teacher.

In the other classroom, where the teacher disliked competitive testing, she stood all the children up and began with difficult sums. A pupil who gave a correct answer was told to sit down. When only pupils who failed to answer remained standing the teacher began to ask simpler sums until eventually no one was left. According to the teacher there was no winner but all pupils in the class realized that the final sums were much easier and that the teacher tended to ask those whom she regarded as the best pupils first. The other children therefore had no way of escaping humiliation. A similar case was described in the observed accounts of class reading where, in the interests of fairness, pupils of low reading ages had to take their turn. Again such children often knew that the teacher gave them the easiest passages to avoid protests from other pupils who were following the story. If she then praised the poor reader excessively in comparison with others this only tended to reinforce the poor self-image of the less able children. In Chapter 8 Delamont reported that the pupils quickly learned their academic standing in relation to the other members of the class and the kinds of classroom treatment described above tended to reinforce their judgments. In such circumstances the only escape for the less able children may be to adopt a 'don't care' attitude so that pupils who have been trying to improve their reading in the primary school lose their motivation and begin to read less and less.

As in the discussion of primary practice, it would be wrong to give the impression that the above examples were common to all the teachers observed. Many created warm, friendly classroom climates of the type suggested by American researchers and if in the accounts of the progressive primary-type transfer schools success seemed more elusive, it was perhaps because the aims that teachers in these schools set for themselves were more difficult and challenging. However, teachers who did succeed in creating an atmosphere where 'fear of failure' among pupils was reduced, so that they were able to learn by their mistakes, also succeeded in promoting challenging open-ended discussion while at the same time completing the routine activities demanded by the syllabus.

11 LEARNING TO TEACH IN THE CLASSROOM

In the previous three ORACLE volumes attention has been directed towards the implications of the research findings for those engaged in the in-service and initial training of teachers. It was argued that one value of the ORACLE research, within a programme of in-service education, was that certain 'teaching problems' which teachers might have thought were the result of personal failings were, in fact, far more common and appeared to arise from the forms of classroom organization and curriculum planning which were to some extent imposed upon them. It was suggested that whereas the 'teacher as researcher' models proposed by Stenhouse (1975) and Elliott et al., (1981) were more appropriate in 'open classrooms' (to use Stenhouse's own words) the creation of in-service training programmes based on the ORACLE findings might be of more help to the less-confident teacher. In initial training teaching tactics used by the most successful teachers in the ORACLE study could be the subject of micro-teaching exercises, while the findings concerning the typical classroom should provide student-teachers with a more realistic picture of the classrooms they train in.

The purpose of this short chapter is not to repeat this previous discussion. Instead the practical implications of the suggested course of action will be considered. ORACLE Phase II, the second stage of the ORACLE programme, monitors teachers' attempts to examine their existing practice in the light of the research findings. The new research phase concentrates on the use of group work since there seem a number of reasons why increasing the amount of collaborative working among pupils could help solve some of the problems of the individual monitors and habitual changers, two of the least successful teaching styles. The work is still in progress but some evaluation of this style of in-service training has already been carried out.

THE ROLE OF THE HEADTEACHER

During the first stage of the ORACLE project some in-service training was carried out during the development of the teacher-based assessment materials (Jasman, 1981). Jasman persuaded groups of enthusiastic teachers to work with her in developing procedures for assessing pupils on skills not normally tested by conventional measures. Over a period of a year, criteria were

specified and curriculum materials which required pupils to
exercise these particular skills were developed. In using the
four rules of arithmetic to solve practical maths problems
worksheets were produced which graded the kind of help
pupils received from the teacher. All children in the class
were assumed capable of 'mastering' the task if they were
given sufficient help. Teachers therefore noted, using a code,
not only the number of times they were required to aid a pupil
but also the type of help given. Children who could solve the
problem without too much help from the teacher received the
highest mark. If the teacher had to repeat instructions or
explain the appropriate rule this was penalized more than helping a child conceptualize a particular problem. Other tasks
used checklists to appraise the child's ability to pursue various
aspects of independent study; at the end of the course these
checklists were incorporated into a scheme for assessing projects and topic work. The teachers were rightly satisfied at
what they had accomplished in so short a time. They claimed
that using the checklists made them look afresh at their pupils
and decided to go back to their schools to convince colleagues
of the importance of such schemes.

Six months later an opportunity arose to evaluate the success
of this in-service programme. The results are described in
Sylvia Leith's (1981) chapter in 'Research and Practice in the
Primary Classroom'. Leith found that none of the teachers
visited were still using the assessment scheme. All still testified
to the value of the in-service course, claiming that it had made
them change both their attitudes to the pupils and their teaching styles. When asked why they were no longer using the
schemes they had helped to devise two main reasons were
given. The first and most important concerned the headteachers,
some of whom showed interest in the schemes but did not appear
to value the ideas enough to incorporate them into the school
in-service training programme. Some headteachers said that
there were more important priorities and directed the teachers
to put their energies into other areas of the curriculum. The
second reason given was failure to convince the other staff
members of the value of these new forms of assessment. Whereas
the teachers who had attended the original in-service course
had lived through a process requiring them to re-think their
own classroom practice, they were unable to re-create the
excitement of this experience at second hand for the other
staff. It would seem that, unless attempts at innovation are
carried out *within the school itself*, insufficient teachers experience the change of attitude which enables existing practice to
be re-examined and modified.

For these changes to happen the headteacher must set about
re-defining the idea of 'busyness' within the school. Unless the
staff feel that it is legitimate to be busy teaching children to
collaborate in groups and encouraging discussion they will
always feel themselves under pressure to continue with routine

activities such as correct writing and setting up displays of the
kind described in Chapter 10 (p. 184). Teachers also need to be
helped to deal with parents who may be worried about 'these
modern practices'.

The manner in which such changes are brought about is even
more important. Headteachers know that within the staff there
may be considerable differences of opinion about methods and
practice. There are obvious dangers in airing such differences
openly as this could lead to friction and destroy rather than
enhance existing working relationships. A very gradual approach
to any scheme of school-based in-service work is advisable,
particularly when it is intended to go beyond the discussion
stage and to concern itself with the evaluation of classroom
practice. The existence of the perception gap described in
Chapter 10 points to the fact that it is not sufficient to talk
with staff about what they do in the classroom.

One headteacher of a middle school in the ORACLE study,
along with his senior colleagues, developed a strategy for dealing with these difficulties. He called the staff together to look
at recent research about problems faced by teachers in similar
schools. This was a conscious decision because he did not wish
to threaten the staff at the start by suggesting they should
question their own school practice. One of the examples chosen
was a film from the audio-visual pack 'Match and Mismatch' by
Harlen et al. (1977a; 1977b; 1977c), concerning Benny, a pupil
who couldn't write very well but could draw a picture of an
internal combustion engine and describe to the other children
how it worked. The headteacher, later in discussion, asked the
staff how 'under our present system we cope with pupils like
Benny?' Eventually teachers decided that to provide adequately
for pupils like Benny they would need to group by ability for
subjects such as mathematics. The headteacher was opposed to
setting but saw that if he were now to impose his view upon the
staff after such lengthy and considered discussion it would
destroy the feeling of co-operation and 'openness to each other's
opinions' which had developed during these staff meetings.

He therefore allowed the mathematics teaching to be reorganized but at a price. Voicing his reservations about ability grouping, he asked in return that staff would agree to monitor the
effect carefully by allowing lessons to be observed. The teachers
agreed and so the beginnings of more direct collaboration
between the staff in the analysis of their teaching was begun,
with the ORACLE research team helping to devise the necessary
procedures for the task.

This pattern of staff development also had another interesting
effect. As in most schools the degree of commitment of staff to
this in-service programme varied. At the beginning three or
four teachers regularly absented themselves from the meeting,
but these same teachers were the first to complain when decisions affecting their classrooms were made. The headteacher
had then to explain that these changes had been arrived at

democratically through staff discussion and that the remedy
was in their own hands should they want to put an alternative
view. By the end of the term all the staff had begun to attend
the weekly meeting.

THE TASK OF THE ADVISORY SERVICE

In the above case the headteacher and his staff were involved
with the ORACLE research and could count on the project's
resources. In other local authorities this kind of help can come
only from the advisory service. However, at the present time
it is very difficult to give this support because of increasing
demands on the advisers' time and energies. Besides general
responsibility for in-service training and participation in staff
appointments, many local authorities now give the advisory
service an inspectorial role requiring school visits with a report.
Others require advisers to introduce competency checklists
and monitoring schemes into the schools (Holt, 1981). This can
only make the advisers' task of encouraging teachers to develop
self-accounting schemes based upon the evaluation of their
own teaching more difficult. If teachers are to respond imagina-
tively to the challenge of researching their own classrooms,
then the role of the adviser is crucial and he will have little
chance of success if he comes to the task in the role of an
external accountant.
   Most authorities now run courses for headteachers and their
deputies dealing with such issues as staff relationships, curriculum planning and more recently, in the aftermath of the
ORACLE research, the evaluation of classroom practice. However, in some local authorities matters have gone further and
from these short courses have sprung up research groups in
which headteachers are invited to bring volunteer members of
staff to a one-day conference after which the participants are
asked to go back to their schools and carry out the following
tasks:

(i)   To pick a lesson or series of lessons and write down as
        precisely as possible what it is hoped will happen during
        the lesson.
(ii)   To single out during the course of the lesson one or two
        groups of children for special attention.
(iii)   To write down after the lesson any evidence that the
        intentions as set out in (i) were achieved. Such evidence
        might consist of overheard snatches of conversations
        between pupils or from direct questioning or as a result
        of work which was produced later.
(iv)   To list any difficulties which were encountered in carry-
        ing out this lesson appraisal and more importantly to
        note any kind of evidence it was desired to collect but
        proved impossible to do so. Finally the teacher records

whether the failure to collect this evidence was due to
unsuitable conditions or because she knew of no method
by which it could be done.*

The next stage of the evaluation takes place at two levels.
First, each headteacher meets with his or her own staff and
discusses the results of the exercise. It quickly becomes
apparent that, whatever the lesson, the same problems of collecting evidence have been experienced. Headteachers in adjacent schools may arrange to hold joint meetings so that eventually staff from each of the schools will be released to work
alongside each other from time to time. Second, the headteachers'
research group meet with the advisers. Together they pool
ideas and decide the next step in the evaluation. Headteachers
needing support receive it from their colleagues as well as from
the advisers, and the staff of the Teachers' Centres can be
brought in as an additional source of manpower for school
visits. In this way an adviser can cut down the number of direct
visits he needs to pay to any individual headteacher, thus
increasing the scope of the scheme.
In local authorities working alongside the ORACLE research
team the first exercise is being followed up by a second during
which each school is trying out one or two particular evaluation
techniques with the help of a specially prepared document
entitled 'Ways of collecting evidence about classroom activities.'
Schools choosing to make use of very specialized techniques
such as systematic observation or tape recordings are provided
with training. Since choice of evaluation technique will be
influenced by the nature of the problem to be considered, each
school or group of schools is requested to focus on a particular
issue and an 'action research' strategy adopted. First, 'recon-
naissance' is carried out to investigate the facts of the issue;
second, proposals are made for solving the problem; and third,
the proposed course of action is evaluated (Elliott, 1980).
When the first groups of headteachers have successfully completed their evaluation they should, with the support of the
adviser, provide a nucleus team helping other headteachers

*Curriculum in Action, a joint project of the Open University
and the Schools Council have produced a series of packs for
the use of teachers who wish to research their own classrooms.
In Block One, 'An Approach to Evaluation', teachers are
presented with six questions.
   (i)   What did the pupils actually do?
   (ii)   What were they learning?
   (iii) How worthwhile was it?
   (iv) What did I do?
   (v)   What did I learn?
   (vi) What do I intend to do now?
These issues are similar to the ones which form the starting
point of the discussion in the ORACLE groups.

in the local authority to set up their own groups.

ORACLE AND INITIAL TEACHER TRAINING

There has also been discussion in previous volumes about the value of the ORACLE findings to those carrying out the training of new entrants to the teaching profession. It was suggested that the development of skills exhibited by the successful teachers in the study, such as fostering extended conversation, giving feedback and developing collaborative group work should be brought about through a course of micro-teaching. General discussion of the issues raised in the study should also give students a more realistic picture of classroom life in the primary school. For example, while discussing the development of creative writing skills in children, the tutor might also point out the use that teachers make of 'correct' writing as a coping strategy. The aim should be not merely to describe how some pupils behave in a more docile manner when given routine exercises than when faced with more challenging work but also to get the student-teacher to understand why this is so. Unless this happens there may be a danger that the student comes to see his tutor's enthusiasms as unrealistic and out of touch with current practice.

Many tutors in both colleges and university departments of education report, however, that it is often difficult to interest their students in such pedagogical issues. Students thrive on method work to do with aims, curriculum content and classroom organization, but any attempt to persuade them to reflect upon examples of classroom practice usually produces less satisfactory responses. At a recent conference of primary-method tutors one participant described how she had given her students vignettes of some actual lessons during which discipline problems had occurred. One of these concerned a teacher who, seeing a boy drop a piece of paper on to the floor, had, without thinking, told him to pick it up, only to have the pupil refuse. Whereas with a group of experienced teachers on a diploma course discussion of how to solve this particular teacher's problem continued for two hours, it occupied only ten minutes of the student-teachers' time. Most of them concluded that the teacher in the story had been foolish and that they would not make a similar mistake!

One explanation for this difference is that the student-teachers lack sufficient experience to feel confident in expressing views about the behaviour of more experienced colleagues. To provide this experience and at the same time educate the student to degree standard is a difficult if not impossible task. A recent survey of primary and middle-school B.Ed. courses reported that students received, on average, 19.3 weeks of block school experience during the four years of the course. The maximum in the colleges sampled was 28.8 weeks. This

works out at less than half a school term per year and the
greatest proportion of this time was spent in the third year.
The smallest amount of school experience was usually offered
in the year before entering the teaching profession (McCulloch,
1981). The situation is made more difficult because of the shortage of specialist primary-trained tutors so that any increase
in time spent in schools has to be supervised by the non-
specialist staff recruited to teach educational disciplines (DES,
1979). This shortage is likely to be exacerbated by the cutbacks in teacher training, with little recruitment into the colleges over the next decade. Supervision will then largely be
carried out by an ageing pool of professional tutors.

NEW FORMS OF TEACHER TRAINING

Although considerable uncertainty surrounds the attempts to
predict the likely future demand for teachers, most commentators have until recently taken a very pessimistic view (Lodge,
1981). This pessimism has led students in the colleges to opt
for three-year degree courses offering other job opportunities,
with a one-year postgraduate certificate course as a second
option. In the last few years numbers on the B.Ed. courses
have declined, while those on the PGCE have risen, and it is
difficult to see how this trend can easily be reversed without
a strong political initiative. There are severe problems, particularly at primary and middle-school level, when training
students for teaching in a single year. If there is to be an
increase in time given to pedagogic issues relating to classroom
practice then the problem of time becomes even more acute.
Over the last decade, the range of skills demanded of new
teachers has dramatically increased. Beside the traditional
role of instructor teachers are now expected to be facilitators
of independent learning, curriculum-developers, record-
keepers and experts in pastoral care. It seems strange that in
the PGCE training model no extra time has been allowed to
enable students to cope with these additional demands. In
theory the probationary year is also available to develop these
skills, but its benefit to many new teachers appears very
limited.
     A smaller teaching profession ought, at least, to be a well-
trained one. There are therefore strong arguments for extending the existing system (whether it be three plus one or two
plus two) to a five-year course, where one year is spent almost
entirely within schools. In effect what is now seen as the
probationary year could be undertaken prior to the postgraduate certificate course of the final year of the B.Ed. so
that the student teachers might feel confident enough to challenge the utterances of the specialist tutors in the light of
their year's experience. In the PGCE pattern, after completing
a three-year degree, a student could receive a short, five-week

general method course to enable him or her to operate at a minimum level in the classroom. The remainder of the year could be
spent in one or two schools under supervision of specialist
teacher tutors. Only a small proportion of time (on this pattern)
would be spent in the college comparing experiences with the
other students and correcting any particular weakness identified
by the teacher tutor. During the school-based year, all students
would carry out a self-evaluation exercise. At the end of this
first year a decision would then be made as to whether the
student should complete his training and receive the qualification.
This second year would be mainly spent in college. The students
would be required to complete their method work, engage in
relevant educational studies and do a further block of teaching
practice during the final term. This is offered as one possible
pattern for a revised, two-year training course for graduates.
Other patterns are, of course, possible, also ensuring a certain
primacy to teaching practice early in the course. A variety of
such patterns could be piloted and evaluated in different institutions.

THE TEACHER-TUTOR'S ROLE IN INITIAL TRAINING

The role of the specialist teacher-tutor is of vital importance
in this revised training scheme. A teacher-tutor is a practising
school teacher who also takes responsibility for the induction of
a student into teaching. It follows that if students are expected
to evaluate their teaching their tutors must have previously
done the same and demonstrated that they are familiar with the
use of the relevant techniques. Ideally, therefore, appointment
as teacher-tutor should follow the completion of a higher degree
course having classroom evaluation as a major component. There
is an obvious danger in giving so much responsibility to the
teacher-tutor. A student placed with a teacher whose lessons
were similar to those described by Delamont would quickly find
her enthusiasm for teaching diminished in such a classroom.
Hence it would be important to link the initial training of the
student to the in-service training of the tutor. Ideally, only
experienced teachers who had demonstrated a proven ability
for evaluating their own teaching and who could maintain lively
and stimulating classrooms would be considered for these posts.
   In return, although the training institutions may not be able
to reward teacher-tutors financially, they can, nevertheless,
offer status and recognition. Recently, medical schools have
increasingly come to adopt a practice whereby doctors to whom
students are sent for training in general practice are given
honorary lectureships by the university. The same status should
be given to teacher-tutors in both colleges and university
departments. With the title should go full rights of membership
of the institution, including the use of facilities and the waiving
of fees for higher degrees. Over the next decade, as it becomes

more difficult for classroom teachers to obtain promotion to
senior posts within the school, even such small rewards of
teaching skill may help maintain the enthusiasm and motivation
of younger members of the profession. Similar attempts to
bridge the gap between theory and practice, involving teacher-
tutor, student-teacher and college lecturer, are currently
being made by the IT-INSET project at Leicester, and appear
to be another obvious way of fostering these developments.

Some might see these proposals to extend the period of training as nothing more than a survival strategy for beleaguered
college lecturers facing prospects of further redundancies.
The ORACLE research, however, demonstrates sufficiently
that young teachers, in particular, are not always equipped
with the necessary teaching skills to develop a wide range of
abilities in their pupils. Children who enter the primary classroom this year will seek their first job in the final years of
the twentieth century and, with luck, can expect to continue
in work until almost halfway through the twenty-first century.
Although it is impossible to predict the kind of world these
children will face, it has been evident for some considerable
time that the ability to evaluate and use information will be more
important than the ability to remember it.

Current classroom practice is, however, still dominated by
the traditional model of learning with the teacher as the prime
source of most new knowledge. To judge by their stated aims
most teachers would wish this were otherwise, but it appears
that, at the moment, the training they receive does not afford
them opportunities to express themselves in the classroom in
ways they would choose if free of constraints. If the current
re-think about education causes the training process to be
reorganized in a way that allows student-teachers the time to
gain some of these necessary teaching skills, it should become
possible to produce an informed and self-critical profession.

FUTURE RESEARCH STRATEGIES

Apart from attempts to engage teachers in collaborative research
there is also a need for classroom researchers to tackle more
fundamental issues. There is no shortage of theories of instruction and learning but little is known about how such theoretical
perspectives are translated into classroom practice. One possibility might be to select a particular topic and set out the
different ways it might be taught in accordance with different
instructional theories. The validity of these lesson descriptions
could be checked by presenting them to teachers and asking
whether they recognized them and used them. If instructional
strategies can be described in practical terms, it becomes possible to observe how they are used with different teaching
styles in differently organized classrooms.

It is also important to try and shift the emphasis of the

research effort towards an understanding of how children set
about learning while in the classroom. Teachers, as their own
researchers, collecting and monitoring examples of their pupils'
work, have an important role to play in this task. The study
by Armstrong (1980; 1981), who with another teacher carefully
recorded and discussed the childrens' work and conversation,
is an outstanding example of what can be achieved. British
classroom research now shows a clear shift of emphasis towards
a greater concern to investigate the conditions which maximize
pupil development. The work on matching the task to the learn-
er's needs currently taking place in Lancaster University, and
the research into teacher-pupil interaction and the quality of
learning at Cambridge are two cases in point.* Even in the
United States there is a movement against the mere mechanical
application of the 'time on task' findings, with greater emphasis
on the appropriateness of the task children are asked to do.

Given these new developments, the time for further process-
product studies, of the kind carried out by ORACLE, may now
be past. Such research has been valuable if only because it has
demonstrated that teachers do matter and are therefore the
most precious resource in the school system. The task of the
research community now is to help teachers develop an understanding of the teaching-learning process so that they can
maximize the effect of this positive influence on all their pupils.
In spite of the gloom and despondency generated by economic
cutbacks, there remains a tremendous enthusiasm among the
profession for improving teaching skills. This is amply demonstrated in the work of the late Lawrence Stenhouse and of John
Elliott and by the numbers enrolling for part-time higher degree
courses and in-service training schemes. Following the publication of the ORACLE findings, this enthusiasm has been amply
demonstrated by well-attended meetings where reports of the
work have been presented, and by consistent demands for
in-service courses from teachers and advisers anxious to use
the observation techniques. Support has also been given by
the teacher unions. There is thus strong evidence that, given
the opportunity, the teaching profession is prepared to develop
its own accounting procedures. The ORACLE findings have
shown that at least in the schools studied most of the criticisms
of modern primary teaching which were voiced during the early
1970s have little foundation in fact. There is no serious indiscipline, basics are not being neglected and children continue
to make progress. The sheer stridency of those critics, however, did much to create the public demand for greater accountability within the school system. It would now be a tragedy if

*'The Quality of Pupil Learning Experiences' is an SSRC
project, no. HR 7496, directed by Professor N. Bennett and
C.W. Desforges. 'Teacher-Pupil Interaction and the Quality
of Learning' is a Schools Council Project, Programme Two,
under the direction of John Elliott.

the attempt to impose a rigid accounting system from outside were to dampen the enthusiastic response among teachers for the new styles of self-evaluation which have arisen out of recent developments in classroom research.

APPENDIX
MAIN DATA-GATHERING
INSTRUMENTS

Table A.1 *The observation categories of the Pupil Record*

Category	Item	Brief definition of item
Coding the pupil-adult categories		
1 Target's role	INIT	Target attempts to become focus of attention (not focus at previous signal)
	STAR	Target is focus of attention
	PART	Target in audience (no child is focus)
	LSWT	Target in audience (another child is focus)
2 Interacting adult	TCHR	Target interacts with teacher
	OBSR	Target interacts with observer
	OTHER	Target interacts with any other adult such as the head or secretary
3 Adult's interaction	TK WK	Adult interacts about task work (task content or supervision)
	ROUTINE	Adult interacts about routine matter (classroom management and control)
	POS	Adult reacts positively to task work (praises)
	NEG	Adult reacts negatively to behaviour, etc. (criticizes)
	IGN	Adult ignores attempted initiation
4 Adult's communication setting	IND ATT	Adult gives private individual attention to target pupil
	GROUP	Adult gives private attention to target's group
	CLASS	Adult interacts with whole class
	OTHER	Adult gives private attention to another child or group or does not interact

Category	Item	Brief definition of item

Coding the pupil–pupil categories

5 Target's role	BGNS	Target successfully begins a new contact
	COOP	Target co-operates by responding to an initiation
	TRIES	Target unsuccessfully tries to initiate
	IGN	Target ignores attempted initiation
	SUST	Target sustains interaction
6 Mode of interaction	MTL	Non-verbal, mediated solely by materials
	CNTC	Non-verbal, mediated by physical contact or gesture (with or without materials)
	VRB	Verbal (with or without materials, physical contact or gesture)
7a Task of other pupil(s)	STK	Same as target's task
	DTK	Different to target's task
7b Sex and number of other pupil(s)	SS	Target interacts privately with one pupil of same sex
	OS	Target interacts privately with one pupil of opposite sex
	SEV SS	Target interacts publicly with two or more pupils having same sex as target
	SEV OS	Target interacts publicly with two or more pupils, of whom one at least is of the opposite sex to the target
7c Base of other pupil(s)	OWN BS	From target's own base
	OTH BS	From another base

Coding the activity and location categories

8 Target's activity	COOP TK	Fully involved and co-operating on approved task work (e.g. reading)
	COOP R	Fully involved and co-operating on approved routine work (e.g. sharpening a pencil)
	DSTR	Non-involved and totally distracted from all work

Category	Item	Brief definition of item
	DSTR OBSR	Non-involved and totally distracted from all work by the observer
	DSRP	Non-involved and aggressively disrupting work of other pupil(s)
	HPLY	Non-involved and engaging in horseplay with other pupil(s)
	WAIT TCHR	Waiting to interact with the teacher
	CODS	Partially co-operating and partially distracted from approved work
	INT TCHR	Interested in teacher's activity or private interaction with other pupil(s)
	INT PUP	Interested in the work of other pupil(s)
	WOA	Working on an alternative activity which is not approved work
	RIS	Not coded because the target is responding to internal stimuli
	NOT OBS	Not coded because the target is not observed for some reason
	NOT LIST	Not coded because the target's activity is not listed
9 Target's location	P IN	Target in base
	P OUT	Target out of base but not mobile
	P MOB	Target out of base and mobile
	P OUT RM	Target out of room
10 Teacher activity and location	T PRES	Teacher present with target through interaction or physical proximity
	T ELSE	Teacher privately interacting elsewhere with other pupil(s) or visitor
	T MNTR	Teacher not interacting but monitoring classroom activities
	T HSKP	Teacher not interacting but housekeeping
	T OUT RM	Teacher out of room

Reproduced from 'Inside the Primary Classroom', pp. 12-13.

Table A.2   The observation categories of the Teacher Record

	Task	Q1 recalling facts
		Q2 offering ideas, solutions (closed)
		Q3 offering ideas, solutions (open)
Questions		
	Task supervision	Q4 referring to task supervision
	Routine	Q5 referring to routine matters
	Task	S1 of facts
		S2 of ideas, problems
	Task supervision	S3 telling child what to do
		S4 praising work or effort
Statements		S5 feedback on work or effort
	Routine	S6 providing information, directions
		S7 providing feedback
		S8 of critical control
		S9 of small talk
	'Silent' interaction, i.e. interaction other than by question or statement	Gesturing
		Showing
		Marking
		Waiting
		Story
		Reading
Silence*		Not observed
		Not coded
	No interaction between teacher and any pupil in the class	Adult interaction
		Visiting pupil
		Not interacting
		Out of room
	Audience	Class, group of individuals
	Composition	Identification of pupils involved
	Activity	e.g. Creative writing, practical maths, etc.

*While it was recognized that the term 'Silence' was in some instances a misnomer, its use for everyday purposes was preferred to the cumbersome term silence or interaction other than by question or statement.

BIBLIOGRAPHY

Aitkin, M., Bennett, S.N. and Hesketh, J. (1981), Teaching Styles and Pupil Progress: A Reanalysis, 'British Journal of Educational Psychology', vol. 51, pp. 170-86.

Allport, G.W. (1961), 'Pattern and Growth in Personality', Holt, Rinehart & Winston, New York.

—(1966), Expressive Behaviour, in Semeonoff, B. (ed.), 'Personality Assessment', Penguin, Harmondsworth.

Anthony, W.S. (1979), Progressive Learning Theories: The Evidence, in Bernbaum, G. (ed.), 'Schooling in Decline', Macmillan, London.

Armstrong, M. (1980), 'Closely Observed Children: The Diary of a Primary Classroom', Writers and Readers, Chameleon Press, London.

—(1981), The Case of Louise and the Painting of Landscape, in Nixon, J. (ed.), 'A Teacher's Guide to Action Research', Grant McIntyre, London.

Ashton, P., Kneen, P., Davies, F. and Holley, B.J. (1975), 'The Aims of Primary Education: A Study of Teachers' Opinions', Schools Council Research Studies, Macmillan Education, London.

Ball, S. (1980), Initial Encounters in the Classroom, in Woods, P. (ed.), 'Pupil Strategies, Explorations in the Sociology of the School', Croom Helm, London.

BEDC (Birmingham Educational Development Centre) (1975), 'Continuity in Education: Junior to Secondary', EDC Project Five, Final Report, City of Birmingham Education Department.

Bennett, N. (1976), 'Teaching Styles and Pupil Progress', Open Books, London.

Berliner, D.C. (1980), 'The Teacher as Executive: Administering a Learning Environment', Presentation Paper to South Pacific Association for Teacher Education, Perth, Australia, May 1980.

Bernbaum, G. (ed.) (1879), 'Schooling in Decline', Macmillan, London.

Bernstein, B. (1970), Education Cannot Compensate for Society, 'New Society', 26 February.

—(1971), On the Classification and Framing of Educational Knowledge, in Young, M.F.D. (ed.), 'Knowledge and Control', Collier Macmillan, London.

—(1975), Class and Pedagogies, Visible and Invisible, in 'Class, Codes and Control', vol. 3, 'Towards a Theory of Educational Transmissions', Routledge & Kegan Paul, London.

Blackie, J. (1967), 'Inside the Primary School', HMSO, London.

Bloom, B.S. (1971), Learning for Mastery, in Bloom, B.S., Hastings, J.T. and Madaus, G.F. (eds), 'Handbook of Formative and Summative Evaluation of Student Learning', McGraw-Hill, New York.

Blyth, W.A.L. and Derricott, R. (1977), 'The Social Significance of Middle Schools', Batsford, London.

Borg, W.R. (1980), Time and School Learning, in Denham, C. and Lieberman, A. (eds), 'Time to Learn', Department of Health, Education and Welfare, National Institute of Education, Washington D.C.

Boydell, D. (1974), Teacher-Pupil Contact in Junior Classrooms, 'British Journal of Educational Psychology', vol. 44, pp. 313-18.

—(1975), Pupil Behaviour in Junior Classrooms, 'British Journal of Educational Psychology', vol. 45, pp. 122-9.

Bronfenbrenner, U. (1974), Is Early Intervention Effective? 'Day Care and

Early Education 2', (November)
Brophy, J.E. (1979a), Teacher Behaviour and its Effects, 'Journal of Educational Psychology', vol. 71, no. 6, pp. 733-50.
—(1979b), Advances in Teacher Research, 'Journal of Classroom Interaction', vol. 15, no. 1, pp. 1-7.
Brophy, J.E. and Evertson, C.M. (1976), 'Learning from Teaching: Developmental Perspective', Allyn & Bacon, Boston.
Carroll, J. (1963), A Model for School Learning, 'Teachers College Record', vol. 64, pp. 723-33.
Cohen, L. and Manion, L. (1980), 'Research Methods in Education', Croom Helm, London.
Coleman, J.S. et al. (1966), 'Equality of Educational Opportunity', Washington D.C., US Government Printing Office.
Croll, P. (1981), Social Class, Pupil Achievement and Classroom Interaction, in Simon, B. and Willcocks, J. (eds), 'Research and Practice in the Primary Classroom', Routledge & Kegan Paul, London.
Delamont, S. (1976), 'Interaction in the Classroom', Methuen, London.
Denham, C. and Lieberman, A. (eds) (1980), 'Time to Learn', Department of Health, Education and Welfare, National Institute of Education, Washington D.C.
Denzin, N. (1970), 'The Research Act', Butterworths, London.
DES (1979), 'Developments in the B.Ed. Degree Course: A Study Based in Fifteen Institutions', HMI series: Matters for Discussion, no. 8, HMSO, London.
Eggleston, J. (1979) (ed.), 'Teacher Decision-Making in the Classroom', Routledge & Kegan Paul, London.
Eggleston, J.F., Galton, M.J., Jones, M.E. (1976), 'Processes and Products of Science Teaching', Schools Council Research Studies, Macmillan Education, London.
Elliott, J. (1980), 'Action-Research: A Framework for Self-Evaluation in Schools', Working Paper no. 1, (mimeographed), Schools Council Programme 2, Teacher-Pupil Interaction and the Quality of Learning Project, Cambridge Institute of Education.
Elliott, J., Bridges, D., Ebbutt, D., Gibson, R. and Nias, J. (1981), 'School Accountability: The SSRC Cambridge Accountability Project', Grant McIntyre, London.
Festinger, L. (1962), Cognitive Dissonance, 'Scientific American, vol. 207, no. 4, pp. 93-102.
Flanders, N.A. (1976), Research on Teaching and Improving Teacher Education, 'British Journal of Teacher Education', vol. 2, pp. 167-74.
France, N. and Fraser, I. (1975), 'Richmond Tests of Basic Skills', Nelson, London.
Gage, N. (1978), 'The Scientific Basis for the Art of Teaching', Teachers College Press, University of Columbia, New York.
Galton, M. and Delafield, A. (1981), Expectancy Effects in Primary Classrooms, in Simon B. and Willcocks, J. (eds), 'Research and Practice in the Primary Classroom', Routledge & Kegan Paul, London.
Galton, M., Simon, B. and Croll, P. (1980), 'Inside the Primary Classroom', Routledge & Kegan Paul, London.
Galton, M. and Simon, B. (eds) (1980), 'Progress and Performance in the Primary Classroom', Routledge & Kegan Paul, London.
Gardner, D.E.M. (1966), 'Experiment and Tradition in Primary Schools', Methuen, London.
Good, T.L. and Grouws, D.A. (1977), A Process-Product Study in Fourth Grade Mathematics Classrooms, 'Journal of Teacher Education', vol. 28, pp. 49-54.
—(1979), The Missouri Mathematics Effectiveness Project: An Experimental Study in Fourth Grade Classrooms, 'Journal of Educational Psychology', vol. 71, no. 3, pp. 355-62.
Gordon, M. and Heller, M. (1903), Appendix C, Chapter XV, in Armstrong, M.E., 'The Teaching of Scientific Methods', Macmillan, London.

Gray, J. (1979), Reading Progress in English Infant Schools: Some problems emerging from a study of teacher effectiveness, 'British Educational Research Journal', vol. 5, no. 2, pp. 141-57.
—(1981), Towards Effective Schools: Problems and progress in British research, 'British Educational Research Journal', vol. 7, no. 1, pp. 59-69.
Gray, J. and Satterly, D. (1981), Formal or Informal? A Re-Assessment of the British Evidence, 'British Journal of Educational Psychology', vol. 51, pp. 187-96.
Grouws, D.A. (1981), An Approach to Improving Teacher Effectiveness, 'Cambridge Journal of Education', vol. 11, no. 1, pp. 2-14.
Halsey, A.H., Heath, A.F., and Ridge, J.M. (1980), 'Origins and Destinations', Clarendon Press, Oxford.
Hammersley, M. (1980), Classroom Ethnography, 'Educational Analysis', vol. 2, no. 2, pp. 47-74.
Hargreaves, A. (1978), The Significance of Classroom Coping Strategies, in Barton, L. and Meighan, R. (eds), 'Sociological Interpretations of Schooling and Classrooms, A Re-appraisal', Nafferton Books, Driffield.
—(1979), Strategies, Decisions and Control: Interaction in a Middle School Classroom, in Eggleston, J. (ed.), 'Teacher Decision-Making in the Classroom', Routledge & Kegan Paul, London.
—(1980), The Ideology of the Middle School, in Hargreaves, A., and Tickle, L. (eds), 'Middle Schools: Origins, Ideology and Practice', Harper & Row, London.
Hargreaves, A. and Tickle, L. (eds) (1980), 'Middle Schools: Origins, Ideology and Practice', Harper & Row, London.
Harlen, W., Darwin, A. and Murphy, M. (1977a), 'Match and Mismatch: Raising Questions, Leader's Guide', Oliver & Boyd, Edinburgh.
—— (1977b), 'Match and Mismatch: Raising Questions', Oliver & Boyd, Edinburgh.
—(1977c), 'Match and Mismatch: Finding Answers', Oliver & Boyd, Edinburgh.
Harnischfeger, A. and Wiley, D. (1978), Conceptual Issues in Models of School Learning, 'Curriculum Studies', vol. 10, no. 3, pp. 215-31.
Holt, J. (1969), 'How Children Fail', Penguin, Harmondsworth.
Holt, M. (1981), 'Evaluating the Evaluators', Hodder & Stoughton, London.
HMI Survey, (1978), Department of Education and Science, 'Primary Education in England: A Survey by HM Inspectors of Schools', HMSO, London.
Jasman, A. (1981), Teachers' Assessements in Classroom Research, in Simon, B. and Willcocks, J. (eds), 'Research and Practice in the Primary Classroom', Routledge & Kegan Paul, London.
Jencks, C. et al. (1972), 'Inequality: A Reassessment of the Effects of Family and Schooling in America', Basic Books, New York.
Kelly, A. (ed.) (1981), 'The Missing Half: Girls and Science Education', Manchester University Press.
King, R. (1973), 'School Organisation and Pupil Involvement: A Study of Secondary Schools', Routledge & Kegan Paul, London.
Lacey, C. (1970), 'Hightown Grammar', Manchester University Press.
Leith, S. (1981), Project Work: An Enigma, in Simon, B. and Willcocks, J. (eds), 'Research and Practice in the Primary Classroom', Routledge & Kegan Paul, London.
Lodge, B. (1981), Bleak Outlook for Primary Jobs, 'Times Educational Supplement', 6 March.
McCulloch, M. (1981), 'School Experience: Patterns and Responses' (mimeographed) Paper Presented to the Council for National Academic Awards (CNNA) Conference: Initial B.Ed. Courses for Early and Middle Years, West Midlands College of Higher Education, 7-8 April 1981.
McDonald, F.J. and Elias, P. (1976), 'Executive Summary Report', (mimeographed) Beginning Teacher Evaluation Study, (BTES), Phase II, Educational Testing Service, Princeton, New Jersey.
McIntyre, D.I. (1980), Systematic Observation of Classroom Activities, 'Educational Analysis', vol. 2, no. 2, pp. 3-30.
Nash, R. (1973), 'Classrooms Observed', Routledge & Kegan Paul, London.

Nisbet, J.D. and Entwistle, N.J. (1969), 'The Transition to Secondary Education', University of London Press.
Peterson, P.L. (1979), Direct Instruction Reconsidered, in Peterson, P.L. and Walberg, H.J. (eds), 'Research on Teaching: Concepts, Findings and Implications', McCutchan, Berkeley, California.
Plowden Report (1967), 'Children and their Primary Schools', (2 vols) Report of the Central Advisory Council for Education in England, HMSO, London.
Reynolds, D. (1976), The Delinquent School, in Hammersley, M. and Woods, P. (eds), 'The Process of Schooling: A Sociological Reader', Routledge & Kegan Paul, London.
Romberg, T.A. (1980), Salient Features of the BTES Framework of Teacher Behaviours, in Denham, C. and Lieberman, A. (eds), 'Time to Learn', Department of Health, Education and Welfare, National Institute of Education, Washington, D.C.
Rosenberg, M.J. (1960), An Analysis of Affective-Cognitive Consistency, in Hovland, I. and Rosenberg, M.J. (eds), 'Attitude Organization and Change', Yale University Press, New Haven.
Rosenshine, B. (1971), 'Teaching Behaviours and Student Achievement', NFER, Slough.
—(1976), Recent Research on Teaching Behaviours and student achievement, 'Journal of Teacher Education', vol. 27, pp. 61-4.
—(1979), Content Time and Direct Instruction, in Peterson, P.L. and Walberg, M.J. (eds), 'Research on Teaching: Concepts, Findings and Implications', McCutchan, Berkeley, California.
Rosenshine, B. and Berliner, D. (1978), Academic Engaged Time, 'British Journal of Teacher Education', vol. 4, pp. 3-16.
Rutter, M., Maughan, B., Mortimore, P. and Ouston, J. with Smith, A. (1979), 'Fifteen Thousand Hours: Secondary Schools and their effects on children', Open Books, London.
Schools Council (1972), Working Paper no. 42, 'Education in the Middle Years', Evans-Methuen, London.
Simon, B. and Willcocks, J. (1981) (eds), 'Research and Practice in the Primary Classroom', Routledge & Kegan Paul, London.
Soar, R.S. and Soar, R.M. (1972), An Empirical Analysis of Selected Follow Through Programs: An Example of a Process Approach to Evaluation, in Gordon, I.J. (ed.), 'Early Childhood Education', National Society for the Study of Education, Chicago.
Solomon, D. and Kendall, A.J. (1979), 'Children in Classrooms - An Investigation of Person Environment Interaction', Praeger, New York.
Spelman, B.J. (1979), 'Pupil Adaptation to Secondary School', Publication no. 18, Northern Ireland Council for Educational Research.
Stake, R. (1978), 'Case Studies in Science Education', vols 1 and 2, CIRCE, University of Illinois at Urbana-Champaign.
Stenhouse, L. (1975), 'An Introduction to Curriculum Research and Development', Heinemann Educational, London.
Sumner, R. and Bradley, K. (1977), 'Assessment for Transition: A Study of New Procedures', NFER, Slough.
Tisher, R.P. (1970), The Nature of Verbal Discourse in Classrooms, in Campbell, W.J. (ed.), 'Scholars in Context: The Effects of Environment on Learning', J. Wiley, Australasia.
UCCA (1981), 'Universities Central Council on Admissions, 19th Report Statistical Supplement.
Whitehead, F., Cadey, A.C., Maddren, W. and Wellings, A. (1977), 'Children and their Books', Schools Council Research Studies, Macmillan, London.
Willis, P.E. (1977), 'Learning to Labour: How Working Class Kids Get Working Class Jobs', Saxon House, Westmead.
Woods, P. (1979), 'The Divided School', Routledge & Kegan Paul, London.
—(1980a) (ed.), 'Teacher Strategies: Explorations in the Sociology of the School', Croom Helm, London.
—(1980b) (ed.), 'Pupil Strategies: Explorations in the Sociology of the School', Croom Helm, London.

Youngman, M.B. (1978), Six Reactions to School Transfer, 'British Journal of Educational Psychology', vol. 48, pp. 280-9.
Youngman, M.B. (1980), Some Determinants of Early Secondary School Performance, 'British Journal of Educational Psychology', vol. 50, pp. 43-52.
Youngman, M.B. and Lunzer, E.A. (1977), 'Adjustment to Secondary Schooling' (mimeographed), School of Education, University of Nottingham.
Zigler, E. and Valentine, J. (1979), 'Project Headstart', Free Press, New York.

INDEX